Entertained or Else

Entertained or Else

Boredom and Networked Media

Tina Kendall

BLOOMSBURY ACADEMIC
NEW YORK • LONDON • OXFORD • NEW DELHI • SYDNEY

BLOOMSBURY ACADEMIC

Bloomsbury Publishing Inc, 1359 Broadway, New York, NY 10018, USA
Bloomsbury Publishing Plc, 50 Bedford Square, London, WC1B 3DP, UK
Bloomsbury Publishing Ireland, 29 Earlsfort Terrace, Dublin 2, D02 AY28, Ireland

BLOOMSBURY, BLOOMSBURY ACADEMIC, and the Diana logo are
trademarks of Bloomsbury Publishing Plc.

First published in the United States of America in 2025

Copyright © Tina Kendall, 2025

For legal purposes, the Acknowledgements on pp. vi–viii constitute an
extension of this copyright page.

Cover design by Daniel Benneworth-Grey

All rights reserved. No part of this publication may be: i) reproduced or transmitted in any form, electronic or mechanical, including photocopying, recording, or by means of any information storage or retrieval system without prior permission in writing from the publishers; or ii) used or reproduced in any way for the training, development, or operation of artificial intelligence (AI) technologies, including generative AI technologies. The rights holders expressly reserve this publication from the text and data mining exception as per Article 4(3) of the Digital Single Market Directive (EU) 2019/790.

Bloomsbury Publishing Inc. does not have any control over, or responsibility for, any third-party websites referred to in this book. All internet addresses given in this book were correct at the time of going to press. The author and publisher regret any inconvenience caused if addresses have changed or sites have ceased to exist but can accept no responsibility for any such changes.

Library of Congress Cataloging-in-Publication Data
Names: Kendall, Tina (College teacher) author
Title: Entertained or else : boredom and networked media / Tina Kendall.
Description: New York : Bloomsbury Academic, 2025. |
Includes bibliographical references and index.
Identifiers: LCCN 2025016472 | ISBN 9798765107591 hardback | ISBN 9798765107584 paperback | ISBN 9798765107614 pdf | ISBN 9798765107607 epub
Subjects: LCSH: Mass media–Audiences | Boredom | Online social networks
Classification: LCC P96.A83 K46 2025 | DDC 302.23–dc23/eng/20250505
LC record available at https://lccn.loc.gov/2025016472

ISBN:	HB:	979-8-7651-0759-1
	PB:	979-8-7651-0758-4
	ePDF:	979-8-7651-0761-4
	eBook:	979-8-7651-0760-7

Typeset by Integra Software Services Pvt. Ltd.
Printed and bound in the United States of America

For product safety-related questions, contact productsafety@bloomsbury.com.

To find out more about our authors and books, visit www.bloomsbury.com
and sign up for our newsletters.

Contents

Acknowledgements   vi

Introduction: Always entertained? Boredom and networked media   1

1. What to do when you're bored: Gendered boredom and networked media   23
2. How to look bored: Bored bodies and the biopolitics of faciality and gesture in short-form video   45
3. Boredom-on-demand: Always-on subjects and television's ambient turn   71
4. #BoredintheHouse: TikTok and the rhythms of #lockdownlife   99

Epilogue: Unworking entertainment: Public boredom and the next normal   133

Notes   137
Index   162

Acknowledgements

Before the following pages take us into the endless looping and listing, the limitless streaming and infinite scrolling of networked media culture, I want to express my gratitude to the people who have resisted the urge to 'click away' from various iterations of this research; each one of you has provided the insight, encouragement and care that have brought this project to fruition. I truly could not have done it without you.

Thank you to Katie Gallof Houck, Stephanie Grace-Petinos and the team at Bloomsbury Academic for giving this book such a wonderful home. The very early stages of the research were supported by a British Academy Small Grant, which allowed me to incubate some of my ideas around boredom, temporality and digital media aesthetics. The book's ideas have also been shaped through discussions at many conferences, workshops and symposia over the years, and I want to acknowledge some of those involved here: thank you to Ellen Rutten and Niels van Doorn, who organized the fantastic 'Bland, Boring, Banal' symposium at the University of Amsterdam way back in 2015, where I presented the very first paper on this topic; to Miriam De Rosa and Darren Berkland for including me in the symposium 'On Gesture' at Coventry University in 2019; to Peter Conlin at the Centre for Postdigital Research at Coventry University for organizing the boredom studies reading group at various inspired site-specific locations, including the cafeteria of the Coventry Ikea. Your support for the research has been more important than I can say, thank you. I am also grateful to Adrienne Evans for including me in the Postdigital Intimacies Research Network and for being such a wonderful supporter of this project. My thanks also go to Marsha Cassidy, Michael Goddard and Zara Dinnen for inviting me to develop my thinking around television's ambient turn at the SCMS in Chicago, at the University of Westminster and at the University of Birmingham. I would also like to thank Neta Alexander for putting together the brilliantly generative SCMS panel on binge-watching after Covid-19 in 2021, and to our fellow panellists, Tanya Horeck and Kartik Nair, for their insight and support for this book's ideas around the pandemic's bored body problem. I owe a special debt of gratitude to the Society for Cinema and Media Studies, which has always felt like an academic family, whose members include Caetlin Benson-Allott, Eugenie Brinkema, William Brown, Lisa Coulthard, Nikolaj Lübecker, Jason Middleton, Lisa Purse, Lindsey Steenberg, Robert Sinnerbrink, Johnny Walker, Austin Fisher, Helen Wood, Helen Wheatley and countless others. I also want to say thanks to Caroline Bainbridge and Susanna Paasonen for being amazing, supportive and lovely!

I owe a huge debt of gratitude to my institution for generously supporting me to travel to these and other important events over the years. In a context of ever-diminishing research budgets, ARU has somehow always managed to prioritize this kind of invaluable support; thank you to Matthew Day and Sean Campbell, both of whom have been so kind and helpful. Thanks to my amazing colleagues in Film & Media, past and present: Sarah Barrow, Jussi Parikka, Milla Tianen, Joss Hands, Seb Franklin, Neil Henderson, Simon Payne, Mareike Jenner, Nina Lübbren, Henry Miller, Sarah Gibson Yates, Jennifer Nightingale, Toby Venables and Harriet Fletcher. I am amazingly lucky to work alongside you all. I am immensely and eternally grateful to Tanya Horeck for her friendship, insight, advice and unwavering support ever since my very first day at ARU. You truly have been an amazing colleague, mentor and friend. Thanks as well to Martin Zeilinger for providing feedback on drafts and for his friendship.

Portions of this book have been published as journal articles, including sections of the introduction and Chapter 1, which was originally published in *New Formations* in 2018 as '"#Bored with Meg": Gendered Boredom and Networked Media'. Thanks so much to Jeremy Gilbert and the editorial team for their help in shaping my ideas at this formative stage, and to Lawrence Wishart for allowing me to reprint the material in this book. Thanks to *Critical Studies in Television* for allowing me the space to test out some of my ideas around binge-watching, sleep and biopolitics in 'On Binge Watching: Nine Critical Propositions' (co-authored with Tanya Horeck and Mareike Jenner) in 2018. A shorter version of Chapter 2 was published in *Necsus: European Journal of Media Studies* in 2019 as '(Not) Doing it For the Vine: #Boredom Vine Videos and the Biopolitics of Gesture', and I want to thank Greg De Cuir and Miriam De Rosa for including this work in the special issue on gesture. A short portion of the material for Chapter 4 was previously published as part of a special dossier on binge-watching in *Film Quarterly*. My sincere thanks go to Neta Alexander for coordinating the dossier, and to B. Ruby Rich, Marc Francis, Rebecca Prime and everyone at *FQ* for their incredible editorial and critical insight.

Lastly, I want to thank the people in my life who have supported me through the process of researching and writing this book. To my family, thank you for always believing in me. Your support is so important. To Jamie Andrews, thank you for being there from the start of this project, for carrying me through it and for making me laugh along the way. And finally, to Hugh McNaughtan, whose unwavering love, care and deep silliness gave me the strength to get this book over the line. Life with you is never boring.

Introduction: Always entertained? Boredom and networked media

Boredom has come to occupy a central, and yet vexed position within twenty-first-century cultural life. In the popular culture of networked entertainment, sites from Bored Panda to Boredom Therapy, and mobile apps such as Bored Button and Bored Chat have consolidated boredom as the ultimate enemy of screen-based 'fun'. Positioning boredom as a global epidemic that may strike anyone, anywhere, at any moment, these sites and apps promise to dissolve boredom in an endless stream of 'must-read viral content'[1] and 'addictive games ... specially selected ... to entertain you'.[2] Popular entertainment site Boredom Therapy, for example, adopts a cod-philanthropic register to inform its readers that the 'media startup' organization was founded 'with the goal of fighting boredom worldwide' by engaging the public with 'incredibly shareable content' and 'inspiring and extraordinary stories from around the world'.[3] In a similar vein, the popular microblogging and social networking site Tumblr entices potential users with the bold promise that, as a subscriber, 'You'll never be bored again', while casual gaming apps Bored Button and Viveport both promote their products through the hashtag #NeverBeBoredAgain.

Like many other forms of media in the twenty-first century, these entertainment platforms discursively construct boredom as a lurking menace that must continually be monitored and managed by users in the pursuit of fulfilled, contented lives. In this context, smart phones and streaming devices have been promoted as tools to fend off boredom, whenever and wherever it may set in. While the 'problem' of boredom and what to do about it is nothing new, this book will show how it has been increasingly instrumentalized as a feeling that drives users back to entertainment networks. As I argue in this book, media users have been interpellated in this context above all as boredom managers: empowered agents who are tasked with the responsibility of curating the affective texture of their own experience as it unfolds in real time, with the aid of networked media tools. And yet, this promise – that boredom can effectively be banished once and for all through our media streams – is routinely contradicted by the sheer volume of boredom-related hashtags that recur daily across these same networking platforms. Indeed, hashtags such as #BoredAsF, #SnapChatMeImBored, #BoredomKills, #BoredomStrikes and others are now firmly entrenched within the affective vocabulary of Internet cultures. In its recent guise as a popular hashtag, #boredom indexes the ubiquitous – and yet often obscured – condition of collective lethargy, flat affectivity and stalled anticipation that we routinely experience, express and seek to displace through our engagements with networked media. As this book will show, boredom is not only managed and assuaged through digital entertainment; it also accrues through and resonates across these same affective networks where, paradoxically, it generates revenue for social and streaming media corporations.

Of course, media corporations have a long history of transforming boredom into capital. But during the global Covid-19 pandemic, as lockdown boredom came to dominate as a widespread topic of anxious speculation, networked media companies doubled down on their promise to alleviate boredom in the home. In response to projected fears about how people would cope with so much newly unstructured time in the confines of their homes, governments, cultural organizations and media outlets across the globe began to issue advice documents, tool kits, watch lists and recommendations for how to cope with boredom during lockdown. Digital home entertainment and home health companies – from Netflix and Animal Crossing to Fortnite and Daily Burn – promoted their products aggressively in this context as tools for managing boredom. Across social media platforms such as Instagram, TikTok and others, hashtags such as #LockdownLife, #StayHomeStaySafe, #QuarantineandChill and #BoredintheHouse appeared, lending visibility to the boredom that was hitherto seen as a trivial concern – something that only adolescents and 'boring people' experienced, as per this Morpheus meme variation (Figure 0.1).

But while it would come to proliferate as a popular hashtag during the pandemic, the experience of being #BoredintheHouse – and the act of sharing, shaping and mitigating this feeling through social and networked media – has a much longer history. One central claim of this book is that social media and other streaming entertainment platforms are, and have long been, technologies of lockdown: both producing and pacifying the bored, housebound subjects that are central to the twenty-first-century digital economy. *Entertained or Else: Boredom*

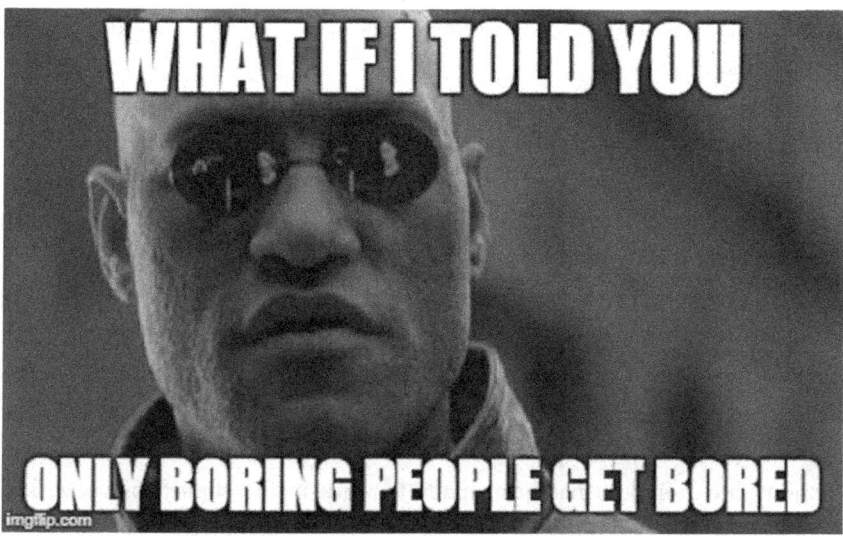

Figure 0.1 Morpheus meme variation by anonymous author © Imgflip 2017.

and *Networked Media* offers a critical examination of #LockdownLife *avant la lettre*, by focusing on some of the latent intensities and affective atmospheres that would come to be openly apprehended, discussed, documented and shared on a massive scale in the context of the Covid-19 crisis.

In a very direct way, this harnessing of boredom to networked forms of participation and active agency takes aim at, and promises to short-circuit, the feelings of powerlessness, apathy, frustrated stuckness and being held captive in time that the emotion has typically been understood to index. In *A Philosophy of Boredom* Lars Svendsen explains that boredom is bound by a 'range of emotional limitations' and a feeling that 'nothing can engender any interest'.[4] There is, furthermore, a sense of time's emptiness in boredom, which is felt intensely by subjects in the present time of its unfolding.[5] Peter Toohey suggests that '[p]redictability, monotony and confinement are all key' to defining boredom.[6] In her seminal book, *Experience Without Qualities: Boredom and Modernity*, Elizabeth Goodstein describes boredom as 'an infuriating, demoralizing, despairing' crisis of meaning that reveals to subjects a failure of desire itself.[7] 'In boredom', she writes, 'there is no distinguishing in here from out there, for the world in its failure to engage collapses into an extension of the bored subject who empties out in the vain search for an interest, a pleasure, a meaning. Self and world collapse in a nihilistic affirmation that nothing means, nothing pleases, nothing matters'.[8]

Such apocalyptic threats to self and world continue in some ways to underwrite the promises of fulfilment that accrue around networked entertainment in the twenty-first century. However, boredom's more weighty existential dimensions are also downgraded in this context, so that it can instead serve as a prompt for what Ludmila Lupinacci calls 'compulsory continuous connectedness': a pervasive and 'socio-technically constructed notion that it is only by keeping always-on ... and actively engaged that one can navigate and thrive in an environment that is purposefully framed as continuously uncertain'.[9] In this context, boredom is imagined as a problem, but a trivial one, which can easily be managed through compulsory continuous connectedness. As this book will demonstrate, boredom has been made to work in the context of networked media above all as a prompt for users to translate incipient feelings of stuckness, stasis and apathy into networked forms of agency. Instead of inciting inward reflection about life's meaning, or prompting change, boredom more frequently acts as an important trigger point, consolidating the specific gestures, habits and embodied practices that feed into and help to sustain the entertainment networks that are proffered as boredom's cure.

This book considers the complex, fraught and often contradictory relations that are forged between boredom and everyday media use in the twenty-first century. As it will demonstrate, the 'entertained or else' ethos of digital capitalism is built on a promise of pleasure through compulsory continuous connectedness, which requires the relentless management and optimization of boredom. The book demonstrates how networked media have developed new technical means of capitalizing on boredom's state of suspension – its frustrated 'wish for a desire', as Adam Phillips memorably puts it – in order to make boredom into a source of value creation for media corporations.[10] It develops in-depth analyses of a range of boredom-themed media made before, during, and after the Covid-19 lockdowns, including YouTube boredom tutorials, Vine videos, reaction GIFs, viral TikTok challenges and boring media aesthetics, focusing on slow TV, ambience videos and so-called 'background TV' available on streaming platforms Netflix and Napflix. Focusing on the discursive, technological and affective structures that encourage users to *be entertaining* and to *remain entertained*, the book analyses how boredom has been increasingly instrumentalized as both an individual mood and a wider structure of feeling that drives participation across media networks. It identifies the range of cultural techniques that have been developed for codifying, classifying, sensing and pre-empting boredom, as well as those that teach users, counter-intuitively, to embrace boring media as a means of coping with the intensities and discontents of always-on existence.

However, if boredom is increasingly instrumentalized in a digital network culture as a feeling that keeps driving us back to our social media feeds, it is important to ask *how else* it might operate. As an incipient force of felt intensity, what else might boredom do? What other actions might boredom prompt if loosened from the tent pegs of habit? While the technological affordances of computational media have put pressure on our ability to conceive of boredom as a radical challenge to digital capitalism, this book attempts to think about the political potential that might still be embedded in 'vulgar boring media' today.[11] It does this by developing an understanding of boredom as a force of suspension that is paradoxically active – what Roland Barthes refers to as 'the neutral' – an affective intensity that works by temporarily unravelling, unpicking, suspending, slowing down, thwarting or neutralizing dominant structures of attention and affect in networked settings.[12] While this force of suspension does not necessarily resist or oppose the capture and commodification of attention and emotion on digital networks, I maintain that it can still make trouble for platform capitalism's fantasies of round-the-clock attentive absorption and its putative pleasures. As I will claim, by taking the time to notice the ordinary micro-expressions of boredom that are entwined with the more intensive affective rhythms of entertainment media, we can begin to sense longings for temporal and rhythmic relations to the everyday that exist beyond the 'monotonous indistinction of 24/7'.[13]

In the remainder of this introduction, I develop the key theoretical arguments that inform the book's investigation of boredom as both a site of bio- and psycho-political control and as a potential force of active suspension. I will begin by unpacking the claim that networked media are precipitating a historically specific relationship with boredom through their ability to place lived experience outside of the conscious and phenomenological grasp of subjects. I situate such claims within a historical overview of critical debates about boredom and entertainment to explore both continuities and differences between modern and twenty-first-century boredom. I then turn to an in-depth discussion of the context of biopolitics and digital psychopolitics and their relationship to boredom and subjectivity in an always-on context. Along the way, I will also introduce the book's case studies and the sub-arguments that I advance through them in individual chapters.

Boredom is everywhere, no one is bored: boredom and computational media

Writing in 2014, the late media and cultural theorist Mark Fisher reflected on the paradox of boredom by observing that while 'the boring is ubiquitous ... no one is bored'.[14] Channelling widespread anxieties about the advent of the smartphone and its capacities for constant distraction, Fisher speculated that the 'intensive, 24-7 environment of capitalist cyberspace' had replaced the boredom of empty or idle time 'with a seamless flow of low-level stimulus', such that there was 'neither an excuse nor an opportunity to be bored'.[15] Fisher's concern over the diminution of a certain experience of boredom in an always-on culture taps into a much wider cultural zeitgeist of this period of rapid technological transformation. For instance, film scholar Nicholas Rombes's pioneering work on digital cinema in 2009 frequently returned to the topic of boredom and its slow erasure by digital modes of making and watching films. For Rombes, the 'boredom of the slow, long takes' of New American Cinema were part of an 'era of boredom' that was channelled by punk anthems, *National Lampoon*'s 1972 special issue on boredom, and Valeria Solanas's *SCUM Manifesto*, amongst other trends. This golden age of boredom as both a phenomenological experience and an expression of revolt from social conformity is encapsulated for Rombes by the 'boring, hot summer days of wandering around the city, taking in a movie to escape the heat in the dark'. Like Fisher, Rombes expresses deep-seated anxieties about what he calls the encroaching 'instant-everywhere of digital', which, he argues, 'leaves no space for boredom'.[16] In both thinkers' accounts of technological acceleration, the oppressive but potentially productive experience of 'empty absorption' in 'boredom 1.0' is subsumed by a culture of compulsive communication. In their view, critical reflection and contemplative absorption are sidelined in this context, in favour of the injunction to interact, generate content and join the debate, to the extent that while everything is now boring, no one is actually bored.[17]

In *Dependent, Distracted, Bored: Affective Formations in Networked Media*, Susanna Paasonen points out that such 'narratives of loss' are a frequent refrain in a network culture. These narratives tend to look back with longing 'for forms of experience that were available before networked connectivity took hold', and when 'the sense of time felt less warped, when attention spans were more sustained, when information took longer to acquire and therefore held more interest, when the imperative of immediacy had not yet come to govern, and when things felt less boring'.[18] As Paasonen suggests, boredom is one common complaint in these narratives, a low-level malaise that is understood to emerge from networked media's emphasis on compulsory connectedness and its monotonous repetition of the same under the sign of 'nowness and newness'.[19] It is worth pausing to ask why Rombes and Fisher would lament boredom's disappearance in their narratives of disenchantment, considering its status as a complaint in garden variety critiques of digital acceleration. This thought that boredom may be a thing of the past is perhaps especially hard to imagine in the wake of the pandemic, which brought boredom squarely into the mainstream as a persistent and pressing concern. By valuing boredom as a feeling worth missing, these thinkers insert themselves into a long philosophical tradition that has acknowledged boredom as both a symptom and a resource.

Indeed, boredom is a highly ambivalent conceptual category, which has been assigned a multiplicity of sometimes contradictory values across its critical history. As a conceptual category that is, according to Patrice Petro, 'at once empty and overflowing',[20] boredom has been interpreted as a passive expression of 'sameness, disinterest, and apathy – a resignation to the status quo', but also as involving 'an uncomfortable yet creative self-consciousness', which might yield 'resistance and opposition'.[21] In the seminal work of Frankfurt School thinkers, from Walter Benjamin to Siegfried Kracauer and Georg Simmel, boredom was interpreted 'not only as a symptom of the breakdown of older ways of being in the world but also a locus of new possibilities'.[22] It featured at once as a psychological reaction to modern urban life and its production of permanent nervous stimulation, as an expression of apathy in the face of both the drudgery of work and the manufactured novelties of entertainment and leisure, and as 'the enabling moment of human creativity'.[23] In his work on mass society, Siegfried Kracauer saw boredom as both a symptomatic response to the disorientating, exhausting lived experience of modernity, and a potential refuge from that same context of ubiquitous stimulation. For Kracauer, boredom was an index of exhaustion that stemmed equally from work and leisure pursuits. He writes about the 'vulgar boredom of daily drudgery'[24] that primes 'little shopgirls' and other modern subjects to seek out more 'pleasant' leisure pursuits in an attempt to 'alleviate the boredom that leads to the amusement that produces the boredom'.[25] But beyond this perpetual feedback loop of vulgar boredom, Kracauer also alludes to an 'extraordinary, radical boredom' which might interrupt the 'state of permanent receptivity' that is demanded of subjects in the context of modernity, allowing them to experience time in a different way. For Kracauer, relief from the vulgar drudgeries of modern life could be found only by learning to embrace the condition of profound boredom that subjects are taught to continually avoid. He describes a process of retreating home, drawing the curtains and abandoning oneself to a rapturous boredom that could be found only in this way, by shutting oneself away from the world of manufactured entertainment. Although he saw vulgar boredom as a symptomatic nervous expression experienced in a context of overstimulation, Kracauer also invested faith in profound boredom to create a space to reflect, and to dream different futures.[26] However, as is evident in the title of one of his essays that touches on the topic of boredom, 'Little Shopgirls Go to the Movies', Kracauer's approach to thinking about vulgar vs. profound boredom maintains many of the social and gendered hierarchies that continue to inform twenty-first-century understandings of boredom as either a trivial or philosophically weighty feeling.

Capturing boredom's subjective dullness and its creative potential, Walter Benjamin famously described boredom as both the 'dream bird that hatches the egg of experience',[27] and as a 'warm gray fabric lined on the inside with the most lustrous and colourful of silks'.[28] For Benjamin, too, boredom was a symptomatic response to modernity's gradual re-structuring of lived experience, as 'the capacity to assimilate, recollect and communicate experience to others is replaced by a sense of life as a series of disconnected impressions with no common associations'.[29] In this context, the individual risks becoming a 'hostage to boredom' in an unstructured world deprived of collectivity and meaning.[30] But Benjamin also invested boredom with critical potential, reading in its work of temporarily holding the subject in suspense a potential to awaken a critical reflectiveness that might break the spell of commodity culture. Of all the Frankfurt School thinkers, Benjamin's work invests perhaps the greatest positive potential in boredom's relationship with the everyday, the ordinary, and in mass cultural objects and practices. While boredom is framed largely from the period of modernity onwards as an individual failing or complaint, Benjamin insists that it is also an 'index to participation in the sleep of the collective'; in other words, it is a shared social symptom, but one that hovers on the edges of collective consciousness.[31] As such, experiences of boredom retain a latent potential to re-ignite collective action if we can learn to see the desires that are buried underneath the boredom that we have learned to merely tolerate.

In the mid-twentieth century, Theodor Adorno would extend some of these critiques in his work on the culture industry, and particularly its production of vulgar boredom. In characteristically cantankerous style, Adorno interprets boredom as a reflection of the 'objective dullness' and 'objective desperation' of the masses who, reared on the endless false pleasures of 'shallow entertainment', no longer know what to do with their spare time and can only keep going back for more of the same. In his view, the culture industry's cultivation of the 'eversame' atrophies the imagination and instils a feeling of powerlessness that fuels feelings of boredom alongside political apathy. Both, for Adorno, are symptomatic expressions of an inability to break free from the tedium of work, the tedium of leisure and the tedium of work disguised as leisure. But for all his crankiness, even Adorno admits at the end of this essay on 'Free Time' that the culture industry's hold on the human imagination is never complete; he concludes with the speculation that in the boredom of free time we can 'glimpse a chance of maturity (*Mündigkeit*), which might just eventually help to turn free time into freedom proper'.[32]

These Frankfurt School thinkers would have a profound influence on subsequent philosophical perspectives on boredom. In what is perhaps one of the twentieth century's most extensive critical treatments of boredom, Martin Heidegger's lectures on metaphysics posited 'profound boredom' as the 'fundamental mood' of philosophy. For Heidegger, boredom is also a multifaceted feeling, which he plots on a spectrum from the relatively short-lived and superficial experience of 'becoming bored by something', to the slightly more obstinate feeling of 'being bored with something', and finally the phenomenon of 'profound boredom', a boredom so all-encompassing that it swallows up the subject, to the extent that in this boredom 'we become an undifferentiated no one'[33] who is 'indifferent to everything and everyone'.[34] For Heidegger, only this variety of profound boredom – a phenomenological process of painful self-reflection in which the subject is 'left empty' and 'held in limbo' – has the potential to attune subjects to the 'authentic' nature of their existence in the world.[35]

For these theorists of modern boredom, the criticality that is borne out of a slow and painful process of self-reflection serves as the crucial hinge between the shallow, complicit boredom of mass entertainment and the more 'legitimate' experience of existential boredom. While for thinkers such as Kracauer, Benjamin, Heidegger – and maybe even Adorno – boredom was still understood to offer a space for critical reflection, reverie or revolt, it is precisely the subject's capacity to *feel bored* that, for Fisher and others, is subject to steady erosion in the era of digital networks. Fisher's claim that 'the boring is everywhere' but 'no one is bored'[36] thus marvellously telescopes the range of contradictory claims that cluster around the experience of boredom in an age of digital networks: boredom is everywhere and nowhere; boredom dominates as a collective affective sensibility, at the same time that human subjects are losing the ability to reflect on, or even *feel* it; boredom coerces our involvement within networked circuits of data and information-processing – even though we are aware that such activities are profoundly tedious and even pointless – but without offering the opportunities for critical reflection or cultural resistance that were once delegated to boredom.

Indeed, what Fisher's account of boredom 2.0 gestures towards is the fundamental shift in human experience that has been catalysed by the emergence of twenty-first-century media technologies that increasingly operate below or beyond the thresholds of human perception. As thinkers such as Mark B. Hansen, Shane Denson, Jonathan Crary, Franco 'Bifo' Berardi, and Bernard Stiegler have suggested, computational media technologies have brought about a decisive shift in the economy of human experience, which is 'increasingly conditioned and impacted by processes that we have no direct experience of, no direct mode of access to, and no potential awareness of'.[37] This marks a significant shift from previous media formats, such as photography and analogue cinema, which corresponded directly to human sensory experience. By contrast, computational media operate 'without any necessary – let alone direct – connection to human sense perception and conscious awareness'.[38] As Shane Denson maintains, this brings about a situation in which '[o]lder relations – such as that between a human subject and a photographically fixed object – are dissolving, and new relations are being forged in the microtemporal intervals of algorithmic processing'.[39] This regime of networked media operates through new micro-temporalities, which place increasing demands on subjects to act in the absence of the time required 'to receive, reflect, and respond'.[40] In a somewhat alarmist register, Dominic Pettman suggests that 'the very *capacity* for critical thinking, or enabling self-reflection, is being steadily eroded, tweet by tweet'.[41] Likewise, Mark Hansen suggests that 'conscious deliberation is increasingly side-lined from the scene of cultural solicitation', and is repurposed to function as part of a 'feed-forward' circuit, in which the human subject's conscious awareness of any given situation is produced only after the fact – once their affective involvement in such circuits has already been solicited and modulated.[42] In this scenario, human experience is marked increasingly by 'a certain degree of cognitive opacity as our consciousness perpetually – and vainly – struggle to "catch up" to what is happening'.[43] This cognitive opacity is mined by media industries in order to extract the maximum profit from time-pressure and from the difference between human and machinic perceptual abilities. For Hansen:

> It is precisely because today's data and culture industries can bypass consciousness and go directly to behavioural, biometric, and environmental data that they are increasingly able to capture our 'attention' without any awareness on our part: precisely because it places conscious deliberation and response out of play, microtemporal behavioral data that evades the oversight of consciousness allows today's data and culture industries to accomplish their goal of tightening the circuit between solicitation and response.[44]

This sidelining of conscious deliberation and the re-tooling of attention and affect by computational media also have important implications for the way that we experience and understand boredom in the present moment. In recent years, under the rubrics of boredom studies, critical attention studies and media and affect theory, scholars have begun to ask how the experience and understanding of boredom have been impacted by twenty-first-century trends, such as the emergence of real-time streaming platforms and imperatives to continuously curate and comment on one's experience online,[45] by neoliberal logics of self-management,[46] by the increasing erosion of divisions between work and play in screen-based media[47] and by the 'real subsumption' of human affect in an age of 'semiocapital'.[48] As these scholars have noted, twenty-first-century developments amplify and extend many of the legacies of modern boredom, but also put significant pressure on the profound variety of existential boredom that thinkers such as Kracauer and Heidegger identified as a critical response to the modern culture of technological acceleration and mass entertainment. Whereas the value of profound boredom for thinkers of modernity was premised on the distinctly human capacities for self-reflection and time-consciousness that the mood was understood to index, it is precisely such capacities that are targeted and restructured by computational media. Downgraded as a privileged form of self-reflection and as an existential mood that indexes extended circuits of lived experience, feelings of boredom now play an important role within the short term 'media-assisted, capitalist operationalization of our desire'.[49]

As I explore throughout this book, networked media increasingly target boredom within micro-temporal circuits, downplaying its value as a mode of critical introspection and repurposing it instead as an agent of value extraction for capitalist industries. They do so in part, as I have suggested, through the discursive framing of boredom as an affective threat that must be swiftly discharged through media engagement and interaction. But they also intervene at a more primary technical level, affecting the experience of boredom through new relationships that these technologies broker between affect, deliberation and action. As I explore in greater detail in subsequent chapters, networked media technologies often work to bracket out the kind of deep contemplative absorption associated with profound boredom by exploiting the gap between what Hansen calls the 'operational present of sensibility' and the temporalized work of conscious awareness and reflection. This 'feed-forward' structure creates a situation in which we can only fully recognize boredom as a feeling that belongs to 'us' after it has been sensed, captured, analysed and modulated by twenty-first-century technologies, and only subsequently fed forward for us to recognize as 'our own'. The relationship between sensory experience and cognitive reflection is thus re-tooled through contemporary networked media, such that an awareness of 'feeling' bored doesn't always coincide (temporally) or align (qualitatively) with the affective sensations and intensities that structure it. Put bluntly, networked media work to ensure that by the time we recognize that we are bored, we are always-already-no-longer bored – or at least not bored in the same way.

In the chapters that follow, *Entertained or Else* builds from this critical discussion of boredom management by showing how video-sharing platforms such as YouTube exploit the 'feed-forward' structure of computational media in their conscription of digitally unbored subjects. Chapter 1, 'What to do when you're bored: Gendered boredom and networked media', focuses on the perennially popular sub-genre of YouTube video tutorials that are addressed largely to teenage female audiences. Reflecting on the blatant gendering of affect in these YouTube tutorials through the figure of the teenage girl, the chapter asks why this work of boredom management should fall so resoundingly to young women to perform. By considering why the figure of the teenage girl has been rendered so excessively visible in these YouTube tutorials, I take issue with the tendency to universalize attention and boredom and to overlook the gendered, racial, class, ethnic and ableist formations that are being reproduced through the labour of boredom management. I argue that the question of *who is bored* – who is constructed as a visible subject of boredom – is a crucial starting point for understanding the entanglements between boredom, networked agencies, power and desire in the twenty-first century.

'Entertainment has got in everywhere': boredom and entertainment on-demand

Alongside boredom, the concept of entertainment has been shaped by a culture of compulsory continuous connectedness, such that new structuring tensions have come to inform its promises of pleasure. As Richard Dyer observes, as a cultural category, entertainment has long depended on 'the notion of escapism' and the 'sense of there being something that is not entertainment, that needs to be escaped from'.[50] In this historical formulation, the encompassing boredom and subjective dullness of ordinary everyday life provide the negative baseline for entertainment's promises of escapism into happiness, pleasure and excitement. In Frankfurt School critiques, the category of entertainment was evoked to describe the repetitive standardization of popular cultural forms, and to differentiate them from the more 'genuinely creative' and demanding works of 'true' art. For Adorno in particular, entertainment's production of pleasure through escapism was highly suspect, in that it distracted away from social engagement and promoted apathy at the expense of critical thinking. For this same reason, Martin Heidegger's philosophy of boredom remains highly suspect of mass culture and what he calls the 'idle talk of the they'.[51] As Byung-Chul Han points out in *Good Entertainment: A Deconstruction of the Western Passion Narrative*, although Heidegger doesn't use the term 'entertainment', his work provides 'the lineaments of a potential phenomenology of entertainment' through its disclosure of the way that mass media attunes subjects to a narrow and conformist worldview. Heidegger writes that in the 'true dictatorship' of 'the they', we can only 'enjoy ourselves and have fun the way *they* enjoy themselves. We read, see, and judge literature and the way *they* see and judge. But we also withdraw from the "great mass" the way *they* withdraw, we find "shocking" what *they* find shocking'. Entertainment thus attunes its subjects to a specific way of being, thinking and feeling in the world based on what Heidegger calls '*averageness*'.[52] This averageness provides a kind of protection and comfort to individuals, even as it distracts from the pursuit of authentic Being, in his view.

As Han puts it, for Heidegger entertainment amounts to a 'depraved form of "care"', in the sense that it is 'an *unburdening of being* that generates *pleasure*' through the feelings of comfort provided by averageness and a kinship with 'the they'. If, for Heidegger, profound boredom provides the attunement necessary for authentic existence, entertainment distracts subjects by making them feel '*at home* in the *present* world. It *maintains the home*'.[53] Boredom constitutes one of the forms of worldly 'suffering' and 'resistance' that we flee in our pursuit of entertainment. As Han points out, Heidegger builds his metaphysics of boredom on a 'highly arbitrary distinction' between enjoyment – understood to be false escapism – and forms of suffering, which are construed as authentic.[54]

In the context of twenty-first-century networks, ubiquitous entertainment has been brought into a different relationship with the everyday and with the concept of escapism. As Dyer writes, while entertainment was classically 'provided by professionals in spaces and times neither domestic nor work-related', in the twenty-first century these parameters have shifted such that entertainment media are 'permanently available' on devices 'that you can take about with you and access at any time'.[55] In addition, Dyer notes that 'changing patterns of employment and rearing really have for some people eroded the separation of graft and care from pleasure that was a grounding of entertainment's aesthetics of escape', to the extent that '[e]ntertainment has got in everywhere'.[56] In this context, 'the subject matter of entertainment is no longer how much more beautiful or exciting life could be but rather an assurance that life as it is is entertaining',[57] and as a result, the 'dynamic of escape, foundational to entertainment, disappears'.[58] For Dyer, this also represents a 'closing of the gap between an awareness of what is and imagination of what could or should be'. In direct opposition to Adorno's position on entertainment, Dyer instead suggests that the waning of entertainment as escapism 'risks threatening the ability to be critical of the way things are by feeling how else they might be'.[59]

As I consider in more detail in subsequent chapters of this book, the success of user-generated video-sharing platforms such as YouTube, Vine and TikTok relies in large part on their promise to transform the boring stuff of everyday life into entertainment for others. As Dyer suggests, social media platforms do not offer an escape from everyday life so much as a means of directly intervening in the temporality of the everyday, shaping it into something exciting or eventful. At their most basic, platforms such as Vine, TikTok, BeReal and others provide an opening onto the 'now' of the everyday, showing people 'simply doing things', as Andreas Treske puts it.[60] By structuring both users and onlookers into a shared, temporalized experience of the socially mediated everyday, these platforms perform an important function of mood modulation – transforming the banality of everyday life into the putatively exciting and eventful rhythms and flows of networked participation. This remit has been especially urgent in the context of the Covid-19 lockdowns, which caused boredom to go viral, not just as an individual complaint, but as a shared, public experience, as I explore in the book's final chapter.

But entertainment has been impacted in other ways by the context of compulsory continuous connectedness. The on-demand nature of digital entertainment doesn't just mean that it is accessible everywhere, but that it is catered ever more closely to, and can anticipate, our needs and desires. This is, of course, a highly problematic idea, which, as Neta Alexander points out, is a covert form of 'censorship in disguise'.[61] Under the promise of endless variety, on-demand models of streaming entertainment are designed to eliminate 'contingency, serendipity, and potentiality' and to keep viewers within the 'comfort zone' of their previous choices.[62] While entertainment is promoted in an on-demand culture as a source of endless pleasure catered to the user's personal taste profile, it eventually acts like an enclosure, restricting our choice and, as Dyer suggests, our ability to imagine otherwise. In a similar vein, Byung-Chul Han concludes his philosophy of entertainment by speculating that as entertainment continues to permeate all spheres of social life – morphing from escapism to infotainment and edutainment – it will form a new *'hypersystem'* that is 'coextensive with the world'. Han notes that through the binary code of entertaining/not entertaining, this new hypersystem 'will determine what is and is not *fit for the world* – indeed, even simply what is'. Entertainment, he writes, 'has been raised to a new paradigm, to a new formula of world and being. In order to *be*, in order to belong to the *world*, it is necessary to be entertaining. Only the entertaining is *real* or *true*'.[63]

As I argue in this book, states like boredom represent the other side of the entertaining/not entertaining binary that Han describes above. One conundrum that I return to throughout the book is how subjects might express, disclose and share boredom on platforms designed around the imperative to be entertaining. Indeed, a key paradox of the boredom-themed content that I analyse in this book is that across networked media, boredom proper – that is to say, its killjoy energies and downbeat sensibilities – is rarely prioritized as an affective, phenomenological experience, even in posts that feature boredom descriptors and tags. While user-generated social media can and does sometimes include gestures, poses and temporal markers that we might intuitively associate with the bodily experience of being bored, a large percentage of such content presents boredom as an alibi for zany activities, performative stunts and high-energy displays that are intended to drive boredom away. In these posts, boredom paradoxically invites participation and charges the ordinary everyday with affective intensity. The most entertaining posts often capture the attention of other media users and sometimes have the power to go viral. Following Han, the binary of entertaining/not entertaining not only determines what floats to the top and hence what is spread, but also dictates what is seen, and hence what *is*.

Always-on media, always-on subjectivity and digital psychopolitics

But while media platforms such as YouTube, Vine and TikTok may present themselves as publicly and freely accessible tools that enable users to express, share or displace feelings of boredom, it is important to remember that they are, in fact, private corporations with hungry shareholders to feed'.[64] Private boredom that is publicly declaimed or performed is therefore bound up in the wider context of networked affective labour, or the transformation of ordinary individual feelings into valuable assets for social media corporations. Indeed, this book is also about the kinds of subjects that are made and reproduced when boredom is instrumentalized in this way as a prompt for networked agency. As I suggest, the notion of continuous compulsory connectedness does not just rely on endlessly entertaining content to feed media streams, but also requires a subject who is imagined as endlessly entertained. The paradigm of always-on computing relies, in other words, on a similar construction of the always-on subject whose appetite for content is imagined as avid and insatiable, often in blatant disregard of the human body's capacity – or indeed the subject's desire – for protracted media engagement. As this book's title suggests, the idea that we must *be entertaining* and *remain entertained*, together with the technical ease of accessing what is framed as satisfying content, helps to sustain media engagement, despite the low-level feelings of boredom that users frequently experience (whether consciously or not) while using media platforms. The era of streaming on-demand entertainment continues to push the fantasy that networked media *actually do* provide pleasurable and satisfying entertainment, even though this pleasure is deeply entangled with the tedious, exhausting work of sorting between the 'truly entertaining' and the vast streams of not-quite-satisfying content that is merely there for us to consume.

One way of understanding digital boredom, as this book will argue, is to see it as the residue that grows out of the interpellation of users as always-on subjects; it is one affective, embodied manifestation of the exhausting work of remaining plugged in and entertained in an always-on culture. This approach to boredom draws from recent work in media theory that has focused on the affective and phenomenological experience of living in an era of always-on media engagement. As scholars such as James J. Hodge and Scott C. Richmond have argued, this era of ubiquitous media has created new embodied experiences and sensibilities, culminating in the new subjects of always-on computing.[65] In this context, networked entertainment platforms are promoted as providing tools for enhancing productivity and supplying endless pleasure, all at once and all the time. Correspondingly, the always-on subject is imagined in relation to the injunction to remain always-on for their social and entertainment networks; constantly 'updating to remain the same', as Wendy Chun puts it.[66] But as Hodge points out, there is 'an exhausting asymmetry between what our technologies ostensively allow us to do and what we actually can do. Machines can be on or off. People are different.'[67] This book considers how networked media address human subjects as avid and insatiable in their desire for entertainment and productivity, in blatant disregard of what bodies can do, and with little concern for what is good for their mental and physical well-being. Boredom, I argue, is one response to this asymmetry between bodies and machines in an always-on culture. Although it is often associated with the experience of having nothing to do, boredom also emerges as an index of overstimulation in a context where we are constantly expected to choose from a staggering array of options through our networked entertainment devices. As James Danckert and John Eastwood suggest in their recent psychological study, boredom arises above all when we are 'caught in a *desire conundrum*, wanting to do something but not wanting to do anything'.[68] What we see in boredom is, as Mark Kingwell puts it, 'desire out of gear – not in the sense of an impasse or stall, such as one might experience in procrastination, but rather in the way that an engine stuck in neutral can red-line its revolutions without producing any traction whatsoever'.[69] As I have suggested, low-level feelings of boredom emerge from the labour of being a subject in a context of compulsory continuous connectedness, even while connectedness is presented as the cure for boredom. As a half-sensed form of disengagement that emerges in an era of ubiquitous media, boredom bears a close kinship with a condition that Tung Hui-Hu describes as 'digital lethargy', which encompasses a 'recalcitrant set of feelings … of being passive, or wanting to dissociate … or avoiding decisions'.[70] Like digital lethargy, digital boredom cuts 'against the sense of agency and liveness that digital platforms produce', describing 'a period before the question "What must be done?" can be fully articulated'.[71] For much of the time, this kind of digital boredom flies under the radar, feeding into a process of what Susanna Paasonen calls 'digital disaffect': 'a sensation of always being about to attain the thing that will bring satisfaction yet finding it lies just beyond reach'.[72] Platforms have largely been able to instrumentalize this boredom because it so often resides below our conscious awareness, just something there, a felt 'grunge of time, the lint that sticks to all things digital', as MacKenzie Wark so memorably describes boredom.[73]

In Chapter 3, I consider the complex relations between boredom, pleasure and viewer agency that coalesce in a context of always-on televisual spectatorship. I advance the term boredom-on-demand to encapsulate the platform strategies, televisual aesthetics and user practices that have converged around boredom in the context of streaming TV. More specifically, my focus is on a range of televisual trends and user practices that have embraced 'boring' TV in a user-directed context: slow, dull or low-intensity televisual content that is made through streaming platforms and marketed as a means of both multi-tasking and pleasantly zoning out. As I argue in this chapter, while boredom is more frequently constructed as an enemy of entertainment and hence of pleasure, boredom has *also* been re-interpreted as a technique of self-care and a means of coping with the pace and intensity of always-on culture. What I call boredom-on-demand – content that is purposely chosen for its downbeat, dull aesthetic qualities – refers us to the downbeat and desultory pleasures of zoning out with TV; pleasures that co-exist with, and help to maintain, the demands of being a subject in an always-on culture.

This book draws throughout on the concepts of biopolitics and psychopolitics to theorize the role that boredom plays in formatting our bodies, emotions and attention as data that are used to tie us ever closer to our digital devices and feeds. Drawing from the work of Giorgio Agamben, Byung-Chul Han and others, it considers how twenty-first-century media technologies extend modernity's biopolitical project of codifying boredom and its bodily norms. While social media platforms enable users to capture the most banal moments of their ordinary lives, they do so within a context that assigns value to human gestures and emotions through their processes of tagging, classifying, ranking and spreading them. As I argue, this process is explicitly biopolitical, sorting human expression along a continuum between the entertaining and the boring, the viral and the invisible.

Chapter 2, 'How to look bored: Bored bodies and the biopolitics of faciality and gesture in short-form video', draws on the work of Giorgio Agamben to consider the biopolitics of boredom and gesture. Taking as its starting point the seemingly simple assumption that we can recognize boredom when we see it – that we can therefore read boredom from gestures, facial expressions and other bodily cues – this chapter traces the historical development of this idea and considers why it has become an increasingly important premise in a digital network culture. It analyses a wide range of media – including nineteenth-century medical treatises, paintings and literary works, boredom-themed reaction GIFs, Vine videos and emergent affective computing applications – which offer a means of visualizing boredom through facial expressions, gestures and bodily movements. I read this process as biopolitical, in that it translates biopower into data that can be observed, ranked and spread. As I consider through an analysis of a range of boredom-themed Vine videos, gesture is often conscripted as a means of synching the bored body up to networked forms of agency, translating bodily states of stasis into patterned performativity, and reclaiming bored subjects for productivity. However, while the human bodies in these videos are bound up within a biopolitical drive to classify, name and fix the experience of boredom, I argue that boredom-themed content on user-generated platforms still retains a degree of opacity that resists its reduction to instrumental, biopolitical ends. This chapter draws on Agamben's understanding of both boredom and gesture as states of suspension that display the human body beyond instrumental ends; it argues that short-form video formats can still demonstrate what Agamben calls the 'pure mediality' of the human body.[74] By focusing on boredom's state of suspended animation in Vine videos, the chapter shows how Vine videos can and do sometimes also make trouble for the affective promise that boredom can be dissolved by entertainment networks.

The book's final chapter builds on and complicates this argument by considering how entertainment networks operate beyond the context of biopolitics, shaping human behaviour by intervening directly into psychological processes.[75] In his elaboration of the concept of 'digital psychopolitics', Han refers to the myriad forms of 'auto-exploitation' that emerge in a neoliberal regime of ubiquitous computing.[76] In this regime, power is not imposed through restrictions and rules, but instead passes through neoliberal 'performance subjects' who have internalized the demand to constantly manage and optimize their emotions, well-being and general health through the aid of digital technologies. Crucially, this psycho-power is underwritten by an ethos of compulsory positivity and achievement, an incitement to continuous pleasure through digital consumption, and a fantasy of freedom from limits and constraints of any kind. But while digital technologies are promoted through discourses of empowerment and freedom, the self-monitoring and control they offer to individuals amount to a stealthy form of surveillance and control by corporations, which produces value out of human affects, emotions and attention. As Han suggests, this fantasy of freedom is a false and damaging one, which contributes to new forms of auto-exploitation and new pathologies, such as burnout, depression, lethargy and boredom.

Chapter 4, '#BoredintheHouse: TikTok and the rhythms of #lockdownlife', considers how the complex relationships between boredom, networked media and neoliberal discourses surrounding attention and mental well-being have been exposed and intensified in the context of the Covid-19 pandemic. While streaming television played an important role in this context as a technology that would help to manage the tedium of #LockdownLife, participatory platforms such as TikTok gained increased visibility in this context as tools for working through the feelings of stuckness, stasis and restriction that boredom indexes. The chapter argues that social media platforms such as TikTok thrived in the period of the pandemic in part because they offer a means of working through a series of thorny tensions that speak to the condition of lockdown: tensions between limitation and freedom, staying put and staying entertained, and between the collective labours of social duty and the solipsistic pleasures of digital connectivity and performative play. Focusing on the #BoredInTheHouse hashtag challenge, this chapter considers how TikTok offered one means of releasing the cramped stuckness of lockdown boredom into the rhythms and flows of contagious memetic participation. The chapter shows how participatory platforms appealed to the 'bored body problem' by addressing users as both performative players and always-vigilant spectators. In this way, they traded on the promise of making boredom eventful, by filling up dead time and synchronizing both bodies and eyeballs to the strange rhythms of #LockdownLife. In doing so, they also help to visualize what a bored public might look like in an age of digital psychopolitics and point towards a desire for new rhythmic relations to post-pandemic time.

The overarching argument that I advance in this book is that while digital technologies seek to capture, modulate and manage boredom, it is also vital to acknowledge the opportunities that these media might also open up for sensing, expressing and reflecting on boredom in a context that promises to displace it. I analyse the pervasive, low-level, ambient forms of boredom, listlessness and tedium that characterize our engagements with contemporary media, finding spaces for criticality and reflection, as well as cultural imperatives for distraction and displacement. *Entertained or Else: Boredom and Networked Media* thus sheds new light on how boredom has been targeted as a key mechanism of biopolitical and psychopolitical control in the age of 'Covid capitalism', and how it might be framed as an affective resource and a form of resistance to the cognitive and physiological pressures of lockdown life.[77]

1

What to do when you're bored
Gendered boredom and networked media

Over its rich and diverse history, boredom has captured the attention of many authority figures. These boredom experts – spanning the disciplines of philosophy, psychology, medicine, mental health, education and parenting – have assigned a wide range of symptoms and root causes to the condition, evaluating it variously as a positive or negative experience and generally brooding over what can or should be done about it. From Blaise Pascal's recommendation that we should all learn how to sit quietly in our own room,[1] to nineteenth-century medical advice regarding ennui as a fashionable 'female complaint' best treated through leeching, injections, cauterization, rest and excessive feeding,[2] boredom has solicited a whole host of prescriptive instructions as to how these feelings should be addressed. Indeed, to admit to feeling bored in our culture is often taken as an unspoken appeal for guidance on the matter, with boredom advice experts seemingly lurking around every corner. This is perhaps even more the case in a digital network culture, which has constructed boredom as a pervasive and unwanted feeling, which can be chased away through the right recommendation systems. As this chapter will explore, in the twenty-first century, digital technologies, coupled with the neoliberal principles of self-management that undergird them, persist in highlighting boredom as a problem that requires and produces new forms of expertise and self-discipline.

Reflecting on the forms of expertise that converge around boredom in a digital network culture, this chapter focuses on the extremely popular 'What to do When You're Bored' sub-genre of YouTube videos, which are produced by young female YouTubers for an audience of mainly teenage girls. Framing the experience of boredom as both an everyday reality of adolescent life and as a lurking affective danger, these videos model a range of activities that are intended to alleviate or chase away incipient feelings of boredom. By offering a variety of recommendations for how to beat boredom, the young YouTubers that I consider in this chapter perform a variety of affective labour that is increasingly required of gendered subjects in the so-called 'attention economy'[3] of twenty-first-century media. As I argue throughout this book, platforms such as YouTube construct users above all as boredom 'managers': agents who are responsible for, and capable of coordinating, the affective texture of their own experience as it unfolds in real time. And yet this discursive construction of boredom overlooks the significant role that such media play, not only in producing and intensifying new cultural forms of tedium, but also in capturing and modulating the subject's affective experience before she becomes aware of it. Reflecting on the blatant gendering of affect in the YouTube boredom tutorial content genre through the figure of the teenage girl, this chapter asks why this work of boredom management should fall so resoundingly to young women to perform. Why has the figure of the teenage girl been rendered so excessively visible in these YouTube tutorials as an ideal conduit for the monitoring and self-management of boredom? Addressing these questions requires a careful evaluation of the constellation of relations between boredom, attention and gendered subjectivity as these are being (re)articulated in a twenty-first-century context. At the same time, it requires a consideration of how human experience – including the experience of feeling bored – is being affected by non-human ways of sensing, and making sense of, the world.

As I suggested in the introduction to this book, twenty-first-century technologies have brought about a shift in human ways of accessing, sensing and reflecting on the nature of experience. In the twenty-first century, computational media have found new ways of accessing and modulating our sensory experience, and new methods for capturing and commodifying our emotions. While previous media formats such as cinema were always invested in emotional experience, computational media have developed ways of processing and modulating the raw material of sensibility on a bodily level that bypasses the threshold of conscious awareness.[4] This re-tooling of attention and affect by computational media also has significant implications for our understanding of boredom in the twenty-first century. While boredom continues to be shaped by many of the same socio-economic and time pressures that conditioned its emergence during the period of modernity, scholars such as Jonathan Crary, Michael E. Gardiner, Mark Kingwell, Martin Hand and Mark Fisher have suggested that twenty-first-century media have put significant pressure on the profound, existential boredom that thinkers such as Kracauer and Heidegger identified as a critical response to the modern culture of acceleration and mass entertainment. As

Mark Fisher speculates, the late capitalist injunction to fill up empty time has 'neutralised boredom'; as a 'state of absorption', he suggests, boredom is 'now under attack, as a result of the constant dispersal of attention, which is integral to capitalist cyberspace'. While the constant circulation of 'entertaining' content produces vast daily archives of boring media, it also disables boredom as a critical response. As he maintains, no one is bored, and yet everything is boring.[5]

Crucially, in the emerging literature around critical attention studies, such anxieties often converge around adolescents and teenagers, who are mobilized to illustrate concerns about shrinking attention spans and to rehearse arguments about what happens when the human capacity to endure boredom is eroded in an era of digital networks. According to scholars such as N. Katherine Hayles and Bernard Stiegler, the new forms of 'hyper' or 'short-term' attention that have emerged in the twenty-first century raise significant questions about 'trans-generational ways of knowing' that impact on the very foundations of humanistic inquiry.[6] According to Hayles and Stiegler, what we are witnessing in this context is nothing more than a battle for the intelligence of youth, against the 'short-circuited' attention and low thresholds for boredom fostered by new digital technologies.[7] Channelling these same fears about the impact of digital technologies on a younger generation's ability to tolerate feelings of boredom, Sherry Turkle notes, 'What concerns me as a developmental psychologist is watching children grow in this new world where being bored is something that never has to be tolerated for a moment'.[8] As Turkle suggests, concerns about both attention and boredom converge around teenagers in particular because of the important role that boredom has long been understood to play within the formation of subjectivity during the period of adolescence.

In his influential account of boredom, psychoanalyst Adam Phillips links adolescent boredom to a specific experience of temporality, defining it as a 'state of suspended anticipation in which things are started and nothing begins' and as a 'mood of diffuse restlessness which contains that most absurd and paradoxical wish, the wish for a desire'.[9] According to Phillips's psychoanalytic reading, the negative affective state of suspended anticipation that boredom indexes may be painful, but it is through the temporal process of enduring it that the groundwork for meaningful and sustained future encounters is secured. As Mark Kingwell has suggested, this psychoanalytic discourse on boredom shares significant ground with previous philosophical accounts of boredom, both of which view it as a 'crisis of selfhood and desire that must be embraced'.[10] In the twenty-first century, a growing sense of crisis relating to the human capacities for attention and boredom has converged in strategic ways around the media practices of teenagers, whose capacity for sustained critical reflection is imagined to be most at risk in the dangerous new regime of hyper-attention.

This chapter suggests that there are also significant gendered implications of these debates, which are often overlooked in the critical literature on boredom studies, and within wider debates about the attention and affect economies of contemporary media. This short-sightedness about the role of gender in recent scholarship has been acknowledged by Angela McRobbie and Jonathan Beller in their respective interventions into debates about affective labour and the post-Fordist attention economy. As McRobbie notes, much of the recent work in the field of radical political theory that has addressed the centrality of immaterial and affective labour within the context of post-Fordism has largely failed to examine the significance of gender, in spite of the fact that what is premised in these trends is a 'feminization of work'.[11] In a similar vein, Jonathan Beller writes that the emerging scholarship on the attention economy of contemporary media has often entailed either a sidelining or an outright dismissal of the 'racial and gendered formations' that underpin the current re-tooling of attention, dismissing such identity markers as 'somehow epiphenominal' to the process.[12] As Beller insists, dynamics of race and gender are not incidental, but rather *constitutive* of the technologies that emerge to manage and discipline attention in the twenty-first century. Although the technical operations that are used to extract value from work and attention continue to evolve in the twenty-first century, the gendered and racial dynamics of the political economy that drives them have remained largely unchanged. As Beller notes: 'the post-Fordist attention economy still depends upon the patriarchal, white-supremacist, imperialist organisation of the global imaginary to maximise returns'.[13] At the same time, it also depends increasingly on the affective labour of female subjects, as Angela McRobbie suggests when she claims that 'the gender of post-Fordism is female'.[14] With these claims in mind, this chapter will now turn to a reading of boredom management as a vital form of affective labour that is routinely undertaken by teenage girls in the attention economy of twenty-first-century media. As I will suggest, the gendering of boredom through the figure of the teenage girl plays an important role in the way that emergent networked technologies seek to capture and capitalize on the attention and emotion of teenage audiences. Young girls are called on to manage boredom in this context *precisely because* they are the subjects who are *most required* to embody and produce value from boredom in an age of networks.

What to do when you're bored: boredom management as affective labour

The series of 'What to Do When You're Bored' videos made by megastar YouTuber Meg DeAngelis on her MayBaby YouTube channel address boredom as a commonplace, if decidedly unwelcome, experience for teenagers. In the period between July 2014 and June 2016, Meg uploaded five boredom-themed videos to her YouTube channel, including: 'What to Do When You're Bored!', 'What to Do When You're Bored', 'What Girls Do When They're Bored!', 'Weird Things Bored People Do' and 'What to Do When You're Bored During Summer Break'.[15] While some of these videos have since been set to private, the two that remain public on her channel, 'What to do When You're Bored!' and 'What to Do When You're Bored During Summer Break', continue to accrue views, likes and comments – with one viewer commenting in 2021 that 'Quarantine has me watching megs videos again' [*sic*].[16]

All of Meg's boredom-themed videos follow a familiar structure. Ranging between six and ten minutes in length, the videos start with a to-camera monologue where Meg briefly introduces and comments on her own experience of feeling bored, before guiding viewers through a numbered list of activities that they can try out when they are bored in a variety of different circumstances. Although Meg's videos explore a range of activities through which boredom might be successfully dispelled – for instance, building a fort, eating donuts, trying to see if you can lick your elbow – those that are either enabled or enhanced by networked media platforms are given a special priority in the MayBaby universe. Indeed, Meg's status as a self-styled 'social media superstar' – with (at the height of her fame in 2017) over 5.6 million YouTube subscribers, 2.2 million Instagram followers and a range of corporate sponsorship deals – is secured through, and depends on, her ability to engage the attention of her target audience of potentially bored teenagers, and to encourage clicks, likes, comments and other forms of networked participation and consumption.[17]

Meg's expertise as a boredom manager is strongly connected to the way that her videos construct an understanding of what is 'normal' for teenage girls to do when they are bored. In other words, through the advice they give about how to dispel boredom, they produce an ideological framework for modelling appropriate ways of desiring, acting, thinking and being for a young girl. It is important to note that while Meg's boredom videos are still amongst the most popular of all the YouTube videos that address boredom in this way (ranging from around 2.3 million to 6.6 million views, and from 67,000 to 274,000 likes), they conform to what is a fairly standard generic formula that can be found in a whole host of other YouTube videos made by, or featuring, *female* teenagers, both before, during and after the Covid-19 pandemic and associated lockdowns. For instance, Australian YouTuber Gillian Bower has produced a range of list-based boredom tutorials on her YouTube channel since April 2016, including titles such as '10 Fun Things to Do When You're Bored! What to Do When Bored!'[18] and 'DIY Room Decor to Do When You're BORED! Easy DIY Room Decor Ideas!'[19] Californian YouTuber Cassie Diamond devotes several posts to boredom, starting with '4 Fun DIY's to Do When You're Bored!' in 2014, and 'What to Do When You're Bored This Fall! Treats, Activities & More!' in 2015, followed by a series of videos all titled 'Fun Things to Do When You're Bored!' made between 2017 and 2019, another called 'What to Do When You're Bored' in 2019 and the pandemic-themed 'What to Do When You're BORED at HOME!' in April 2020.[20] Like MayBaby's YouTube boredom tutorials, these videos picture young, conventionally attractive women in mainly domestic settings, who address boredom as a familiar problem for teens, before guiding their followers through a list of activities that they should try. The videos rely strongly on the connection between boredom and 'bedroom culture' to establish the vlogger's authenticity and expertise.[21] At the same time, these YouTubers are anything but ordinary; they embody aspects of aspirational personhood that are central to the ideological and affective work that these videos perform through boredom.

Before we move on to consider how MayBaby's boredom-themed content performs this work of boredom management and ideological inculcation, it is worth pausing to explore how these 'What to Do When You're Bored' YouTube tutorials build upon, but also differ in significant ways, from some of the earliest boredom-themed content uploaded to YouTube. Since its launch in 2005, boredom has been a popular topic on the platform, with boredom-related terms used to comment on videos featuring a wide range of activities and subjects. For example, Lilwaybabe's thirty-four-second-long video '2006 Bored and Reading Anything Out Loud' features what appears to be a Black British mother and daughter sitting in a waiting room. Flicking through a glossy magazine, the daughter asks, 'Mum, can I take one of these?' This is then followed by an indistinct but disgruntled-sounding response from the mother as we see the daughter tear a page from the magazine. The camera is shaky, and the video is very low-quality, in keeping with the period and context in which it was produced. This video captures some of the feelings of boredom that occur in spaces like waiting rooms, with the camera's presence presumably playing a role in helping the video's creators to pass the time. But while it comments obliquely on ordinary boredom, it certainly does not position the subjects of the video as experts in the arts of boredom management, as the later YouTube boredom tutorials will do. Rather, it simply observes an everyday scene of boredom as it unfolds.

Similarly, a video by 19film80, 'Bored (2005)', begins with a title card that reads 'Bored', followed by the words 'April & May 2005'; the caption in the description box says simply: 'A boring day'. This video pictures a young Latino man in a series of vignettes captured at different locations in his home: at first, we see him staring off into the distance and hear the sound of a television in the background; later, we see him drink water and then Gatorade; we see him take out his flip phone and pronounce the date 10 April 2005; later, he tries on a straw sunhat and then sits on the floor, again staring into the distance. Like the previous example, 19film80's video conveys a strong sense of boredom and time passing, without any clear attempt to shake off the boredom that the video takes as its subject. PsychoMetalFreak's '14 August 2006 Me Being Bored' is a vlog-style video featuring a teenage girl who is seated on the back porch of her house, speaking directly to the camera. She touches on the topic of boredom a few times, but mostly she shares updates, shows us her pets and her Converse, and discusses other details of her family and school life. The tone is intimate, but the video is diffuse and disorganized, conveying in this way a sense of what it feels like to experience boredom as part of the flow of ordinary adolescent life.

Early videos that adopt the title 'What to Do When You're Bored' start to show some of the characteristics of the later boredom tutorial videos but demonstrate a much broader range of styles, subjects and activities than appear once the format is consolidated as a specific content genre on YouTube. For example, Vividedge06's 'What to Do When You're Bored', which is described in the comments box as an 'artistic spin on boredom', focuses on the daily routine of one British teen as he wakes up, showers, looks out at the street outside, brushes his teeth, gets dressed, applies hair gel, does homework, spins a globe around and around, lies listlessly on his bedroom floor, channel surfs, does sit-ups and so on. ThisisJessandViki's ten-second-long video, 'What To Do When Your Bored' [sic] starts with the caption 'What do we do when we get bored?' The frame then cuts to a shot of two teenage girls in a hard-to-decipher domestic setting, perhaps a bedroom. One of the two girls pretends to strangle the other, and just as both fall out of frame, an end card appears with the word 'THAT!' written on it. By 2008, a range of boredom-themed videos such as Erinbechtold's

'What To Do When You're Bored?' and TheLessThanThrees' 'Episode 2: What To Do When You're Bored' begin to adopt more of the key features of the YouTube boredom tutorial content genre by featuring young, conventionally attractive teenage girls who run through a numbered list of suggestions for how to keep from feeling bored. But in contrast to the tutorials made later by megastar YouTubers such as MayBaby and Cassie Diamond, these are markedly less professionally produced, are more whimsical and seem less invested in promoting the expertise of the YouTuber as boredom manager. If boredom was quickly established as a recurring topic of YouTube videos from the platform's early history, by 2014 the 'What To Do When You're Bored' YouTube tutorial had become firmly established as a distinct content genre for mainly affluent, often white, gender-normative and conventionally attractive young women to share tips with their followers for activities to try whenever they feel bored. But why should this be so?

The gendering of boredom through the figure of the young girl is a very significant part of the boredom tutorial content genre on YouTube and plays a role within the wider mechanisms of discipline and control that structure power relations in a digital network society. As Anita Harris argues, 'Young women have taken on a special role in the production of the late modern social order and its values. They have become a focus for the construction of an ideal late modern subject who is self-making, resilient, and flexible'.[22] In the attention economy of networked media, women and young girls are increasingly called upon to produce value for media corporations, through the deployment of highly 'gendered skills of flexibility, networking and affective labor'.[23] As Jacqueline Arcy notes, although women have 'historically been tasked with affective and relational work', this expectation for women to perform emotion management 'is intensified in the digital realm'.[24] It is important to add here that such expectations have expanded in the twenty-first century to include younger women and girls, who are a key demographic for platforms such as YouTube and Instagram. While social media platforms have created exciting new prospects for entrepreneurial young women – aspirations for attainment that are 'often physically embodied in the blogger, the vlogger, or the Instagrammer'[25] – these opportunities are accompanied by new forms of surveillance and discipline, which define the terms of their success. As scholars such as Wendy Chun, Brooke Erin Duffy and Amy Shields Dobson have suggested, widespread cultural anxieties about digital culture have also been framed in gendered terms, piggybacking onto long-standing stereotypes of teenage girls as either promiscuous and vulnerable, or 'whimsical and inconstant, flighty and narcissistic',[26] and hence in need of protection from the lurking dangers of networked sociality. As Dobson notes, 'girls and young women are seen as active users and media producers in the social media landscape, but they are often judged as being active in the "wrong" ways – thought to be engaged in projects of self-representation driven by vanity, or incessant communication driven by insecurities and trivialities'.[27] The attention of young girls is thus commodified as an important source of value for media corporations, at the same time as it is derided through perceptions of girl culture as trivial, shallow, narcissistic and flighty. In turn, such perceptions function to disguise the affective labour of boredom management as so much internet 'fun', reproducing instead the problematic idea that the young, entrepreneurial women who increasingly sustain the post-Fordist economy through their immaterial labour are only in it for the 'lolz'. The trenchant reality of this situation, as I will argue, is that while the post-Fordist attention economy feeds off of the young girl's ability to perform the affective work of boredom management, it also frustrates a mobilization of boredom as an active critical response.

The boredom-themed videos that I examine in this chapter are concrete examples of the kind of affective labour that has been outsourced to young women in the context of post-Fordism. By relegating the affective labour of boredom management increasingly to young girls, these videos also re-activate historical gendered divisions between 'a higher-valued form of boredom understood as male and a lower-valued boredom understood as female'.[28] As Patrice Petro and Allison Pease have suggested, this specifically gendered understanding of boredom helped to catalyse important feminist responses in the early twentieth century, amongst modernist writers who described boredom as both a 'chronological descriptor of women's lived experience in time, but also as the dilemma of accessing a subjectivity that was without previous definition'.[29] As such, in literary modernism, boredom serves as an important 'gauge of the feminist struggle' and the 'tremendous difficulty women experienced in realizing and pursuing their desires, and thus in realizing themselves as anything other than bored'.[30] While boredom has often been treated as an individual complaint or even a personal failing of those who are unable to properly direct their passions or attention, as both Petro and Pease suggest, this atomization of bored women works to disguise the shared, structural factors that condition it. As Pease suggests, in the modern novel it is acknowledged as a shared condition, a 'structure of feeling' that expresses the conflict between women's nascent desire for autonomy and agency in this period, and her realization of how limited, relative and contingent her newfound freedoms were.[31] In doing so, the modernist novel performed an important form of political work by showing women as collectively bored – not as a result of a personal deficit, but as a reflection of their position under patriarchy. These novels hence produce an intimate public, or a 'place of recognition and reflection' where women could recognize themselves collectively as bored.[32]

Meg's videos and their treatment of boredom as an experience through which young women learn to navigate their new place within a post-Fordist attention economy suggest significant parallels with the context of literary modernism and the nascent feminist politics of boredom. Indeed, the boredom tutorials that I consider in this chapter also index the tensions and contradictions that young women face as they enter into a networked digital economy as desiring entrepreneurial agents. On the one hand, the 'What to Do When You're Bored' YouTube content genre creates an intimate public space through which young women are able to recognize and reflect on their own experiences of boredom, to sound out the contours of their future desiring selves and to produce themselves as aspirational agents. On the other hand, in the post-Fordist attention economy, the performance and labour of aspiration rely on, and continue to reproduce, highly circumscribed understandings of gender, race, class, sexuality, ethnicity and ability, which in turn limit the forms that this desire might take.[33] While I want to take seriously the role that YouTube boredom tutorials might play in opening up a collective space for sounding out boredom and desire, this potential is held in tension with the platform affordances, norms and ideologies that mitigate against a recognition of boredom as a shared, structural condition. I will argue that as examples of boredom management, these videos work mostly to neutralize the critical work of boredom and to disable it as a politicized feminist response.

A conspicuous but key feature of all of these videos is that while they are devoted to the topic of boredom and call on a shared understanding of the experience amongst their audiences, they do not prioritize the recording function of the YouTube platform in order to capture and reflect on the sensory and affective processes at stake in an experience of boredom. On the contrary, although the videos use boredom as a seemingly universal point of identification for their audiences, the sometimes complex and ambivalent sensations, feelings and thoughts to which boredom might give rise are rarely, if ever, alluded to, and never addressed in any great detail; instead, these videos evoke boredom only briefly for the sake of moving viewers past it. In these videos, then, boredom is targeted precisely for its value as a transitional state; videos such as these capture the attention of teenage audiences by intensifying and capitalizing on the 'wish for a desire' that Phillips suggests is inherent in the mood, and by rapidly supplying the various authorized forms that this desire might take. The temporality through which these videos work plays an important role in this process: rather than highlighting boredom's value as a mode of hesitant introspection, these videos seek to rework its temporality within the decidedly short-term circuits of networked desire, whose ephemeral objects of attention are endlessly re-invented and re-invested.

Like other boredom-themed YouTube tutorials, Meg's videos stage-manage this temporality of boredom in particularly interesting ways. While the bulk of the running time in her videos is given over to illustrating activities through which her viewers might avoid boredom, they tend to feature brief segments in which Meg verbally describes, or even physically acts out, what it feels like to be bored. For example, in Figure 1.1 below, we see Meg with a laptop cradled in her lap; she is lying upside down on a chair, her head thrown back in frustrated ennui, seeming to have reached the end of her tether. Figure 1.2 shows Meg posing in another classic boredom pose, her dejected face cradled in a fist held to her temple, while in Figure 1.3 she takes action by messaging her friends to inform them that she is bored.

These segments call on audiences' previous familiarity with boredom, but also work to shape specific ways of thinking about and responding to it. In her first video, 'What to Do When You're Bored!', Meg addresses her audience by saying: 'Hey Guys, it's Meg. So, it's summer, and I don't know about you, but I'm bored of being bored because being bored is really boring; and also, I'm bored of being told that I'm a boring person because I'm bored. You feel me?' What is noteworthy about this preamble is the emphatically tautological description of boredom it provides: she feels bored of being bored because being bored is boring. On the level of content, Meg's description – and the expression of slightly disgusted consternation that accompanies it – evokes boredom's condition of stalled agency, and the feelings of 'dreary agitation' and 'cramped restlessness' that it often arouses.[34] These sequences gesture towards a phenomenology of boredom, in which Meg's vlog camera is charged with the task of conveying what boredom feels like: picturing the sensations, bodily postures and affective intensities that are implicated in the experience. In some ways, this short opening sequence is reminiscent of the early boredom-themed videos on YouTube that I

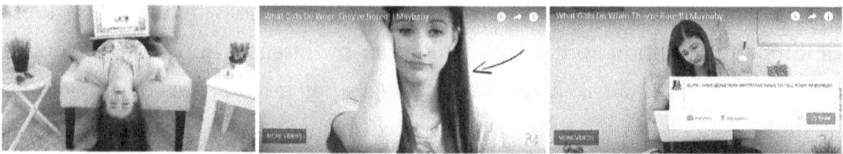

Figures 1.1–1.3 'What Girls Do When They're Bored' by MayBaby © YouTube 2015.

discussed at the beginning of this chapter. However, Meg's performance of what it feels like to be bored is relentlessly stage-managed, in ways that are clearly intended to shore up the idea of the bored subject as a bad subject: the condition of being bored is so unambiguously negative that it threatens to transfer its abject negativity onto the subject, defining the bored subject as boring – a quality that is clearly not sought-after within the MayBaby universe. In a similar vein, Meg's second video, 'What to Do When You're Bored', begins with her account of a 'special kind of bored' when 'you know you have stuff to do, but those things that you have to do are also boring … and I know that if I do those things they'll just be boring too and I'll stay bored'. As with the tautological definition of boredom offered in Meg's first video, this evocation of boredom hints at the feeling of temporal suspension implicit in boredom: the idea of 'staying bored' evokes an image of stalled anticipation that continually circles back around to more boredom, rather than moving past, or away from, it. Like networked entertainments sites such as *Boreburn* and *Boredom Therapy*, these videos mark out boredom as the enemy of enjoyment, framing it as a problem that can and should be expediently managed through networked forms of attention and interaction. By contrasting the bored subject with the perpetually entertained subject, the videos also construct Meg's highly idealized lifestyle as both desirable and attainable for her teenage viewers. While the boredom-avoidance advice offered by Meg may seem relatively mundane, it serves an important role in establishing Meg's authority as a lifestyle expert – someone who embodies the image of the 'good life' to which her audience can aspire. As Tania Lewis notes of the emergence of 'lifestyle media' in the early twenty-first century, '[w]hat lifestyle programming sells to the audience are not just products but ways of living and managing one's life'.[35] As such, she notes, lifestyle experts 'represent a mode of collective identity that brings together optimal forms of consumption with a kind of rationalization or informationalization of everyday life'.[36] Caught up within this informationalization of everyday life, these videos may allow us to glimpse at boredom's downbeat sensibilities, but they do so in order to frame boredom as an object for lifestyle management – as an unruly feeling which must be properly addressed by their teenage viewers if they are to avoid being reduced to the abject status of the 'boring bored' person.

But while these descriptions evoke the idea of being bored and mark it out as an unambiguously unwelcome experience, the dominant affective mode through which the videos perform boredom is anything but dull and listless. Rather, the videos double down on their promise of dissipating boredom right from the very start through the excessively positive affectivity that they work to produce at every level. This positivity is communicated through Meg's distinctively upbeat delivery style, which contrasts starkly with the performed boredom that we see in the opening sequences. She often remarks in these and other videos, for example, that she has had 'way too much coffee, again', and frequently speaks so quickly that her thought processes seem to lag behind her stream of words, to the extent that she often loses her place or gets tongue-tied. Boredom's sense of dullness is also countered by the bright, candy-coloured mise-en-scène of her bedroom settings, which are frequently updated and taken as the subject of other YouTube tutorials, such as '10 DIY Room Décor Project Ideas You NEED to try!', and 'DIY Room Décor Tumblr Room Makeover!'[37]

The fast-paced editing style and quirky sound cues also play an important role in affectively modulating boredom by eliminating any sense of dead time and producing a sense of pace, rhythm and future-oriented anticipation within the static frame of Meg's vlog camera. Quite apart from the activities that these videos prescribe to alleviate boredom, the affective tone that they generate plays a key role in modulating boredom's sense of stuckness or ambivalence – translating it into the kind of positive affective encounter that is more likely to encourage continued viewer engagement and to be spread through networked screens. In short, although Meg introduces boredom as the topic of these videos, feelings of boredom are scarcely found in them, since the point of these tutorials is precisely to find ways of making boredom disappear.

Indeed, as Meg swiftly reassures audiences towards the end of her prologue in 'What to Do When You're Bored', she is 'here to help'. Her goal, she says, is to get viewers 'unbored', by showing them 'silly little things' they can do when they are bored. The carefully constructed temporal structure of the videos also plays an important role in this process of affective modulation. In the first of her boredom videos, Meg's description of boredom is interrupted mid-flow by an extra-diegetic intervention in the form of a text pane (with accompanying harp music), which is inserted while the video is momentarily paused, to inform viewers that Meg is 'going through a face sticker obsession, so if you're wondering what is under neath [*sic*] my eyes they're stickers okay thanks bye!' (Figure 1.4).

Even while Meg is rehearsing what it feels like to be bored, this performance of boredom's downbeat, killjoy affectivity is interrupted in favour of a (celestially inflected) extradiegetic commentary from a present tense in which boredom has already been successfully displaced. This temporal disruption contributes to the processes of affective modulation that are the very *raison d'être* of these videos. Here, it has the effect of reassuring bored viewers that boredom can be easily upgraded into a more intensive affective experience – traded in, in this case, for a face sticker obsession. Other videos in the series seek to modulate the affective and temporal experience of boredom in slightly different ways. 'What to Do When You're Bored' and 'What to Do When You're Bored on Summer Break' contain short montage sequences that in each case *precede* Meg's ensuing verbal accounts of what she feels like when she's bored. In these opening sequences, we see in preview format a montage of the activities that will feature later as items on Meg's numbered lists. These brief segments use a rapid editing style and an upbeat soundtrack to illustrate 'future' Meg happily whiling away her time through various tasks that she is about to recommend to viewers in the tutorial. In 'What to Do When You're Bored', Meg first addresses audiences by telling them: 'Hey guys, it's your girl Meg, and I'm here to help you when you're bored'. This is followed by an eight-second montage which pictures Meg dancing

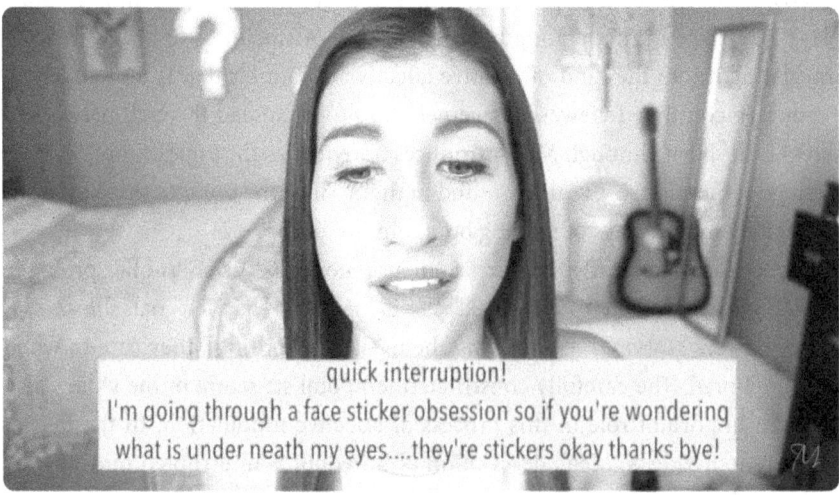

Figure 1.4 'What to Do When You're Bored!' by MayBaby © YouTube 2014.

around her room wearing a pair of bright pink Skullcandy headphones; Meg watching a video on her MacBook Pro while drinking a cold beverage out of an oversized Mason jar, Meg making coffee from her Mr Coffee-branded Keurig coffee brewer, Meg posing for iPhone selfies, Meg making iTunes playlists on her iPhone and so on. Aside from the obvious point that the activities pictured here are thoroughly branded and eminently 'Instagrammable', the fact that they precede her description of what boredom feels like is crucial to the way that these videos seek to modulate this feeling: by the time we hear her talk about it, boredom's sense of temporal suspension and its location within the mundane everyday has *already* been modulated by the affective anticipation of a time *after* boredom. In this way, the videos work to ensure that from the moment they commence viewing, audiences are always-already-no-longer bored. This mood of affective anticipation, meanwhile, is bound up with, and helps to reproduce, problematic ideas about gendered subjectivity in a social media context. The affective promise of no longer being bored is explicitly tied to the putative pleasures of presenting oneself as an object of socially mediated perception – an idealized and gendered object of the Instagram gaze.

However, this strategy of dividing the temporality of boredom into shorter and shorter micro-temporal circuits, which can be endlessly re-ordered and refreshed, also comes with a catch: while these videos send out the reassuring message that boredom can always be evaded through lists, they also imply that, once the video ends, boredom might return. In this way, boredom is produced as a looming future threat at the same time that it is foreclosed as a possibility within the present. Indeed, the nature of the video series itself suggests that the work of boredom management is never done but needs to be continually refreshed through repeatedly renewed acts of networked interaction. In short, these videos produce a temporality in which boredom is relegated to the past (evoked as an experience that is already in the process of being left behind) and projected into the future (as a looming threat, which might return), but is never available in the real time of viewing. As Mark Fisher suggests, they produce a time in which '[n]o one is bored, everything is boring'.[38]

If these videos succeed in their aim of converting bored viewers into swarms of what we might call digital 'unbored' – a term whose association with the undead usefully describes a state of being bored and incapable of feeling bored at the same time – they do so through a promise that they can protect viewers from the negative affectivity of boredom, by re-directing its obstructed agency and suspended temporality outward, dissipating it into the short-term circuits of networked participation. In the process, the complex negativities at play within the restless affectivity of boredom are captured and modulated *before* the viewer has time to fully process them; boredom is evoked in a brief window that is, following Mark Hansen's understanding of twenty-first-century media, 'long enough for viscerality but not long enough for contemplation'.[39] What counts most here is not the camera's ability to capture a time in which Meg *was* bored, but its ability, as Hansen suggests, to anticipate the future, and to thereby facilitate connections that are the foundations of social media. While these videos downplay the value of recording as a means of 'capturing durational traces of human experience', they rework it as a means of constructing 'the connections that underlie contemporary media networks'.[40] Far from rendering an experience of boredom visible and palpable for their audiences, these videos work to disperse it into an amorphous structure of feeling that is everywhere and nowhere, and which belongs to everyone and no one. As such, the boredom that is specific to the exhausting and tedious forms of affective labour that are demanded especially of young girls in the context of YouTube is not legible as either a symptom of, or as a response to, the material conditions that produce it. These videos therefore work to disable a collective politics of boredom as a gendered condition, by re-working its temporality: making it appear generalized and subjectless.

A crucial factor in the success of Meg's videos is the way that they seek to capitalize on the affective feedback loop that is established between viewer and video by translating viewer agency into specific interactive commands. The videos exploit the affordances of networked media, explicitly enlisting audiences in the promotion of the MayBaby brand, by asking viewers to help get the videos to a specified number of likes – a gesture which bookends most of the videos. Similarly, many of the activities that Meg recommends for becoming 'unbored' refer viewers back to platforms and products with which Meg is associated. For example, items six and eight on the 'What to do When You're Bored!' video instruct viewers to watch all of Meg's videos and to follow her on Twitter or Instagram – an operation which, as she tells viewers, will take 'eight seconds' if they already have an account and 'sixteen seconds' if they need to create an account before then following her. It is significant that this video quantifies the gestural activities of liking and following in such specific terms, as part of its address to viewers as potentially networked agents. By framing these gestures as both quick and effortless, the video frames boredom within an explicitly networked attention and affect economy, in which reflex action is privileged over deliberation. In so

Figure 1.5 'What to Do When You're Bored' by MayBaby © YouTube 2014.

doing, as Hansen suggests, videos such as these play a role in helping 'today's data and culture industries to accomplish their goal of tightening the circuit between solicitation and response'.[41] Similarly, the 'What to Do When You're Bored' video provides details about how viewers can create animal avatars of themselves using the 'Pocket Avatar' mobile app. Then, viewers are invited to upload their avatars onto Twitter using the hashtag '#BOREDWITHMEG' which appears across the bottom of the screen in the screenshot pictured below (Figure 1.5).

Others announce meet-ups at which her fans will have the opportunity to 'come hang out, chill, and take fun selfies' with Meg.[42] This possibility of *being bored with* is both a decisive and deceptive aspect of these videos' appeal. On the one hand, the idea of being *bored with* Meg taps into one of the primal fantasies of networked communication: namely, that networks bring people together; that they forge communities that might overspill the boundaries between online and off; and that they might thereby compensate for, or eliminate, feelings of boredom and loneliness that are commonplace amongst teens. Indeed, the video 'What to Do When You're Bored!' makes this connection between boredom and loneliness explicit, as Meg recommends starting a YouTube channel when her viewers are bored, telling them: 'You can be lonely in your room, or you can be lonely in your room with a cam and internet friends, and I think the second option is a lot better'. As Meg indicates here, boredom and loneliness are often intertwined in adolescence, and networked media are framed increasingly as a means of attenuating both unwanted experiences. While most of the viewers of these videos will not necessarily follow Meg's advice about setting up their own YouTube channel, many of them do use the technical affordances of the MayBaby YouTube page, and other media channels that are linked through it, to comment on the videos and to share them with others. Through these comments pages, users are able to generate a sense of being *bored with*, as opposed to simply being bored. Beyond the content of what is exchanged through such gestures, the activities of interactive multitasking – watching, scrolling, reading, commenting, sharing, liking – help to produce new rhythms that work to break up boredom's sense of cramped listlessness.

In this respect, the content of these videos is perhaps secondary to the connections they promise to foster, and to the sense of 'networked publics' that they may thus help to create. As danah boyd suggests, social media 'allows contemporary teens to envision themselves as part of a collectively imagined community'.[43] As an affective experience held in common, boredom holds the potential to operate as a very powerful social glue, bringing a diverse audience of teenagers together and connecting them through the range of communicative interfaces that are associated with the MayBaby brand – from online discussion forums and social media platforms, to live appearances at which fans can mingle with each other, and meet Meg in person.

However, as Wendy Chun reminds us, we may want to remain wary of the 'banal and impoverished notion of friendship' that often underwrites such promises of connection.[44] As Chun points out, the 'imagined connections' fostered by social media are grounded less in an established sense of solidarity *with* others than they are in the formation of specific *habits* – 'projected links based on frequent and potential repetition'.[45] In this context, she notes, 'the strength of a friendship – its weight – is gauged by the frequency of certain actions' rather than on more qualitative measures, such as a mutual sense of trust and support that might be tested and confirmed over time.[46] In this way, networked media platforms such as the MayBaby YouTube channel capitalize on both the 'wish for a desire' that Phillips argues is at stake in boredom, and on the desire for connection that many teenagers experience as a normal part of their everyday lives. Although it is crucial to recognize this 'wish for a desire' as an important part of negotiating one's sense of self in adolescence, it is also vital to see how platforms such as YouTube keep this search moving forward, never letting the viewer's attention rest for too long on any one object. Indeed, as Hansen and Pettman suggest, today's 'data and culture industries' profit largely from the sense of cognitive opacity that is produced as people vainly struggle to keep up with the rapid, short circuits of digital networks. Downplaying the value of boredom and loneliness as modes of critical introspection, which might help teenagers imagine and test out their relationships to the world and to other subjects and deflecting the value of being *bored with* as a genuinely collective experience, the videos considered here discursively frame these feelings instead as unambiguous threats that must be quickly discharged through endlessly renewed, individualized acts of media engagement. In the process, the very complex affective and sensory experiences of feeling bored or lonely in adolescence are captured, modulated and rendered functional, translated into actions and gestures of staying in touch, constantly updating, contributing to the conversation. Framed in this way, the hashtag '#BOREDWITHMEG' may resonate less as a collective expression of a shared affective experience, than it does a mode of (micro-)celebrity branding, which monetizes boredom by converting potentially bored teens into swarms of digital 'unbored' – networked subjects whose engrained habits, gestures and actions create value for both the MayBaby brand and the YouTube corporation. It is also important to acknowledge that these gestures of sharing are anything but gender-neutral, as Kyra D. Gaunt suggests when she notes that 'numbers of views are the new currency in a digital attention economy, and girls are becoming this economy's free distributed laborers'.[47] At the same time, the work performed by these young women is consistently disguised through the problematic notion that young girls are driven through some kind of 'natural' gender imperative to socialize on these platforms. In other words, the visibility of this work *as work* is compromised through the pre-established gendered infrastructures through which it is framed. This is something that Kimberly Ann Hall acknowledges when she writes that 'the labor of performance within networked sociality … is rarely characterized as labor, because it is typically theorized as social, or communicative, and thus outside the sphere or labor'.[48]

On a representational level, then, YouTube video tutorials such as these consolidate an affective grammar of twenty-first-century boredom, which teaches teenage audiences to remain vigilant against signs of incipient boredom and models appropriate and inappropriate ways of managing it. However, on an operational level, media platforms such as YouTube are able to intervene at a level prior to sensory or cognitive awareness, re-tooling the relationship between affect, deliberation and action. In this sense, Fisher is right to affirm that 'there is no longer any subject capable of being bored', since digital networks protect the subject from the full force of this affect and work to dissolve boredom's constitutive negativity and its condition of obstructed agency into the injunction to interact. However, what the critical literature on boredom in the context of twenty-first-century media has failed to address is the gendering of this experience. As I have suggested, video platforms such as YouTube work through attention to also perpetuate highly traditional ideas about gender and to circumscribe the terms of the young girl's participation within this context. In doing so, they work to produce the category of young girlhood as inherently communicative and perpetually networked, and to disguise this affective labour as so much internet 'fun'.

Fisher's otherwise prescient account of boredom 2.0 falls short of engaging with the full implications of his own argument, perhaps because of the sense of nostalgia that his account conveys for a time when boredom was still commensurate with a (male) subject who could feel it, and who could, in turn, draw from it to 'produce something' of cultural value.[49] Aside from their implicit devaluing of a 'shallow' boredom that is gendered female, these responses also run the risk of reducing a highly complex media attention ecology to a 'moral critique of the psychological subject' who 'can never pay *enough* attention to what *really matters*'.[50] Indeed, as I have shown in my analysis of the MayBaby YouTube boredom tutorials, it is precisely this idea of the subject as fully commensurate with her own thoughts and emotions – and hence responsible for properly managing them – that the media and culture industries exploit in order to keep young girls ensnared within the attention and affect ecology of digital networks. Such networks rely on girls as attention and affect 'managers', responsible for, and capable of coordinating, the affective texture of their own experience as it unfolds in real time. Social media platforms in particular thrive on this idea of the subject as fully commensurate with, and responsible for reporting back on, her own emotions and experiences. Young girls are positioned as the ideal subjects of boredom management precisely because the affective labour that they are called on to perform in this context can be passed off as just 'what girls do'. The shallow boredom that we experience increasingly in a networked culture is thus transferred over onto young girls, whose role it is to manage.

And yet, as I have also suggested, this overlooks the significant role that such media play, not only in producing and intensifying new cultural forms of tedium – for example, the boredom that is involved in endlessly scrolling through feeds and navigating a potentially infinite system of networked links – but also in capturing and modulating the subject's affective experience before he or she becomes aware of it. Indeed, on a non-representational level, such videos also have the potential to expose us to a different kind of boredom and tedium, one that's connected to the technical affordances of streaming platforms such as YouTube, where videos with similar content are joined together to form their own self-sustaining feedback loops. Over time, teenage viewers who subscribe to channels such as the MayBaby YouTube channel may find themselves exposed to the structural boredom that is generated by YouTube's endlessly listing, endlessly looping aesthetic. Although digital media platforms such as YouTube rely on strategies of repetition and reiteration in order to hook audiences and to intensify our engagements with screen-based media, they can also, as Carol Vernallis notes, produce a distinct feeling of being 'stuck in a loop', as the pulse of excitement or interest sooner or later segues into boredom, which is in turn re-invested in the search for new intensities, anticipations and attachments.[51] Trying to keep up with, or make sense of, the pulse of networked media is in itself exhausting and profoundly tedious, and as David M. Berry claims, 'the constant flow of real-time streams of information and data that rush past us in increasing volumes' in a digital network culture can also produce a pervasive mood of bland indifference, as we try to make sense of our data feeds through something like what he calls a 'bureaucratic process of classification or filing'.[52] In a similar vein, Richard Grusin notes that while the 'anticipatory temporality' that is established through networked media can produce a heightened sense of alertness, it can also generate 'a muted or low-level affect of waiting or passing time'.[53]

As a result, the networked subject is faced with a double bind in which she is expected to manage feelings of boredom increasingly through the very same technical processes that produce and perpetuate them in the first place. As Mark Hansen suggests, these processes of affective mediation also take place well beneath the threshold of human perception, impacting on our experience in ways that are sometimes, but not always, available to conscious awareness. Because twenty-first-century media have, as Shane Denson aptly puts it, 'a direct line to our innermost processes of becoming in time', we can no longer frame boredom as a resource that is somehow beyond, or resistant to, these forms of mediation.[54] Rather, it is only by acknowledging the distributed nature of boredom in the twenty-first century that we can begin to assess its impact and possibilities, as this hybrid experience of boredom is fed-forward for human consciousness to grapple with and to act on. At the same time, it is important to focus on how these technologies that target boredom through micro-temporal circuits are still stitched into a patriarchal imaginary, which relies increasingly on the labour of young women at the same time as it reproduces problematic gendered hierarchies and divisions. A vital task for both 'boredom studies' and 'critical attention studies' lies in acknowledging the significance of gendered subjectivity for the constellation of relations between attention and boredom as they are emerging in a twenty-first-century context. Indeed, as I have suggested, an important first step towards re-imagining what a collective feminist response to boredom might look like today consists of rendering visible both the experience of boredom and the work of boredom management that teenage girls are regularly required to perform in a network culture, rather than passing it off as so much Internet fun.

2

How to look bored

Bored bodies and the biopolitics of faciality and gesture in short-form video

Have you ever had occasion, while speaking to a friend or significant other, to pause and ask yourself: *am I boring them*? For anyone who has ever felt overcome by this type of uncertainty, the instructional website WikiHow provides step-by-step advice in an article entitled 'How to Know if a Person is Getting Bored of You'. Amongst other methods, the piece advocates scrutinizing your companion's body language to detect tell-tale signs of boredom: is your interlocutor 'facing you head on' and mirroring your body language, or are they 'slouching or hunching, crossing [their] arms or looking down or away'? Are they 'evasive, downcast, or wandering around the room' with a 'spacey, far-away look'? Do they nod continuously (more precisely, do they nod more than three times) without meeting your gaze? Or maybe they seem calm, 'standing quite still, with few gestures, flourishes, or pronounced facial expressions'.[1] After reading this advice, the uncertain reader may understandably feel even more uncertain, given how commonplace, context-dependent and open to interpretation many of these bodily expressions are.

Under the auspices of demystifying boredom, this WikiHow article instead illuminates some of the difficulties of locating this complex emotion as an object of knowledge. Indeed, across the growing field of Boredom Studies, the one thing that researchers seem to agree on, despite their many differences of approach and opinion, is that boredom is slippery and hard to define. As Wendell O'Brien puts it: 'There is a problem of identifying what boredom essentially is – a part of which is the problem of determining whether it is one thing or something that comes in a variety of importantly different forms or modes'.[2] As psychoanalyst Adam Phillips memorably notes, 'we should not speak of boredom but of boredoms, since the notion itself includes a multiplicity of moods and feelings that resist analysis'.[3] In his *Philosophy of Boredom*, Lars

Svendsen complicates the matter further when he points out that when asked, many people have difficulty knowing whether they are bored or not. If they do admit to feeling bored, people often find it very hard to say *why* they are bored.[4] In short, boredom is a slippery condition that throws up challenges to both objective and subjective scrutiny.

And yet, despite these epistemological challenges, there persists a culturally constructed idea of what boredom looks like. For example, when asked to draw 'a bored person', the AI image generator *Dall-e Mini* returns images that picture boredom as a (white male) condition that involves a slumped posture and one or both hands cradling the chin or forehead, or – in a somewhat less conventional

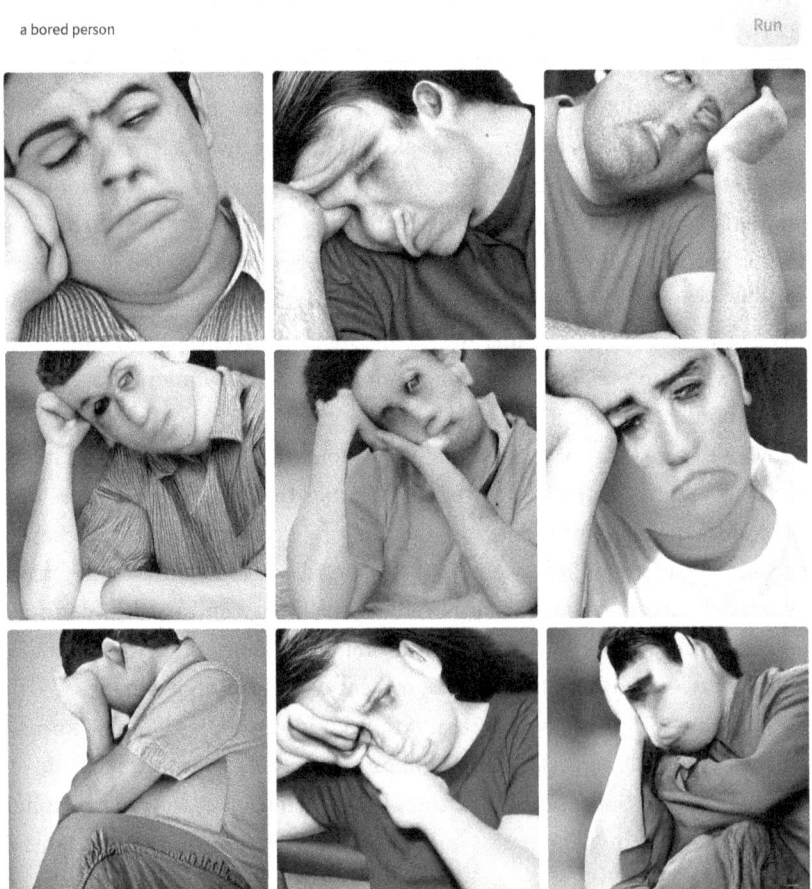

twist – fingers plunging into the eye or mouth (Figure 2.1). A second request to picture 'someone who is bored' reveals a few additional dimensions: boredom is black and white, a world leeched of colour; it has something to do with cats (Figure 2.2). A third prompt in the form of a question, 'what does boredom look like' conjures up a more nervous atmosphere dominated by the colour green, with line drawn figures whose heads are placed on desks or slumped in front of laptops; some figures with large round eyes appear to be juggling handheld devices or wielding other hard-to-decipher objects (Figure 2.3). Trained on a dataset gathered from millions of images and corresponding text descriptions

Figures 2.1–2.3 'A Bored Person', 'Someone Who Is Bored' and 'What Does Boredom Look Like?' Images returned from a search generated by the author © *Dall-e Mini* 2023.

scraped from the internet, social media, search engines, image-hosting websites and other sources, *Dall-e Mini* offers an intriguing snapshot of boredom as it is imagined by, and intersects with, twenty-first-century digital technologies.[5] As this chapter will explore in more detail, this cultural construction of what boredom looks like is being rehearsed, catalogued and revised daily in a post-digital culture that is obsessed with emotions and their relationship to the lived, expressive, gesturing body.

This chapter takes as its starting point the seemingly simple assumption that we can know if someone is bored; that we can, therefore, recognize boredom by reading it on the body. It traces how this idea came about and considers why it has become an increasingly important premise in a digital culture. Such speculations about how we might read boredom through bodily movements, posture, gesture and facial expression have a long-established history in Western cultures. During the period of modernity, boredom and the study of human movement and gesture co-evolved as part of a much wider biopolitical drive to classify and understand human interiority through outward signs. In the twenty-first century, the assumption that our emotions can be observed and indexed to bodily movements and facial micro-expressions has been central to many technological developments, including affective computing applications that claim to provide privileged insight into human emotions, behaviour and desires. It is also this premise that drives much of the communicative activity that takes place across digital network cultures, through reaction GIFs and user-generated social media formats, which offer a means of sharing contagious emotion through facial expressions, gestures and bodily movements. As this chapter will go on to explore, this process is biopolitical, in the sense that it attempts to make the human body and emotions available as data that can be captured, tagged and spread – put to use across a wide range of digital contexts.

The chapter will focus on a selection of short-form videos made on the (now archived) social media platform Vine, which use boredom-related hashtags – including #bored, #boredom, #BoredomStrikes, #BoredomKills and #BoredAF – to classify bodily movements and gestures, and to link them to a situation, mood or state of mind that is thereby linked to boredom. The chapter will place these #boredom Vine videos within a historical continuum, analysing them as part of a long-standing biopolitical process through which the bored body's recalcitrant energies have been surveilled and managed, disciplined and shaped. Tracing a line through these various historical endeavours to capture and fix the experience of boredom and drawing from Giorgio Agamben, the chapter will go on to situate #boredom Vine videos within the emergent attention economy of twenty-first-century media, which aims to extract profit from even the most mundane of our daily gestures and experiences, including the experience of being bored.

Like other digital media formats, Vine videos display a particular obsession with facial expression and with the 'division of bodily movements, actions, and gestures into discrete parts'.[6] In #boredom Vines, Viners commonly turn their cameras on themselves, attempting to capture what the experience of boredom feels like through (micro-)gestures and facial expressions, before spreading their videos through the app's social network, ostensibly in an effort to drive boredom away. Gesture and faciality are thus positioned in these Vines as communicative interfaces that disclose an internal mood or affective state, and as a physical means through which this same affective state might be forestalled or discharged into action. This chapter analyses the often-uncomfortable tensions that emerge in these videos between digital network culture's demand for both entertaining content and sufficiently entertained subjects, and the obdurate state of lethargy and stalled agency that these videos sometimes, but don't always, express. In general, I am interested in thinking about what happens to our understanding of boredom – what Elizabeth Goodstein calls 'an experience without qualities' – when we focus on it alongside gesture and facial expression, tracing its relation to the lived body.[7]

Boredom and the biopolitics of gesture

This chapter draws from Giorgio Agamben's understanding of gesture as a crucial site through which human experience is disciplined and converted into biopower. In his essay 'Notes on Gesture', Agamben describes a 'generalized catastrophe of the sphere of gestures',[8] which he locates at the end of the nineteenth century, in the wake of the medical and proto-cinematic experiments of Gilles de la Tourette, Edweard Muybridge, Jules-Étienne Marey and others. These experiments attempted to analyse human movement by breaking it down into discrete patterns, fixing it as a series of frozen images and thereby estranging subjects from a kind of gestural commons. Gesture is thus bound up with modernity's biopolitical attempts to investigate, systematize, map and classify the human body. As Deborah Levitt points out, although Agamben does not mention them specifically in this essay, Frederick Winslow Taylor's time and motion studies are another key example of this same method of subjecting human movement to scientific scrutiny. His time-lapse photographs of workers' movements aimed to discover 'any individual expressivity contained in the gestures of factory workers – and to excise it in favour of perfectly homogenous and efficient movements synchronized with the hands of the clock'.[9] In a similar vein, Jules-Étienne Marey's physiological investigations of human motion are driven by a utopian belief that even interior states and movements invisible to the naked eye could be studied and made more productive through scientific visualization. It is this context that Agamben has in mind when referring to a widespread 'loss of gesture', which entails both a 'shift in the means of knowing the body', and a transformation in human embodied experience: no longer private, interior and intimate, experience and understanding of the self is henceforth inextricably bound up in 'the public display of images'.[10] According to Agamben, this process of breaking down human movement and subjecting it to scientific rationality had the effect of alienating humans from their gestures, causing a traumatic rupture in the way that people experienced and understood the body in its gestural capacity.

During roughly the same period that Agamben diagnoses a 'generalized catastrophe of the sphere of gestures',[11] Walter Benjamin locates an eruption of boredom, which, in his words, 'began to be experienced in epidemic proportions during the 1840s'.[12] According to Elizabeth Goodstein, boredom would slowly come to be understood during this period 'in physical rather than metaphysical or moral terms'[13] as a form of exhaustion that 'could be blamed on the weak individual unable to keep up with the demands of modernity upon the body'.[14] In tandem with the study of gesture and human movement, many scientific thinkers set out to study boredom with a view to improving economic productivity and social hygiene. Although a full discussion of nineteenth-century medical understandings of boredom as a 'pathology of the will'[15] is beyond the scope of the current chapter, what is significant for the present discussion is the way that these concerns would come to be indexed in part to the expressive, gesturing body as a site on which the subject's pathologically recalcitrant energies could be observed and managed. A range of discourses during this period – from medical and social to literary and artistic – would focus on the bored body's gestures, movements and facial expressions, in an attempt to both represent and alleviate the condition of stalled agency that boredom represents in this context.

One noteworthy example is Émile Tardieu's 1903 medical treatise, *L'Ennui*, which offers a taxonomy of different types of boredom. The aim of his study was to produce a psychological understanding of boredom and to suggest a variety of treatments for each type. Tardieu's book focuses at key points on the 'physical signs' of boredom that might allow medical professionals and others to diagnose it, including a range of distinctive gestures and bodily movements, including: 'yawns, grimaces, [and] tics'; a 'blank look', 'weariness of [the] gait', 'inert, static facial expression' as well as a generalized 'stupid' or 'ghost-like appearance'. In addition to these outward visible signs, Tardieu notes that boredom can express itself through a range of co-occurring physiological and mental symptoms, such as a 'sensitivity to cold, syncope, loss of appetite, weight loss, apathy' and 'mental turmoil, immature or irrational impulses, monomania, hypochondria, lunacy, stupor'.[16]

Although Tardieu's treatise focuses on boredom as a predominantly psychological or even moral condition, it nonetheless invites a reading of *ennui* through outward bodily symptoms. In this discussion, boredom's internal affective pressures are indexed to, and given visibility through, external bodily cues. It is precisely this attempt to visualize boredom through gesture that re-makes the bored body into an object of scientific management in the nineteenth century, and which thus targets it as an ongoing site of biopolitical production. However, even in Tardieu's treatise, this effort to correlate internal psychological processes with external visible signs is fraught with tensions and ambiguities that remain unresolved, partly because of the constitutive blankness that Tardieu assigns to the symptomology of *ennui*. What, exactly, is the medical classification of a 'blank look', let alone a 'stupid appearance'? How might a trained observer distinguish when a yawn or weary gait point to chronic boredom, as opposed to the effects of a bad night's sleep? While the passage above begins as an effort to describe the symptomology of boredom in relation to the body, it quickly slides into metaphorical terms that strain the basis of Tardieu's scientific method, as he goes on to describe the boredom sufferer as someone who looks as though he were 'six feet underground, stranger to his surroundings, forever isolated in the world of the living', and, further, describes boredom as a 'millstone round the neck' and as springing from the 'inexorable circle in which we are all trapped'.[17] Arguably, the same qualities of affective blankness and physical inertia that make boredom difficult to diagnose also help to shape it into a perfect screen for the projection of anxieties about the rapid changes taking place in this period of modernity at full throttle.

This rendering of the affective life of *ennui* through bodily attitudes of torpor and lassitude would also find echoes in a range of literary and artistic representations in the long nineteenth century, which participate in a similar attempt to interpret what was at stake in the new phenomenon, in part by mapping boredom on the body.[18] In his 'epic of modern boredom',[19] *Madame Bovary*, Flaubert visualizes Emma's intractable state of boredom often in physical terms, through a specific set of gestures and physiological symptoms: 'She grew pale and suffered from palpitations of the heart … On certain days she chatted with feverish rapidity, and this over-excitement was suddenly followed by a state of torpor, in which she remained without speaking, without moving'.[20] Similarly, boredom is famously embodied in Baudelaire's poem 'To the Reader' as a monstrous figure whose subdued gestures, gaping yawn and crocodile tears conceal a thirst for violent destruction.[21] In his remarkable illustration for the 1896 version of *Fleurs du Mal*, Jean Vebert pictures this crouching figure as a vortex of inky blackness that sits atop the author who looks forlornly down onto a blank page, as if waiting to be swallowed up by monstrous boredom (Figure 2.4).

Figure 2.4 'l'Ennui' by Jean Vebert © Bibliothèque nationale de France, 1896. Reproduced with the permission of BNF.

Walter Sickert's painting entitled *Ennui* (1914) figures the experience of domestic boredom through the dejected and slumped bodily postures and unfocused stares of both the husband and the wife, who are confined to a single room seemingly without much to occupy them (Figure 2.5). The painting reproduces some of the physical symptoms of boredom identified by Tardieu's treatise by the same name: the blank looks, inert facial expressions, weariness of movement. Their languid, torpid gestures – the smoking of a cigar, the act of leaning wearily against a set of drawers – are frozen in time, immobilized for the viewer's inspection.

Figure 2.5 *Ennui* by Walter Sickert © Tate Modern 1914.

In his 'Notes on Gesture', Agamben makes sense of these kinds of artistic and literary representations by claiming that the 'age that has lost its gestures is, for this reason, obsessed by them'. In the extreme and overwrought gestures embedded in aesthetic works, from 'Isadora Duncan and Sergei Diaghilev, the novel of Proust, [and] the great *Jungendstil* poetry from Pascoli to Rilke', Agamben diagnoses 'a society that ... tries at once to reclaim what it has lost and to record its loss'.[22] Aesthetic works like Flaubert's *Madame Bovary* or Sickert's *Ennui* are similarly shot through with a sense of ambivalence concerning the shift between private and public ways of interpreting and experiencing the body and its emotions. But while the gesturing bodies in these works help to visualize emotions such as boredom, they retain a degree of opacity and particularity that also demands the work of interpretation. In them, boredom is perhaps legible, but only just. As a condition that resists analysis, boredom lends itself well to expressing the essential ambiguity that Agamben sees at work in the domain of gestures.

As Agamben goes on to note, cinema emerges from this same context as a technologico-aesthetic tool, which both documents and attempts to reclaim this crisis of gesture. As Janet Harbord writes, cinema is complicit with the wider scientific logic that purports to diagnose interiority through the observation of gesture and facial expression: 'The grammar of cinema in this early period comes into line with the proliferating range of discourses concerned with reading traces of the subject on the exterior of the body, traces that reveal the inner workings of the subject in whatever codified form'.[23] Moreover, as Harbord suggests:

> Far from being simply an entertainment complex, cinema is aligned with a properly modern set of practices that, according to Foucault, capture, reproduce, and administrate bodies through the inculcation of the care of the self. Under the sign of the biopolitical, the modern subject is produced through a newly dispersed power moving through the populace as techniques of self-management are cross-referred to statistically rendered classificatory norms.[24]

But while cinema can and does contribute to the reification of gesture, it also holds the potential to resist it and to reveal dimensions of human experience that have been alienated through this same process. This is because, as Agamben claims, 'cinema has its centre in the gesture and not in the image'.[25] In contrast to scientific ways of knowing – which attempt to visualize human bodily experience by freezing and studying it as individual images – cinema liberates gesture as potentially 'a moment of life subtracted from the context of individual biography as well as a moment of art subtracted from the neutrality of aesthetics'.[26] In this way, cinema retains the potential to disclose the essential element of the human gesture: namely, '*the exhibition of a mediality*' that exceeds a rational logic of means and ends.[27] By exhibiting itself as 'pure mediality',[28] gesture sets itself apart from the sphere of instrumental action and communication, preparing for the 'emergence of the being-in-a-medium of human beings' and thus opening 'the ethical dimension for them'.[29] For Agamben, the full ethical potential of human life can be glimpsed in moments where the ready-made meanings that have become sedimented within gesture have been emptied out, neutralized or rendered inoperative. By referring to itself only as a medium – that is to say, a *means of communication*, rather than a specific message – gesture is transformed into 'a carrier of potentiality'; a force of neutralizing or suspending that might open onto the ethical possibility of re-making relations, of 'acting-otherwise'.[30]

I want to suggest that there is a productive affinity between boredom and Agamben's understanding of gesture as indexing a state of 'ontological suspension'[31] in which 'nothing is being produced or communicated, but rather something is being endured and supported'.[32] Although Agamben does not pursue this affinity between gesture and boredom directly, his chapter on 'Profound Boredom' in *The Open: Man and Animal* elaborates boredom's condition of 'being-held-in-suspense' in terms that are strongly compatible with his understanding of gesture as 'the proper sphere of that which is human'.[33] As he notes, 'profound boredom' discloses the human in its openness, its 'pure potentiality', which is a 'suspension and withholding of all concrete and specific possibilities'.[34]

As I shall now consider, social media platforms emerge from cinematic technologies, extending their dual potential to reify or to redeem both gesture and boredom in the twenty-first century. Although the suspended or stalled state that Agamben associates with profound boredom is not prioritized – either discursively or technically – by twenty-first-century media, I want to claim that this state of ontological suspension *can* still be expressed through gesture in short, networked video formats such as Vine. In what follows, I develop an understanding of boredom as a temporalized affective and embodied experience of stalled agency that is closely aligned with the notions of suspension, incommunicability and endurance that inform Agamben's reading of what is disclosed through the sphere of gesture.

'Doing it for the Vine': boredom and the attention economy of networked media

Commonly thought of as an experience of distended, vacant or repetitive time, boredom has come to epitomize a pervasive, default state of negativity that digital network culture promises to manage through its unlimited supply of entertainment on demand. The *OED* defines boredom simply as 'the state of feeling bored', listing a range of synonyms including lack of enthusiasm, excitement, interest or concern; apathy, languor, sluggishness, frustration, dissatisfaction; and repetitiveness, flatness and blandness.[35] In recent psychological research, boredom has been described as 'the aversive experience of wanting, but being unable, to engage in satisfying activity'.[36] Significantly, this research re-classifies boredom to privilege its relationship with attention rather than existential meaning, which was the basis of measure for previous medico-psychological definitions. In the context of late capitalism, the question of what counts as 'satisfying activity' has been culturally constructed through the category of entertainment, as Julian Jason Haladyn suggests when he writes that boredom can be viewed in this context 'as an assumed response indicative of anyone who is not fully engaged or, more precisely, *entertained* at a given moment or by a given object or event'.[37]

As I discussed in this book's introduction, computational capitalism's direct targeting of the human body's capacities for sustained attention has been a major preoccupation of recent media theory, featuring as a concern in the work of Franco 'Bifo' Berardi, Jonathan Crary, Mark B. N. Hansen, Jonathan Beller and many others.[38] In this context, states such as boredom and fatigue – which point to the limits of the human body's capacity for sustained attentiveness and productivity – have been pre-emptively targeted as key sites of biopolitical experimentation and production.[39] This chapter adds to these ongoing discussions by considering how gesture has been requisitioned in this context as perhaps *the* primary means through which boredom – and the problematic suspension of attentive engagement that it indexes – can be managed and put to work.

In recent decades, the field of affective computing has seized on this cultural logic of boredom as a failure of attention and has developed artificial intelligence systems trained to 'see, read, listen, feel, classify, and learn about emotional life'.[40] Across this highly competitive field, AI Start-ups have developed proprietary facial recognition and biometric sensing systems that are being trained to detect incipient boredom, amongst other emotions. Technical systems for 'reading' boredom through gesture and facial expression are currently being tested for use across a range of educational and commercial settings, with the aim of rescuing flagging attention spans from the perceived perils of boredom. For example, the multi-national Noldus Information Technology corporation has developed a proprietary 'FaceReader' facial expression analysis software that 'quantifies all possible movements a person can make with his or her face', with a view to analysing and influencing consumer behaviour. Like most other facial expression analysis software, Noldus's FaceReader is based on the Facial Action Coding System developed by anthropologists Paul Ekman and Wallace Friesen in 1978. In addition to the six basic facial expressions that Ekman claims are universal – anger, disgust, happiness, sadness, fear and surprise – FaceReader 7.1 (launched in 2017) includes the 'commonly used affective attitudes' of interest, boredom and confusion.[41] In a blog post that helped to publicize the launch of FaceReader 7.1, Noldus points out that in the emerging field of 'neuromarketing', it is vital to know whether potential customers are bored, so that their attention can be rescued for commercial exploitation and profit. According to Noldus, boredom is indexed to facial expressions such as dimpling, lip pressing and tightening, and closed eyes (Figure 2.6).[42]

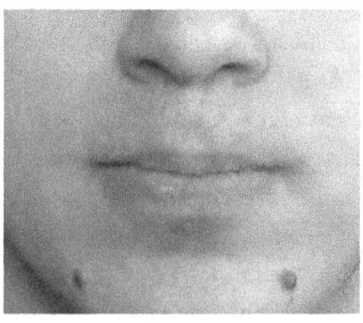

AU 23. Lip Tightener

Contributes to the emotion anger, and to the affective attitudes confusion and boredom. Muscular basis: orbicularis oris.

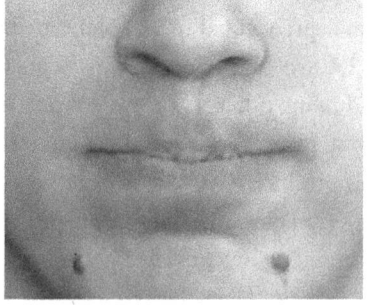

AU 24. Lip Pressor

This Action Unit contributes to the affective attitude boredom. The underlying facial muscle is orbicularis oris.

Figure 2.6 Some boredom-related facial action units © Noldus IT bv.

Similarly, Affectiva's biometric research platform 'iMotions' combines 'facial expression data with measures of physiological arousal, brain activity, eye tracking, and more' to 'build up a complete view of human behavior, action, and thought'.[43] For example, in the burgeoning field of EdTEch, startup companies such as Little Dragon[44] and Auto Tutor[45] deploy Affectiva's facial recognition technologies to detect boredom in real-time educational settings. Affectiva and Little Dragon both frame this application as a means of enhancing the quality of education by keeping students engaged. As Affectiva puts it, the software is 'designed to sniff out the emotional response of users and reflect it back to them through UI choices'.[46] While flagging attention spans have long posed a potential problem in the field of education, this idea has gained a particular traction in a twenty-first-century attention economy, where boredom is indexed to fears about 'hyper' versus 'deep attention'.[47] In the context of the Covid-19 pandemic, these types of fears reached fever pitch, with many start-up companies quickly developing boredom-detection software to 'remedy problems of presence, engagement, and teachers' difficulty in "reading the room" online'.[48] What is novel about these technologies is the idea that they can read micro-movements and gestures *before* or *better than* humans can, making it possible to develop technological systems for pre-empting this 'dangerous' flagging of attention. These applications of emotional detection are explicitly biopolitical, raising 'clear *mental integrity* questions regarding conditioning and impact on child subjectivity, more so given the presence of both surveillant and hyperreal emotion'. As Andrew McStay points out, these technologies filter emotional life through 'economic, psychological, statistical, and calculative expert frames of what emotional life is, using APIs and attractive data visualization to hide the truth that what emotions are is unclear'.[49]

This central fantasy that human emotions are indexed to, and legible through, gesture is also central to the appeal of many of the image-based memes and viral videos that circulate across our networked platforms and devices. While bored people do not always make for the most entertaining of subjects, in GIF culture in particular, boredom-themed animations abound, offering users ways of commenting on situations that are thereby interpreted as boring. Functioning as what Jason Eppink, digital curator for the Museum of the Moving Image, calls 'gestures of the Internet',[50] many reaction GIFs like these have entered a 'common lexicon'[51] where they're woven into communicative exchanges as readily identifiable short-hand emotions that draw on gesture as their material support. For example, the bodies in many reaction GIFs are often used in forums or in online exchanges to signal a user's weariness, apathy or frustration; to condemn a particular topic as not worthy of one's attention; or to urge an interlocutor to move a conversation along. While scholars such as Hampus Hagman, Iris Cuppen and others have argued for the GIF's potential to restore the fullness of the gesture by pulling it from its narrative framework,[52] these examples show that GIF reaction gestures such as these may just as easily settle down into convention and cliché. These GIFs frame boredom's state of suspended animation as an aversive experience, while providing a means of dispelling it through the networked actions of searching, finding, copying and posting. When used in this way, the bored body's gestures are conscripted to work not as a force of suspension, but as a productive part of networked media, which speeds communicative activity along.

As I will suggest, in the context of twenty-first-century media, gesture has come to accrue specific communicative functions; but just as significant is the way that particular gestures are engrained within, and become a habituated part of our engagement with, platforms such as Vine. In the case of #boredom Vines, gesture is often conscripted as a means of unblocking the bored body's stalled agency and channelling it back into communicative networks, where it can continue to produce value for media corporations. Simply put, habituated or semi-automated gestures that are required to participate in a digital network culture reclaim the bored body for productivity. But while the bored body is increasingly drawn upon, paradoxically, as a source of productivity, it still retains the ethico-political potential that Agamben ascribes to gesture and to cinema: to suspend, to oppose the sphere of action and communication and to resist fixed intention or goals. Through their exposure of bodies that are held in the grip of inertia or indecision, caught in a liminal zone between stasis and movement, repetition and change, #boredom Vines highlight boredom as a potential problem for digital network culture's fantasies of 24/7 productivity and unbroken attentive engagement.

The remainder of this chapter will focus on a specific configuration of boredom and gesture that flourished in the brief period between 2013, when the Vine platform was launched, and 2017, when it was archived by parent company Twitter. While social media platforms such as Vine enable users to capture even the most banal and seemingly unremarkable aspects of their daily lives, they do so within the context of an attention economy, which assigns value to these human embodied gestures and movements through their processes of naming, classifying, ordering, ranking and spreading them. This process is explicitly biopolitical, working to distinguish gestures 'at the fleeting limit between the normal and the pathological',[53] sorting gestural expression along a continuum between the entertaining and the boring, the spreadable and the unspreadable.

In the case of Vine videos, this framing of the bored body as the site of potential productivity often works somewhat differently. Unlike GIFs, which are more frequently based on material extracted from previously existing moving image media, Vines enlist users to create their own content. This conscription of users in the production of content is, of course, a key feature of a range of social media platforms but has a particular significance in the context of #boredom Vines, as I suggest below. During its four-year lifespan, Vine's app for smartphones allowed users to create six-second looping micro-videos, to upload them to the video-sharing platform, where they could describe them through captions and tag them using hashtags; followers could like or comment on the Vines or re-Vine them. As with other social media networks, the Vine platform therefore works by reducing the fullness of a user's embodied agency into a set of specific gestural possibilities aimed at generating maximum traffic on the site. Vines were also frequently shared across other video-sharing platforms, notably YouTube, where many users created compilations to store their favourite Vines before the site was archived. The most popular Vines went viral and inspired other Viners to re-iterate, re-mix and riff on the original – as, for example, in the *What are Those?*[54] and *Ryan Gosling Won't Eat His Cereal*[55] memes that originated as Vine videos. Vine encouraged a specific relationship to gesture through its in-app editing feature, which recorded video when the user's finger was on the screen, and automatically paused, or 'cut', when the finger was lifted.

Perhaps because the app was designed for use on personal mobile devices – permitting videos to be filmed and uploaded with ease – Vine quickly established a close connection to the habitual, the banal, the ordinary, often depicting 'users simply doing things',[56] frequently in domestic settings. Indeed, when I first began researching Vine in the early stages of this project, I was initially struck by the banality of the content that was posted to the platform in general, and the seeming lack of any distinction between the kind of posts that used boredom tags and those that did not. In other words, Vine seemed to have a special relationship to the boring outside of any separate conceptual category that might name and contain it. If anything, boredom hashtags seemed to be used most often simply to indicate an experience of struggling to name and lend meaning to the content that was being shared – to name and qualify an 'experience without qualities'.[57]

Read in relation to gesture, what is at stake in many Vines that use boredom hashtags to index this diffuse, amorphous state is potentially, following Agamben, nothing other than the 'communication of a communicability'. It has precisely nothing to say because what it shows is 'the being-in-language of human beings as pure mediality'.[58] Rather than pointing to anything specific *about* boredom, gesture in Vine videos is potentially shaped by the affective pressures that are at stake in the experience of having, precisely, nothing to say – in a context in which we are constantly being entreated to communicate.

However, there is a complex biopolitical process of inculcation at work here that merits further scrutiny. While Vine displayed a particular affinity for the mundane, its success relied on its ability to elevate even the most unremarkable aspects of human experience into entertaining content that could drive traffic to its website and spread it to others. Nathan Jurgensen notes the paradoxical way that Vine and associated platforms such as Vinepeek were able to transform boring, average, everyday material into a feeling of excitement and anticipation, writing: 'Dog sushi computer baby bowling buy beer concert train cooking kid cat shot-glass sports video game eating fireplace cab-ride thinking about what comes next feels a bit addictive'.[59] This process of affective modulation – whereby the mundane and boring is translated into a feeling of anticipation and entertainment – is central to the biopolitical management of boredom and attention through twenty-first-century networked media. Indeed, although I was initially struck by the diversity of content that #boredom Vines seemed to name, after a while, specific patterns began to emerge, many of which foregrounded this process of affective modulation at work on Vine. It quickly became apparent that while there were hundreds of Vines being uploaded with boredom hashtags every month, the most popular were those that re-interpreted banal settings and gestures as either humorous, or surprising, or both. Viners who wanted to capitalize on the visibility that the platform afforded them did so by making sure that the content was engaging, unique, memorable and above all not dull. They also tended to mimic or riff on previous posts that had gained widespread circulation, sorting content into unspoken categories or genres.

For example, many #boredom Vine videos feature gags or comedic performances, which may hint at boredom's state of suspension, endurance or incommunicability, but are expressly intended to move both the user and the viewer past this stasis. The popular 'When Happy Cloud Gets Bored',[60] 'Ghetto Names'[61] and 'When boredom strikes w/Izzy Dinma'[62] all operate in this way, framing boredom as a pretext for comedic gags or madcap antics aimed at making viewers laugh, and thereby accruing value in the form of loops, likes and re-Vines. 'Ghetto Names' – a brief comedic monologue riffing off the names of household bathroom cleaners – acknowledges this goal of accumulating views through a sub-caption that reads, 'I'm blowing up y'all's feed tonight'. Here the hashtag 'bored' undercuts the blatant attention-seeking that is hinted at in the sub-caption, reinforcing boredom as the great motivator for all manner of comedic, off-beat or zany performances. 'Happy Cloud' highlights this relation between boredom and zaniness by picturing in close up YouTuber Daz Black's head, which is entirely encased in soap suds, save for the eyes and mouth. Holding an electric toothbrush up to the camera, Black says (in a cartoon voice), 'Look what I can do', before simulating some kind of drilling action or electric shock therapy as the toothbrush burrows into his cloud-head as seen in the frame grab below (Figure 2.7). This zany performance is framed in relation to boredom's powerful sense of suspended agency, which has seemingly driven Black to seek out this new and highly unusual way of passing the time. Many #boredom Vines work in this way, displaying acts that are so irrational or offbeat that they sometimes border on, and seem to validate, sheer stupidity.

Many #boredom Vines try to manage boredom through zany performances that aim to shock. For example, 'Fun Pain Tazer Boredom' (which has since

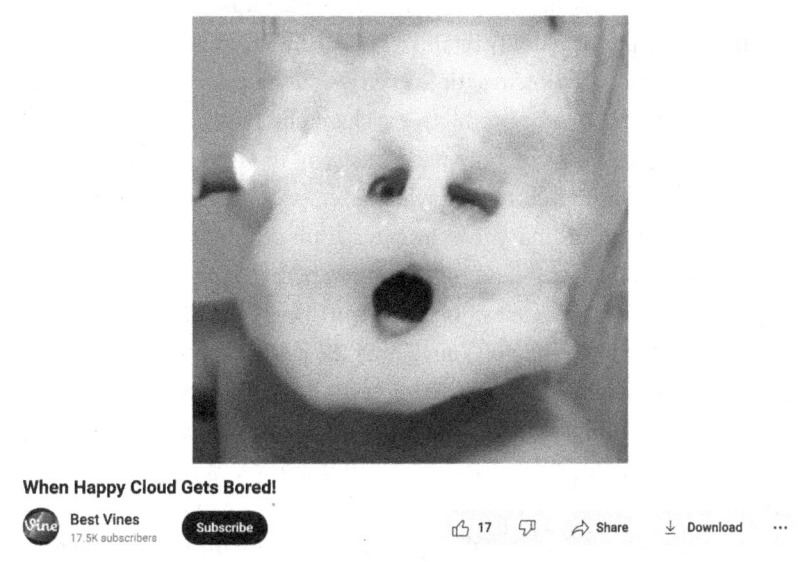

Figure 2.7 'When Happy Cloud Gets Bored' by @Daz.Black © Vine Video 2013.

been taken down by its producer) takes this remit literally, as an unseen camera operator's hand is seen holding a taser, which he uses on a second man's upper thigh. The about-to-be-tasered man can be heard breathing in a rapid and exaggerated pattern – in through the nose, out through the mouth – as if preparing physically for the ordeal; once tasered, he emits what sounds like a genuine cry of pain before falling backwards into the bathtub, laughing. While this Vine doesn't make it clear how the content relates to boredom *per se*, it can be assumed that boredom is once again identified as motivation for the senseless stunt, which seems to have no goal – except, perhaps, the goal of staving off boredom. This Vine also unwittingly re-enacts a much-publicized 2014 psychological experiment that found that people would 'rather be electrically shocked than left alone with their thoughts', effectively choosing pain over boredom and 'inner reflection'.[63]

As Sianne Ngai suggests, zany performances such as these navigate tensions that are symptomatic of the '"perform-or-else" ideology of late capitalism, including its increasingly affective, biopolitical ways of meeting the imperative to endlessly increase productivity'.[64] This Vine offers insight into what this imperative to increase productivity might look like in the context of an attention economy, which generates value from these sorts of zany, hyper-performative or reckless stunts. However, as Ngai points out, 'for all its spectacular displays of laborious exertion, the activity of zaniness is more often than not destructive; one might even describe it as the dramatization of an anarchic refusal to be productive'.[65] For Ngai, then, zany performativity retains a critical dimension through its hyperbolic displays of pointless or violent action, even if – in the context of #boredom Vines – this seeming refusal to be productive is channelled back into networked forms of productivity. In this way, zany performativity in #boredom Vines highlights the tensions at stake in a context in which users are conscripted into performing every aspect of their ordinary lives as entertaining content for others to view. In terms of Agamben's understanding of gesture, perhaps the hyper-performativity of these videos might work to exhibit, or put on display, the mediality of the human being. However, the framing of Vine within the attention economy of networked media mitigates against that, as the fullness and ambiguity that both boredom and gesture have the potential to disclose are reduced to a set of hashtags and descriptors that are calculated to promote Viner profiles. #Boredom posts may hint at boredom as a state of 'doing nothing' – what Agamben calls 'Nothing as pure, absolute potentiality'; but their inscription within the performance cultures of networked media puts this 'nothing' to work.[66]

Aside from modelling the categories of performativity that are most productive for the management of boredom, #boredom Vine videos also frequently intervene into the temporality of boredom, using the technical affordances of the Vine app to break up and enliven an experience of distended or vacant time. Two extremely popular Vines, 'Bored as Shiiiiii'[67] (Figure 2.8) and 'VINE VIDEO | BORED IN CLASS!!'[68] foreground the gestural and in-app possibilities for piercing or shaking up boredom's painful state of duration. 'BORED IN CLASS!!' names a highly recognizable situation, with which many young viewers can surely identify, of feeling trapped in a tedious and dreary lesson. While this painful experience of situative boredom is alluded to in the Vine's title, what is noteworthy about the Vine is that the temporality of boredom is never given a chance to unfold. The video begins, rather, with a loud, shrill shriek that pierces through the class, sending shockwaves and reverberations through the room that cause fellow classmates to whip around in alarm. This is followed by a reaction shot of Viner JackSepticEye's face, frozen in a rictus grin. If the 'bored' of the title hints at boredom's sense of intolerable, extended duration, the shriek pre-empts this unwanted temporality before we even have a chance to experience it. Similarly, the shriek also models one means by which

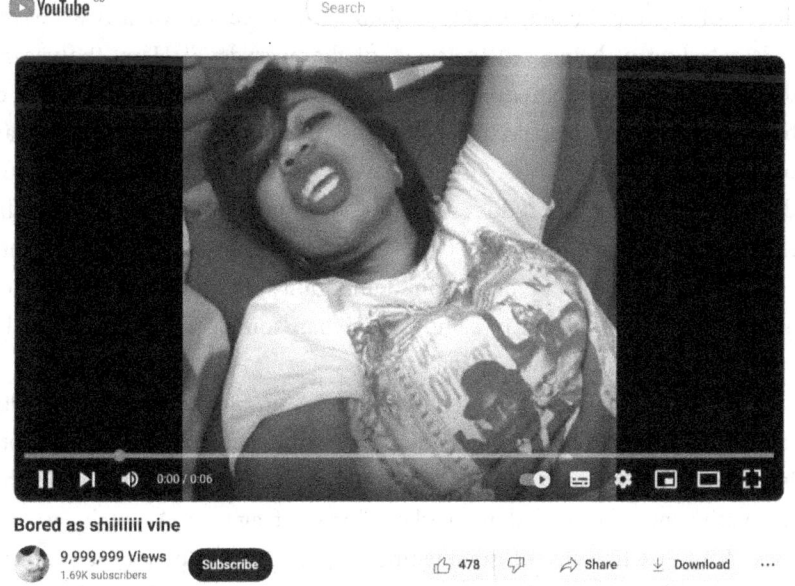

Figure 2.8 'Bored as Shiiiiii Vine' by Daneisha Powell © YouTube 2017.

the painful condition of blocked or suspended agency associated with boredom can be discharged into potent sonic action.

'Bored as Shiiiiii' works in a similar fashion but begins with the Viner Daneisia Powell in a classic boredom pose, as pictured in the screen shot above. The mise en scène of the bedroom, the positioning of Powell's body lying supine on a bed, and her blank or unimpressed facial expression all convey an atmosphere of domestic boredom that is easily recognizable and relatable (see Figure 2.8). This condition of boredom is framed as so easily legible, in fact, that this shot only lasts for one second before cutting to reveal a head and shoulders shot of Powell, now standing upright, performing a dance to Jay-Z's 'Big Pimpin'', her lips pressed forward in a comedic pout. This transition, combined with the rhythm of the music and Powell's slightly jerky movements, cut into the distended, dead time of boredom, enlivening the mood into one of playfulness. This video has enjoyed an extremely long afterlife on Instagram and YouTube since its original posting on Vine in 2014. Judging by the user comments on YouTube, the popularity of this video seems to have something to do with the powerful and effective way that it stages its transition from bored stasis to playful excitement. Many of the user comments re-contextualize what happens at second two in light of their own experience, for example: '0:02 when they cancel school for a week',[69] or 'When your crush finally texted you back'.[70] What the video offers viewers, then, is a means of shaping the temporality of their experience into what Anna Munster calls a feeling of being '"in-the-now" of the everyday'.[71] Here, the vacant or diffuse temporality of boredom is re-structured as an affective event, with a clear before and after punctuated by the cut. As Munster suggests, while this shaping of experience through short viral videos entails a 'contouring of this moment's duration as presentness', it does not offer 'duration full of presence', but rather 'a shaping of the temporariness … of the everyday'.[72] Following Munster, what this Vine offers is a means of structuring temporality such that boredom becomes an event with a clear end in sight, rather than something to be 'endured and supported', as Agamben would have it.[73]

While boredom might present a potential problem for network culture's demand for attentive engagement and entertaining content, here that problem is being worked through gestural efforts of users to translate boredom's lethargy or apathy into recognized networked forms of agency. As such, gesture in these Vines participates in the ongoing biopolitical production of boredom as a site at which subjects might be re-invested back into networked circuits of value. The platform's motto, 'Do it for the Vine', exemplifies this logic whereby users are conscripted into the ongoing production of their own mundane lives as potential entertainment for others. But what happens in Vine videos that *refuse* the affective modulation and temporal re-structuring outlined above? What about the #boredom videos that refuse to 'Do it for the Vine', focusing instead on the embodied, temporal phenomenon of boredom, without making a concerted effort to manage or modulate it? While #boredom Vines that aim to disperse or dispel boredom abound, there are also several examples that avoid the strategies outline above, and which use the technical affordances of the Vine platform to reveal something of the state of suspension and endurance that is at stake in both boredom and gesture. These Vines also take a number of different forms. Many focus on gestural movements that are repeated through the Vine's auto-looping function: foreheads are repeatedly bashed against desks, walls or pillows; groaning bodies fall onto beds and endlessly bounce back up again; hand gestures such as snapping, clapping or puppetry animate the dead time that permeates boredom, but without quite translating it into an event. Others picture faces or mouths in close-up, often emitting inarticulate noises instead of words; there is a lot of sighing, yawning and rhythmic clicking, inhaling, chomping of teeth. A smaller number of Vines feature completely still or quasi-still bodies, slumped back or supine, suspended ambiguously between stasis and movement – a state that is extended potentially indefinitely through the Vine platform's auto-loop function.

For example, in both Annarigatoni's video entitled 'Bored'[74] and in 'on the floor – Boredom kills' (which has since been taken down), the bodies of the respective Viners are positioned in front of the camera and remain unmoving for the duration of the six-second loop. Each one activates a slightly different temporalized feeling that invites the viewer into an experience of boredom, rather than working to dispel it. In 'Bored', the temporality of boredom is produced through a slightly different relationship to the loop. In this video, the stillness of Annarigatoni's body contrasts with the perpetual, moderate motion that is produced by the spinning chair in which she is sitting. Ambient noise from a television set in the background provides a sense of banal everydayness, a stagnant temporal flow that refuses to move on, even as it keeps flowing. This video produces a pronounced feeling of boredom's stuckness, its condition of stasis, through the circularity that it produces through the spinning of the chair, and through the loop, which extends this movement with no end in view. In 'on the floor – Boredom kills' we see a figure lying belly-down on the floor with his head resting on the carpet and face peering into an ill-defined distance. While his body and position within the frame remain static, his unblinking eyes move somewhat slowly, without a clear target or motive. We hear the ambient, muted sound of a segment of big band era music, which repeats for as long as the Vine loops. The overall feeling of watching this video as it loops is akin to what Elena Gorfinkel describes as 'an experienced, sensed temporality' that is produced in the context of slow art cinema, from the relation between exhausted on-screen bodies and the bodies of weary spectators.[75] While the time structure of a six-second Vine video might seem to preclude any meaningful transference between on-screen bodies and Vine users, in this case, the loop function helps to convey a sense of boredom's suspended, ambiguous temporality. Although gesture can act as a kind of physical supplement that helps us to decipher the 'content' or meaning of human experience in these videos, in Laura Mulvey's words, it also 'hovers on the brink of meaning, suggesting but resisting and remaining closer to the ineffable than the fullness of language'.[76]

It is important to add that when viewing Vines, the actual duration of the loop is determined by the gestural activities of users who either disrupt them or allow them to continue playing. Thus, an experience of boredom's obdurate, protracted or frustrated temporality would depend on a viewer whose gestures also remain suspended – at least for a time – to allow the videos time to accrue through repeated loops before moving on to the next Vine. In Vines, duration thus accumulates through repetition, creating a temporal interruption that is at odds with the speediness and forward motion that is more typical of networked exchanges. In this sense, both the gestures of Viners and those of the wider community of Vine users are stitched into what Agamben understands as a potentially ethical relation – one which would apprehend this state of suspension as a fundamental part of the 'being-in-language of human beings'.[77]

While these Vines do potentially frame boredom as a negative experience that is being worked through the gestural possibilities provided by the Vine app, they admit to a greater degree the sense of stasis that Agamben attributes to gesture. Although the human bodies in these Vines are bound up within a biopolitical drive to classify, name and fix the meanings of gestures, many of the gestures that we see in these Vine videos retain a degree of opacity that resists their reduction to instrumental ends. Here, hard-to-decipher bodily gestures and inarticulate vocal expressions convey a sense of boredom at a state of incipience, before it has been mapped, disclosed, understood, before its sense of obstructed agency has been dispelled and re-invested back into networks. Although the hashtags and descriptors used help to classify what we are seeing, these Vines amplify the ambiguities of both boredom and gesture, featuring subjects whose gestures remain suspended and uncertain, before boredom is codified or translated into an event, and before it is dislodged from the body. These examples interest me because in them the gesturing body is not quite legible, and as a result, it is not as *functional* in the sense of displaying its power to spread through, and hence produce profit for, networked platforms. Indeed, it is important to note that another feature of these Vines, in contrast to the earlier Vines discussed in this article, is their modest or extremely small loop counts (many have been looped fewer than twenty-five times). These Vines are *not* the Vines that spread across different platforms; many of them have been taken down and so can't be accessed at all through a traditional web search. I would suggest that this unspreadability has to do with the way that these Vines resist the late-capitalist injunction to translate gestures into entertainment for others. Instead, they put boredom's state of suspension on display, drawing on the gestural potential that Agamben invests in gesture to show the body as supporting and enduring something, rather than as 'doing it for the Vine'.

By exposing embodied and temporal experiences of not-quite-doing-it-for-the-Vine, these videos thereby open up the potential that Agamben invests in gesture to reveal the 'endurance and the exhibition of the media character of corporal movements'.[78] Similarly, in their inarticulateness, they foreground the dimension of incommunicability that Agamben ascribes to gesture when he suggests that 'the gesture is always a gesture of not being able to figure something out in language; it is always a *gag* in the proper meaning of the term'.[79] What these videos highlight through both boredom and gesture is the potential for resistance that both yield within the spheres of communication and action. These videos do not unquestionably take the alleviation of boredom or the entertainment of others to be an end goal but foreground their own mediality and the process of making a means visible as such: *here I am, simply bored.* In this way, these Vines make trouble for the affective promise that boredom can be dissolved by twenty-first-century media technologies, or that we might be endlessly entertained by the boredom of others. This has implications, in turn, for the kinds of hopes that we invest in media platforms, and the sorts of ethical relations that we might hope to forge through them. While gesture in these videos clearly solicits some kind of attention, recognition or relation, the terms of what is being expressed, and what kind of relation might thus ensue, remains uncertain. The sense of suspension or uncertainty that is manifested in the recalcitrant energies of boredom is, as I have suggested in this chapter, a potential resource for Agamben's gestural politics, which would recognize boredom not as a problem for individual subjects to manage, but as storing energies that might refuse inscription within a neoliberal logic of means and ends, to disclose a commons founded on the human gesture as pure mediality. While boredom is not a default form of resistance in a digital culture, it retains a degree of ambivalence because through its gestures, the question of means and ends may be delayed, suspended or short-circuited.

3

Boredom-on-demand

Always-on subjects and television's ambient turn

So far, this book has explored how digital entertainment has mediated boredom by framing media users as boredom managers – agents who are responsible for optimizing the affective texture of their own experience as it unfolds in real time. As we have seen, boredom has been framed as a negative experience and a persistent threat within the context of networked media. This discursive and technical framing drives engagement across entertainment and social networks, which are widely promoted as tools for combating boredom. But if boredom has typically been constructed as the enemy of networked entertainment, it does not *only* operate in this way, as I shall now consider. This chapter focuses on the context of streaming on-demand television, which offers viewers a wide selection of programming that is algorithmically catered to their personal taste profiles. As television and media scholars have documented, the shift to the mobile, multi-screen streaming on-demand model of television involves viewers in new ways, both in the selection and curation of viewing content and in decisions about when and where their viewing takes place.[1] As Chuck Tryon notes, cultural discourses for these digital delivery systems have 'tended to focus on issues of mobility, flexibility, and convenience', linking digital viewing platforms to 'the hectic schedules of "on-the-go" workers and families, giving them the ability to watch wherever and whenever they like'.[2] Digital platforms are also promoted through discourses of plenitude. These frame on-demand television as an endlessly renewable stream of viewing pleasure, which can keep subscribers 'engaged for hours on end'[3] and thus liberate them from 'mundane aspects of everyday life',[4] including – or perhaps especially – interfacing with everyday boredom.

While television has long played a role in managing ordinary boredom, in a post-network era there is a renewed emphasis on the viewer's participation and agency within this process. Dominant cultural discourses around streaming TV re-imagine the viewer in this context as 'active and engaged', both 'in control of' and 'empowered by' their media consumption.[5] As Elena Pilipets notes, Netflix and other streaming platforms have managed to position the idea of 'attentive, culturally informed spectatorship' at the heart of on-demand culture, in ways that disregard the tensions that structure viewership in an always-on context.[6] In this framework, boredom serves as an incitement for the viewer to make informed decisions about the kind of programming that might best keep her entertained or mildly distracted, rather than acting as a prompt to disengage completely. The transition to post-network television has thus promised to make viewers into ever more empowered boredom managers, with streaming platforms framed as enhanced technological tools for 'managing one's time in front of the television rather than succumbing to a television schedule'.[7]

But what happens to the pleasures of mindless, spaced-out viewing in the context of user-directed television? Has television – a medium long associated with the pleasures of relaxation and just 'vegging out' – been completely co-opted into the intensified rhythms of 24/7 capitalism, leaving no space for the reverie that scholars such as Jonathan Crary lament as lost?[8] As I will suggest in this chapter, although the flourishing landscape of multi-channel networks and streaming platforms has arguably facilitated more attentive and impassioned forms of viewer engagement, it has also strategically promoted opportunities to simply zone out. In what follows, I consider the complex relations between boredom, pleasure and viewer agency that coalesce in a context of always-on televisual spectatorship. I advance the term boredom-on-demand to encapsulate the platform strategies, televisual aesthetics and user practices that have converged around boredom in the context of streaming TV. Boredom-on-demand refers us to the downbeat and desultory pleasures of zoning out with TV – pleasures that co-exist with, and help to maintain, the demands of being a subject in an always-on culture.

The chapter is structured as follows: firstly, I sketch a brief history of low-intensity modes of televisual spectatorship, from the 'couch potato' to today's era of user-directed viewership and the multi-tasking 'background TV' viewer. The second half of the chapter considers how a televisual aesthetics of boredom has been used to promote slow and banal TV in a user-directed context: slow, dull, or low-intensity televisual content that is made for, and/or distributed through, on-demand streaming platforms including Netflix and the 'siesta video platform' Napflix.[9] Through an analysis of content from online user forums and news and promotional material, I discuss the specific user practices that construct boredom as an instrumental mood in a context of always-on entertainment. I outline and problematize the ways in which low-intensity televisual aesthetics – alternately characterized as boring or fascinating, depending on the viewer and the context – have been positioned as helping to produce an ambience conducive to absorbed attentive engagement, to mindless productivity, to relaxation and sleep, or to all of these at the same time.

Drawing from scholarly work on ambient media and atmosphere, I suggest that what is at stake in these trends is an ambient turn in television, which emphasizes the medium's ability to transform the affective atmospheres of the viewing environment.[10] As a mode of ambient mediation, boredom-on-demand is marketed to, and embraced by, viewers for its capacity to dull, de-intensify and becalm the atmospheres in which viewing takes place. While ambient television has long served as a potentially 'soothing palliative'[11] in public spaces like waiting rooms, I am interested in thinking about what happens when this palliative function is framed more directly in relation to the viewer's agency, desire and control in personalized viewing contexts. Overall, the chapter considers how framing boredom-on-demand as a technique of ambient mediation can illuminate some of the paradoxes of agency and power dynamics that are worked through both switched-off spectators and their switched-on counterparts in the age of always-on capitalism.

Zoning out, 24/7: from the couch potato to the multi-tasking background TV viewer

While I frame the phenomenon of boredom-on-demand in the context of the twenty-first-century attention economy, it is important to recognize that the pleasures of slackened or low-intensity spectatorship are by no means specific to this context. Across its history, television has long been imagined as providing viewers a satisfying means to relax and unwind. Indeed, the idea that television might promote a condition of lethargic disengagement has long been the focus of suspicion amongst cultural and media theorists worried about the ideological effects that might follow from this position of pleasantly spaced-out spectatorship. One important early point of reference for thinking about a slackened or de-intensified mode of televisual reception might be John Ellis's assertion that the medium 'belongs to the everyday, to the normal backdrop of expectations and mundane pleasures'. Emphasizing television's close kinship with the everyday, Ellis describes televisual spectatorship as 'a casual experience rather than an intensive one. The consumption of TV is often described as "relaxation", indicating a process that demands little concentrated attention and is concerned with variety and diversion rather than enlightenment and excitement'.[12] In his much debated take on what has come to be known as 'glance theory', the television viewer is 'cast as someone who has the TV switched on, but is giving it very little attention'.[13] Compared with the cinematic 'gaze' which 'implies a concentration of the spectator's activity into that of looking, the glance implies that no extraordinary effort is being invested in the activity of looking'.[14] Glance theory has since been widely critiqued for its assumption that the television's domestic location creates a viewer who was by nature distracted and inattentive, only ever half-engaged. In this opposition between casual, distracted viewing and concentrated, effortful spectatorship, Ellis channels the Frankfurt School's concerns about the dangers of relaxation, along with Adorno's suspicions concerning the Culture Industry's cultivation of a television spectator who craves familiarity and eschews cultural content that is innovative or challenging.[15] Despite its scepticism about the cultural value of relaxation, Ellis's work is highly attentive to the television's material and symbolic situatedness within a domestic setting, and its capacity to involve viewers within the ordinary rhythms and pleasures of the everyday. Ellis's theory thus provides a useful entry point for thinking about television's low-intensity appeal to the viewer, its ability to promote states of pleasurable detachment alongside the stronger emotional or identificatory attachments that the medium also encourages.

In popular culture, similar suspicions around distracted viewing would come to be concentrated in the figure of the TV viewer as 'couch potato': the impassive and often 'comically vegetal'[16] viewer who slouches mindlessly on the sofa, bathed in the ambient glow of the TV set, idly switching channels, hoping for something to hold her attention, or waiting for sleep to set in. As William Uricchio informs us, the term couch potato was first coined in 1976 and came to prominence in the 1980s as a way of articulating some of the paradoxes of spectatorship that emerged alongside the shift to multi-channel programming. The term couch potato 'reflects a widespread understanding of television as breeding an extreme degree of passivity'[17] or as a 'misdirection of one's passions'.[18] The concept channels anxieties about economic and social unproductivity and ambivalence about which types of laziness might be considered permissible within the capitalist system's division of work and leisure time. However, the couch potato is not only associated with lifeless inattention, as Uricchio notes. On the one hand, the couch potato is 'seemingly passive, drawn from one time block to the next'. On the other, as a figure armed with a remote control, a VCR, a stack of tapes, and a *TV Guide*, the couch potato is also imagined as an 'active zapper and zipper engaged in viewing activities that were highly mobile and unpredictable'.[19]

During the historical transition between the TVI and TVII eras, the couch potato would come to encapsulate a central ambivalence around passive versus active modes of viewership – an unease that has persisted into our current era of user-directed television. And yet, as television scholars have noted, the couch potato has fallen out of favour as a dominant cultural metaphor, signalling 'a shift in our moral attitude toward life lived in front of a screen'.[20] As Laurence Scott writes, in our era of always-on digital engagement, 'the archetype of the beached sluggard on the couch has been smuggled into a portrait of diligence. As a result, the old-school sheepishness about watching television, especially during the day, has been replaced by a sense of pride in our new technological capabilities'.[21] This is not to suggest that total disengagement is now endorsed outright within the attention economy of digital capitalism; rather, the television viewer as couch potato has been replaced by a multi-tasking viewer who can distractedly stream television whilst also engaging with a variety of other screen-based activities.

Enter the era of so-called 'background TV': television that is turned on as white noise and half-watched while performing other tasks. According to aficionados, background TV helps to produce feelings of comfort and companionship, whether standing in for 'all the hustle and bustle of the office' for those working from home, or masking more distracting household sounds and enabling enhanced task concentration.[22] For background TV enthusiasts, semi-watching shows is framed less as a guilty form of loafing and more as a positive means of optimizing productivity, by helping to achieve the ideal atmospheres in which work can take place. As we have seen, this enthusiasm about TV viewers as empowered through digital technologies has been championed by streaming providers as a means of nudging viewers to 'be active in order to create [themselves] as users'.[23] In this shift from television viewer to multi-platform streaming on-demand user, the already tenuous divisions between passive and active modes of viewership that the couch potato embodied are further compressed into a construction of the viewer as potentially always simultaneously engaged and distracted, switched on and spaced out. As media scholar Tun-Hui Hu puts it in his 'Brief History of Disengagement':

> Perhaps the main difference between the couch potato and the user is simply that it is almost impossible to opt out of the work of being a user. Users now interact even when they want to space out – that is, they now *actively* space out – meaning that the division between activity and passivity has become even more tenuous than ever before.[24]

Whereas the couch potato's sloth-like apathy was previously imagined as a potential threat to capitalist ideals of productivity and sociality, today passivity is, according to Hu, 'just another way to interact with the systems of digital capitalism'.[25]

Indeed, what needs to be recognized in this context, as Elena Pilipets asserts, is the role that streaming platforms such as Netflix play in producing 'simultaneously unfolding intensities of attention and inattention'. In this updated matrix of televisual spectatorship, the viewer's body is often '[c]aptured in a state of attentive distractedness ... simultaneously excited and bored, separated from the world and reciprocally engaged in the networked process of value generation'.[26] Here boredom is not unambiguously associated with disengagement, but is repurposed as another type of relational attachment, a de-intensified modality through which to experience and engage with computational media. This is a point that Scott C. Richmond makes, writing that 'vulgar boredom' – of the sort that might occur while 'veg[ging] out in front of *Top Chef*, playing *Candy Crush* as we do' – is a central, if culturally devalued, aesthetic experience that comes to prominence in digital media culture. Unlike the 'profound' boredom of modernist classics like Andy Warhol's *Kiss* (1963) or *Empire* (1965), 'vulgar' boredom implies a relation between the always-on subject and the media object that is 'slackened, diffuse, lateral'.[27] Where profound boredom requires effort and is a test of the viewer's ability to pay attention and be present to the media object, vulgar boredom operates at a different perceptual and affective level. If there is a pleasure in vulgar boredom, as Richmond suggests, it comes from the slackened, de-intensified way that 'boring media allow us to be with ourselves for a while, in a way that is neither overorganized, subjected to productivity ... nor intensive'. Vulgar boredom, for Richmond, 'merely allows us to detach from the here-now enough to be with ourselves in ... an *ordinary* way'.[28] What this kind of vulgar boredom allows is a means of modulating the intensities and rhythms of spectatorship in an always-on context. There is, in other words, a compensatory value in the type of inattentive viewing sensibility that glance theorists such as Ellis were quick to dismiss. In a context of ever-intensifying rhythms of consumption, 'vulgar boring media' offers one way to think about 'the decoupling between technics and human experience' and 'the shifting texture and rhythm of the ordinary'.[29]

As Richmond and Pilipets imply, boredom plays a complex yet increasingly important role within the construction of spectatorial agency and desire in the context of always-on digital entertainment. As a mood associated with the sloth-like passivity of the couch potato, boredom represents a potential drag on the discourses of intensity, plenitude and speed that help to construct the idea of spectatorial pleasure in this context. What is more, boredom's restlessness is a potential economic problem for what Netflix terms 'survivorship' – the metric that tracks sustained viewer engagement across a given series.[30] And yet, as we shall see, in this context of 24/7 multitasking, boredom's associations with blankness,[31] emptiness,[32] stretched-out time[33] and eventlessness[34] have been repurposed to serve as a homeopathic cure – a way of coping with the asymmetry between bodies and machines that is at the heart of always-on culture. This chapter will now consider the wider cultural logic that has re-framed boredom as a tool for resisting, ameliorating or coping with perceived discontents in an era of ubiquitous communication.

Boredom and slow media

Although boredom has been assigned both positive and negative values across its history, in an always-on culture, it has been widely constructed as a feeling to be avoided or displaced through streaming entertainment. However, over roughly the past fifteen years, boredom has also been re-framed across a range of contexts as a well-being practice and quirky form of countercultural resistance to our 'hectic, hyperactive, overstimulated age'.[35] Through organizations such as the Idler Academy (2010–) and The School of Life (2008–),[36] events such as the sell-out annual Boring Conference in London (2011–20),[37] and a prolific list of popular psychology and self-help titles published between 2014 and 2019,[38] boredom has been enshrined as a mood to embrace as an antidote to a world that is 'always telling [us] to be busy,'[39] while 'leav[ing] us feeling depleted and oddly undernourished'.[40] Framed through the serious disciplines of literature, philosophy, psychoanalysis, art history and classics, these organizations emphasize boredom's philosophical pedigree and associations with art, culture and 'the good life', pitting the vulgar boredom of cheap and flimsy digital entertainment against the more existentially meaningful profound boredom that, it is claimed, can be found through idling and other contemplative and often outmoded practices and hobbies. In these contexts, boredom has been given a pedagogical function, featuring as a technique of self-care and as a mode of resistance to the pace and intensity of always-on society. Whether the aim is better self-knowledge, better sleep, a better work/life balance or a fascinated absorption within the mundane, boredom is positioned as the lynchpin in a structure of temporal experience that is understood to be under threat.

Boredom has likewise frequently been invoked as a feature of the 'slow cinema' and 'slow TV' trends, which have gained traction over the past fifteen years as important alternatives to dominant media aesthetics. As Tiago de Luca and Nuno Barradas Jorge note, while slow cinema has its roots in mid-century European art house filmmaking, the paradigm achieved widespread popularity around 2010 as a tendency in global art cinema with links to various other global slowness movements. Referring to a 'contemplative' filmmaking aesthetic defined by its use of protracted, self-reflexive temporal devices such as the long take, loose narrative structures, minimal editing and an emphasis on real time and the everyday, slow cinema shares with the wider slow cultural movement the aim of 'rescu[ing] temporal structures from the accelerated tempo of late capitalism'.[41] Through its embrace of an 'aesthetics of boredom',[42] slow cinema has predominantly been understood as a historical refusal of, and a revolt against, a countervailing tendency in contemporary popular cinema towards intensification, speed and the spectacular, which are framed as dominant features of always-on entertainment.

In the context of television, the term 'slow TV' has been used to refer to a similar approach to programming that explicitly rejects dominant televisual conventions and embraces an aesthetics of boredom with the aim of carving out an alternative viewing experience. First popularized in 2009 after the Norwegian Broadcasting Corporation (NRK) broadcast its seven-hour and twenty-minute 'Train Ride from Bergen to Oslo', the paradigm of slow TV has been used to refer to extremely long-form event coverage, including an eleven-and-a-half hour boat journey in 'The Telemark Canal'; twelve hours of sawing, splitting and stacking firewood followed by a live stream of a burning fire in 'National Firewood Evening'; seven hours and twenty-three minutes of 'Salmon Fishing' in the programme by the same name; eight hours and thirty-nine minutes of knitting in 'National Knitting Night', amongst other titles. These shows gained immense popularity amongst Norwegian viewers when they were first broadcast by the NRK, with much-vaunted viewing figures of up to 40 per cent of the market share tuning into the original broadcast.[43] Through subsequent widespread international media coverage, the idea of slow TV quickly gained traction outside of Norway, inspiring similar programming in other countries, with one-off variants appearing in Australia, Belgium, China, France, Iceland, New Zealand, Spain, Sweden and the United States.[44] In the UK, the BBC launched their *BBC Four Goes Slow* season in May 2015 – a five-episode collection of 'deliberately unhurried programmes' modelled on the Norwegian model.[45] Seeking perhaps to capitalize on the popularity of slow TV, in August 2016 Netflix jumped on the slow bandwagon, acquiring eleven episodes of NRK content, and promoting them under the special 'Slow TV' collection banner.

In keeping with other slow cultural trends, these programmes have routinely been marketed through discourses of cultural speedup, which frame the experience of watching as both a relaxing alternative to more conventional televisual formats and a form of self-care in a rapidly accelerating society. As the commissioning editor of the *BBC Four Goes Slow* series, Cassian Harrison explained, 'We are so used to the conventional grammar of television in which everything gets faster and faster, we thought it would be interesting to make something that wasn't continually shouting at you and coming up with the next climactic moment'.[46] A key element of slow TV across all of its iterations is an emphasis on mundane, extremely long-form events in real-world locations, which are depicted in simulated real-time structures, from start to finish, filmed from mostly fixed camera positions, with little or no commentary, minimal editing, music or other such interventions. This distant, observational entry point onto highly over-determined activities such as knitting and woodworking, and on stunning natural settings such as Norwegian fjords and the British countryside, makes for what Helen Wheatley calls 'distinctly unspectacular spectacular television'.[47] Through its embrace of protracted temporal structures and uninterrupted processes, slow television embraces boredom as a means of carving out a 'space freed from eventhood', which, as Wheatley argues, facilitates a more contemplative viewing experience than television normally allows.[48]

Across slow TV's press reception, the image of an 'attentive, culturally informed' viewer has often been emphasized as one way of explaining the appeal of shows that are extremely long and distinctly boring.[49] In Thomas Hellum's influential TED Talk on what he calls 'the world's most boring television', the slow TV co-creator works hard to account for why a format that is so patently boring, which seriously strains any viewer's capacity to watch attentively across its unrelenting durational structures, might have resonated so strongly with audiences. One of the conclusions he draws is that slow TV's 'unbroken timeline', with 'all the boring stuff in there' produces a heightened expectation that 'something might happen, though it probably won't'.[50] His talk cites a Tweet from one viewer of 'Train ride from Bergen to Oslo' that reads: 'I am 76 years old and have just watched the best television program ever. I watched all the way until the train stopped. Just before the end station, I rose from my seat to get my luggage. I hit the curtain rod and realized I was in my own living room.'[51] This quote attests to slow TV's production of spectators who are intensively absorbed through boredom into the here and now of the show's representation. In a similar vein, NRK's slow TV press release accounts for the format's allure by explaining that it produces 'a unique experience, the feeling of being present in real time and space. Whether the arena is onboard a train or a boat – or in a venue where knitting pins are clicking away for 24 hours straight, both Norwegian and international viewers are captivated'. Musing over the seeming paradox of pleasurable, captivating boredom, the press release goes on to question: 'Could this be a counter-reaction to our stressed everyday life?'[52]

This framing of boredom as a gateway to intrigue evokes John Cage's much-cited adage that anything that is boring after two minutes becomes less so the longer you look at it. Kenneth Goldsmith calls this 'unboring boredom': the sort 'that we surrender ourselves to ... as a way of getting around ... the vapid "excitement" of popular culture' by immersing ourselves in the 'purposely boring'.[53] As Goldsmith notes, this unboring boredom has its roots in avant-garde experiments with duration, such as *Empire* (1964) and *Sleep* (1964), Andy Warhol's great monuments to eventlessness. These have often been framed as what Pamela M. Lee calls 'cinematic endurance test[s]', films that are 'more frequently discussed than seen', their profound boredom so taxing as to offer up 'resistance to spectatorship'.[54] As Erika Balsom writes in her evocatively titled essay 'Watching Paint Dry', throughout much of the experimental cinema of the 1960s and 1970s, this demand that the viewer should 'look differently, harder, longer' was nestled inside a 'utopian promise' that boredom might allow the viewer to 'inhabit a different economy of signification and attention'.[55] Drawing on Crary's concerns about the 'dispossession and acceleration of time' in the era of 24/7 capitalism, Balsom's piece doubles down on the promise of unboring boredom in the present day, by musing that '[t]o watch paint dry, to watch for the unspectacular, to strain at the edges of perception: this might offer just the pedagogy of attunement needed' in the 'numbing blizzard' of 24/7 screen-based media.[56] She concludes with a sentiment shared by many experimental and slow cinema proponents that the physical space of the cinema might provide the haven of boredom that we need to reinvigorate a lived experience of time that is under threat. In the face of digital media's 'all pervasive glare', Balsom urges us to 'turn away from the plurality of screens and toward the single rectangle: the movie theatre, once aligned with distraction, now sweeps away the pings of real-time communication. Where else can we be so blissfully offline?'[57]

The widespread media coverage of slow TV systematically reinforces this same idea: that an active embrace of unboring boredom in a televisual context might provide a refuge from the stresses and pressures of everyday life, enacting a much-needed temporal re-calibration. Slow TV's aesthetic features work along these lines, cultivating restorative atmospheres that viewers can tune into as a temporary respite. And yet, while slow TV may incite some viewers to 'look differently, harder, longer' in a disciplined effort of waiting for something eventful to happen, this is not the way that these shows have typically been embraced by viewers. Indeed, the discursive construction of slow TV as a refuge from the pressures of always-on culture overlooks the multiple and overlapping ways that this show's much-publicized slowness is threaded into other temporal practices in a digital network culture. From its original NRK broadcasts, slow TV was framed as 'event television', emphasizing the importance of collective and indeed *connected* viewing. During the first broadcast of 'Train Ride from Bergen to Oslo', the show's producers encouraged viewers to react in real time, via a dedicated chat forum on Reddit and through the designated social media hashtag #Bergensbanen on Facebook, Twitter and Instagram.[58] While the episode embraces slowness as an aesthetic strategy, the live broadcast repurposed this slowness within the collective rhythms of networked media, giving it an intensity that it might otherwise lack in isolated viewing contexts. Moreover, the NRK has made each episode of slow TV available on their website, both for streaming and as a downloadable torrent file that is shared under a Creative Commons license. While some viewers may still watch the episodes at their own leisure, they have a range of options as to how, when and for how long they access the content, and what they choose to do with it. From its inception, then, slow TV has been more complexly woven into the intensifying rhythms of screen-based media than is often recognized. And yet, within this context, it offers viewers embodied experiences that feel comparably less frenetic, less intense, less demanding. As we shall now consider, it does so primarily by foregrounding television's capacity to affect the moods and atmospheres of viewing through strategies of ambient mediation.

Boredom-on-demand and television's ambient turn

Through its downplaying of narration, its evocation of gentle, drawn-out processes and its amplification of soothing ambient soundscapes, slow TV embodies features that are characteristic of the wider aesthetic category of ambient media. As Paul Roquet argues in his book *Ambient Media: Japanese Atmospheres of Self*, ambient or atmospheric media have become more common in post-industrial societies since the 1970s, emerging as key technologies of self-care in a neoliberal culture that places increasing demands on subjects to regulate their own moods via atmospheric modulation. As ambient and atmospheric media scholars have argued, the context of ubiquitous computing has further intensified ambient aestheticization, enshrining it as a key feature of everyday life.[59] While all media play a role in generating mood, as Roquet notes, ambient mediation is 'concentrated at the intersection of therapy culture and more recognizably aesthetic pursuits'.[60] Ambient media prioritizes the production of calming moods and restorative atmospheres via an increasing focus on 'background forms of attention', which act on the viewer's bodily presence in space and time, seemingly without her conscious effort.[61] While 'ambient television' has long played a role in cultivating particular atmospheres in public spaces, as Anna McCarthy has documented, in the context of user-directed media, this work of tuning the atmosphere via media objects has devolved onto privatized subjects, who do so via streaming platforms.[62] This requirement for ambient mediation and calming affect has been paralleled by the rise of new aesthetic formats and new viewing practices, including what Helle Breth Klausen calls 'self-medicating media'.[63] Klausen notes that digital media objects such as ASMR videos, ambience videos – a genre of YouTube video that pairs relaxing soundscapes with slow, comforting animated scenery – Spotify playlists of soothing sounds, and meditation apps all work along these lines, to produce atmospheres of sensory calm and ontological security: 'As soon as you have entered this universe, you don't have to give it any more thought. There are no sudden sounds. There's no narrative you have to keep up with in order to be a part of it … You know what's going to happen, and it's predictable in a very safe and soothing way'.[64]

The slow TV phenomenon fits nicely within this description of self-medicating media. Although it has been constructed as an alternative to the pressures of cultural acceleration, its appeal is entirely in keeping with an ambient aesthetic that is now dominant across digital and especially social media, which privileges vibes, aesthetics and 'feels' over storytelling or narrative conventions. Participating squarely within this ambient turn, slow TV co-exists with a range of other low-intensity formats and genres, from ASMR videos, casual games and sleep podcasts to ambiance videos, white- and brown-noise videos[65] and good old-fashioned 'rerun TV', as resuscitated by streaming providers such as Pluto TV.[66] Across this spectrum of boring and soporific media, low-intensity aesthetics work to produce less concentrated and demanding relational attachments between the beleaguered always-on subject and her media objects. In this specific context, the boredom that is elsewhere castigated as the enemy of contentment is re-invested as a potential source of spectatorial pleasure. As Scott Richmond and James Hodge acknowledge, the pleasures of always-on subjectivity are decidedly not those gained from 'concentrated attentiveness' or 'hyper-productivity'. Rather, 'the pleasures of being always on are the pleasures of being otherwise, of managing, of finding relief' from the burdens of being a subject, of paying attention 24/7. As Hodge maintains, the 'dominant (but also quiet) pleasure of always-on subjectivity is one that engages the full body and its sensorium, offering a different form of relationality than the one ruled by liberal personhood. Its pleasures do not engage the mind so much as they solicit the skin'.[67]

Slow TV's aesthetic strategies work along these lines, through ambient techniques that invite viewers to tune into its atmospheres of full-bodied restorative calm. The format's deployment of regular, gentle sensory cues that are clearly locatable within its comforting settings beckons the viewer to participate in an atmospheric surround that feels qualitatively different to the staccato rhythms of daily life under late capitalism. For example, 'National Firewood Evening' summons up feelings of warmth and the pleasant smells and sounds associated with burning, crackling wood. 'Train Ride from Bergen to Oslo' and other transport-based variations on slow TV induce the gentle sensation of smoothly gliding through lush and magnificent landscapes. 'National Knitting Evening' conjures a powerful impression of co-presence induced through the regular background murmur of people idly chatting, set against the steady syncopation of knitting needles. Slow TV's embrace of strongly embodied feelings in fixed settings provides what Roquet describes as '*imaginary sensory landscapes*', which work to '*filter, unify,* and *stabilize* existing environments'.[68] The show's emphasis on real-time structures and the 'unedited timeline' is crucial here, producing a felt continuity between the viewer's pacified body, and the unbroken continuity of the televisual body that is implied through the (nearly) real-time structure. This temporary feeling of unbroken continuity, of gently syncopated or smooth, flowing rhythms is a central feature of these shows' appeal for spectators, whose rhythmic relations to the rather more chaotic, fragmented tempo of 24/7 capitalism feel anything but gentle, predictable or regular. By providing a unified, stable and gentle sensory surround, slow TV's aesthetic formula conveys a sense of ontological security in a context otherwise marked by fragmentation and anxiety.[69]

As Roquet points out, the appeal of ambient media needs to be approached not in terms of 'what it *means*' but rather 'what it *affords* as a technology of self'.[70] As a technology of self, slow TV offers boredom as a kind of sensory-affective filter bubble – a space and time of protection and restorative calm in a context of intensification and overload. The press coverage of slow TV's arrival on Netflix repeatedly reinforced this connection between boredom and relaxation, describing the shows as boring *and yet* 'hypnotic, calming and entertaining',[71] 'very relaxing', 'soothing',[72] 'meditative'[73] and as 'The TV Trend That Will Chill You the F Out'.[74] From its inception on the NRK network, slow TV was discursively framed as offering a boredom-induced respite from a culture of acceleration. But after its acquisition by the streaming platform Netflix, there is a renewed emphasis on the user's active involvement in this process of zoning out. In the context of on-demand viewing, the expansive duration and boredom of slow TV enter into a new economy of signification where they are assigned a different set of use-values as a technology of self. Although viewers *might* choose to watch intensively for long periods of time, in a user-directed viewing economy this potentiality is now framed above all as an extension of the individual viewer's agency and self-determination. This point is made in a tongue-in-cheek way by MTV's live blog commentary used to promote the Netflix Slow TV collection, when it points out that the '25 hours of incredibly boring, incredibly soothing reality TV … is not for bingeing or being a completist. Watching a slow TV show all the way through is like eating a king-size bag of Skittles and not throwing out the disgusting purple ones'.[75] In other words, watching slow TV on Netflix alters the nature of 'incredibly boring' programmes by placing a set of tools for altering a show's tempo and duration at the viewer's disposal. In this user-determined context, the boredom that durational formats have hitherto imposed or inflicted on viewers as a test of their attentional capacities is repurposed as a mood that can be dipped in and out of according to the viewer's self-determined needs.

What I am calling boredom-on-demand encapsulates an understanding of boredom as having been brought under the viewer's control and assigned a use value. In this framework, boredom no longer functions as a test of endurance but as a reflection of an active and informed decision-making process about the viewer's specific needs at a given moment. While slow TV might be watched intensively, as evidenced in the example of the rapt seventy-six-year-old viewer alluded to by Hellum, its ambient aesthetics and availability via on-demand streaming platforms also lend themselves to less intensive, spaced-out viewing. The idea that these shows might be repurposed as background fare by some viewers has been a source of unease for many slow TV purists and other cultural commentators. As Mark Lawson anxiously commented in relation to the *BBC Four Goes Slow* series, '[w]hile showing a 120-minute bus journey without commentary may be innovative in its way, such programmes might be seen as positioning the channel as background activity while you drink, rather than "a place to think"'.[76] Lawson's comment betrays a long-standing anxiety about how cultural objects – especially those that are framed as having an artistic pedigree – are used by individual viewers. It also points to a more specific distinction at the heart of slow media, between a framing of media as entertainment, versus an understanding of media as a therapeutic form of self-care.

As a technology of self, slow TV caters to both because it offers both 'hard' and 'soft' types of fascination. According to the 'Attention Restoration Theory' developed by environmental psychologists Stephen and Rachel Kaplan in the late 1980s and early 1990s, hard fascination is 'focused on tasks, entertainment, and reducing boredom', and is a type of fascination that grows out of voluntary attention.[77] Soft fascination, by contrast, is a type of involuntary or backgrounded attention that is diffuse, makes fewer demands and is less stimulus-rich than hard fascination. As Paul Roquet notes, where voluntary, directed attention will gradually deplete, soft fascinations are understood within this paradigm to 'relieve attentional fatigue' by 'resting the inhibitory function' and providing 'a reflective space for attention to wander freely'.[78] The soft fascinations of ambient mediation are thereby able to 'support various levels of attention while generating restorative moods'.[79]

Slow TV's uneventful, durational, gently stimulating environments lend themselves to being experienced in this way, as soft fascinations that stimulate involuntary attention while supporting task-based voluntary attention. As

Seattle-based slow TV viewer Molly Maloney reports, slow TV is perfect when she is 'engaged in mundane but necessary household tasks that require only a small portion of her interest', such as going through bills or folding laundry. She explains that 'Slow TV is good for making the room feel more alive, while at the same time not competing for my attention'.[80] Of course, as feminist media scholars have recognized, television has long been used by female spectators in this way, as a means of making the rhythms of domestic labour tolerable and even pleasurable. Tania Modleski links this pleasure to broadcast television's creation of a feeling of intermittent flow that smooths over the joins between moments of attention, distraction and interruption that characterize the domestic workday.[81] Maloney is quoted in a *Daily Beast* article that frames the appeal of slow TV on Netflix in a different context by linking it to the 'ongoing political nightmare that is 2016'. In a year that gave us Brexit and Donald Trump, slow TV is here promoted as a means of pacifying, de-intensifying, narcotizing the bodily experiences of political turmoil.

The soft fascinations provided by slow TV arguably perform a similar function of atmospheric and temporal modulation for a beleaguered army of today's home workers in a pandemic and post-pandemic context. In her blog post entitled 'Easiest Shows to Watch While You Work from Home', Isobel Moore recommends Norwegian slow TV for the 'familiar noise of a train going along tracks', adding that '[g]lancing up from your work to see snowflakes fluttering down over a beautiful mountain range with those iconic red-paint houses' is 'magical'.[82] Both of these responses frame the appeal of slow TV in relation to the specific aesthetic hallmarks of soft fascination, which include '*being away* (the feeling of being outside everyday space and time), *extent* (the feeling the environment extends beyond the horizon of perception), and *mystery* (the promise of further intrigue)'.[83] Slow TV amplifies these affects by inviting viewers to inhabit a space-time that doubles and expands the physical location in which it is viewed. Moore's post also points to the sense of 'mystery' that the formula produces, through its evocation of the 'magical' feeling of registering something that exists out there beyond the mundane, monotonous atmospheres and rhythms of WFH.

In these examples, boredom-on-demand is closely indexed to the low-intensity aesthetic qualities that are seen to support the production of relaxing moods. However, boredom-on-demand is not limited to slow media content but can also be established through specific user practices regardless of media aesthetics. Indeed, while slow TV and similar formats can cater to a desire for calm and soothing atmospheres through their low-intensity aesthetics, viewers use a wide variety of televisual formats to induce a state of pleasantly neutral boredom. In a range of internet forums from Reddit and IMDb to Mumsnet, users passionately debate the most boring Netflix shows to watch just before bedtime, or to put on as background TV while doing homework or household chores. These forums identify an extremely broad range of shows and genres that they can access on demand – from *Fear the Walking Dead* and *Futurama* to BBC Documentaries and *Kim's Convenience* – as personal and specific to their own tastes and work or sleep routines. Many of these shows deploy elements that individual viewers identify as 'peaceful' and 'soothing', such as 'PBS' or 'National Geographic' documentaries. The series *How it's Made* comes up consistently, often for the narrator's voice, which user LilyNova describes as 'soothing as fuck', adding: '10/10 would fall asleep again. Not sure if it's still on Netflix though'.[84] Soothing voices and 'consistent monotonous volumes and tones' are by far the most frequently noted characteristic of background or sleep-directed television, with David Attenborough and Werner Herzog being two firm favourites amongst forum contributors.[85]

Although viewers often call attention to specific features of these shows that they find soothing, overall, the type of shows that come up in forums focused on television that can be used as a work, study or sleep aid are not very different in kind from the shows that are recommended for entertainment purposes in other television-themed forums. Instead, the advice given frequently focuses on *how* the shows should be watched to achieve the desired atmospheres. For example, in a television sub-Reddit discussion entitled 'What is the best "Background Noise" TV show?', TicTocTac recommends '[a]ny TV show that you've already watched many times and already know what happens in the episode. This is so that you're not drawn to distraction by watching it to find out what happens; you already know'.[86] This advice is echoed repeatedly across user forums and in an extensive range of popular entertainment sites via listicles that recommend 'Ambien TV: Boring Shows That Put You to Sleep',[87] '11 Netflix Shows to Fall Asleep To, Since You Already Know What's Going to Happen',[88] '20 Best Netflix Shows to Fall Asleep to Because Wow We Need Some Zzzzzs'[89] or '50 Best Shows on Netflix to Fall Asleep To'.[90] Like many of the discussions in user forums, listicles frequently focus not only on what kind of shows to watch, but also on how elements of the platform interface and device settings can be personalized to achieve the optimum atmospherics for a given activity. One listicle instructs users that '[boring] shows should be watched at a low volume so as not to wake you once you've fallen asleep', noting that 'you can always re-watch later if you miss something'.[91] In many forums and listicles, the allure of boredom as an appropriate mood for sleep is in an uncomfortable tension with feelings of FOMO that permeate the atmospheres of digital culture. This tension between needing to zone out and wanting to remain plugged in is one of the central features of what Linda Stone calls 'continuous partial attention', an 'always-on, anywhere, anytime, anyplace behaviour' that is motivated by a 'desire to be a LIVE node on the network … to connect and be connected', to 'scan for … and optimize for the best opportunities, activities, and contacts, in any given moment'.[92]

This same volley between tuning in and zoning out is also at work in entertainment news items that discuss the phenomenon of background TV as a work aid. In a piece entitled '8 Netflix "Chorecore" Shows to Watch While Doing Something Else', *Paste* magazine declares that we have arrived in 'the age of Chorecore TV, the type of audiovisual pig slop that has come to dominate Netflix's business model'. Described as 'background noise and … content (not art)', Chorecore is not something viewers '*watch*', 'talk about' 'tweet about', or 'ever really think about … ever again … It's just kind of *there*, soulless drivel built for the smartphone era and the current anxiety epidemic'. Rather than calling for a return to quality storytelling, or urging viewers to break up with Netflix and their devices altogether, the article proposes another use for this mediocre fare by dubbing it Chorecore TV – 'TV to do chores to', and assigning it a use-value as the ideal accompaniment for mundane tasks, from vacuuming to filing taxes.[93] *Stylist* magazine's piece on the topic of background TV similarly emphasizes 'easily digestible' content that makes for 'easy watching' while working from home, or 'even a show that's slightly boring … not so boring that you can't stand to have it going on in the background, but unchallenging enough to not be sucked into the story'.[94] In other words, the pursuit of calming atmospheres conducive to work calls for boredom, but not *too much* boredom. In these examples, boredom is sought after as both a sure-fire sleep and work aid, but knowing how to select the right kind of media content and watch it in just the right way to achieve just the right dose of boredom is an issue that proves highly fraught and subject to personal taste.

Indeed, what discourses of self-determined viewing and televisual abundance often mask is the hard, exhausting work that goes into finding the right media objects to suit our viewing needs, particularly in a culture of abundance. As Caetlin Benson-Allott writes, while televisual discourses have presented TV as 'easy to use, always available, and always entertaining', the task of scrolling endlessly through and across digital platforms looking for just the right thing runs the risk of generating the wrong kind of viewerly ennui and threatens to turn entertainment into labour. We may live in an age of unlimited choice, but televisual plenitude does not always lead to 'complete televisual satisfaction'. Instead, it encourages what Benson-Allott calls a logic of 'comparative evaluation' that generates a lurking suspicion that 'there must be something better on somewhere else'.[95]

By embracing what Derek Kompare calls 'just-see TV' over 'must-see TV'[96] and settling for the 'good enough'[97] over the truly good, boredom-on-demand thus rejects the foundational fantasy of endlessly entertained subjectivity that is promoted by streaming media providers. However, it does so, as we have seen, by framing always-on subjects as diligent and efficient managers of their own affective experience as it unfolds in real time. Swapping entertainment-on-demand for self-medicating media does not disrupt the systems of digital capitalism, as Richmond, Ilu and Pilipets maintain. Rather, boredom-on-demand functions as a strategy that normalizes and helps to maintain these same temporal and economic systems by providing users with different affective and atmospheric intensities that they can modulate and manage at their own behest.

Napflix and always-on subjectivity

In this context of decision fatigue, a range of niche streaming platforms have emerged to address a situation where viewers are increasingly expected to *actively choose* how they zone out. One example is the streaming video platform Napflix. As its name implies, Napflix models itself very closely on Netflix, but its founders describe it as a 'non-profit enterprise' that aims to help busy people sleep. Since its launch, press reports have routinely emphasized the value of the platform as a technology of self in an always-on culture in which sleep is increasingly under threat. One piece in the Health section of the *Metro* newspaper endorses Napflix as a tool for addressing the problem of chronic sleep deprivation in work environments, citing the statistic that '[i]n the US, 29 per cent of workers report falling asleep or becoming very sleepy at work – costing companies $63 billion … each year in lost productivity'.[98] If sleepiness is a clear and present danger of the multi-tasking gig economy, Napflix is promoted through such discourses as a tool for securing the kind of 'intelligent' sleep that beleaguered workers crave.[99]

Boredom is central to the way that Napflix has been discursively constructed, both through its popular reception and the platform's own promotional media. When it was launched in 2016, international press headlines described Napflix as 'The World's Most Boring Channel',[100] 'The New Online TV Channel so BORING it Will Send you to Sleep with Hours of Latin Mass and Quantum Physics',[101] and the streaming platform that features 'the Internet's Dullest Videos'.[102] A promotional video produced by Napflix shortly after its launch describes the platform as 'a free video streaming service designed to bore viewers to sleep. Instead of streaming entertaining movies and TV shows, Napflix aggregates the most relaxing, slow-paced, and downright boring videos from across the Internet ... The idea is to make entertainment boring'.[103] According to founders Víctor de Tena and Francesc Bonet, the platform is a response to an intensified 'content culture' where '[w]e spend hours updating our Facebook timelines, seeing stories on Snapchat and playing boring games on our smartphones'. Instead of emphasizing its value as a space set apart from the frenzy of vulgar boring media, the founders note that 'Napflix understands that boring entertainment exists, and we have given a place where you can enjoy it!'[104] Napflix thus leans into the uses and pleasures of boring media as both a marketing tactic and a means of mood and atmospheric regulation in an always-on context. Through Napflix, viewers are presented with a set of tools for de-intensifying and smoothing out the jagged intensities of everyday life.

The design and layout of the Napflix site play an important role in helping viewers to tune their atmospheres, presenting an element of choice and personalization within a highly structured and easy-to-use interface. The landing page presents several different ways of accessing content, each of which entails varying degrees of effort on the viewer's part in making the selection. The main page features one randomly selected video that can be accessed directly through the play button without the need for decision-making of any kind. This main video feature plays on a carousel that changes every six and a half minutes, and just below it, there are thumbnail images and titles for an additional six randomly selected videos that can easily be played with a single click. Like Netflix's short-lived 'Surprise Me' feature, which was 'quietly dropped' due to 'low use by customers',[105] this option frees the viewer from the burden of 'mindless browsing', forestalling the comparative logic that might lead to (the bad kind of) viewerly ennui.

At the top of the screen, there are two further options: a 'new content' category and a dropdown menu featuring the ten main content categories that can be

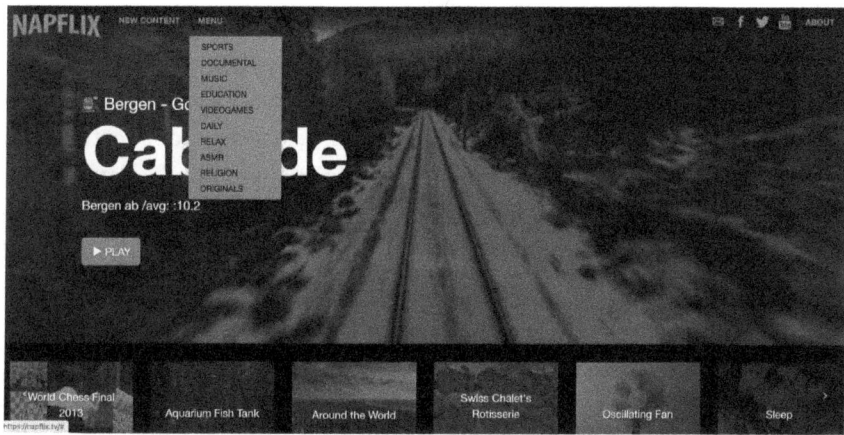

Figure 3.1 Landing page and dropdown menu on Napflix.tv © Napflix 2016.

seen in the screenshot above (Figure 3.1). These offer the viewer slightly more control over the content selection, allowing them to optimize their experience according to their personal taste and viewing needs, while keeping the range of options in each category to a minimum. Whereas many other streaming services design interfaces to create 'an *illusion of content abundance and user agency*',[106] on Napflix, the more selective model of content curation creates a contrasting sense of limited choice and a restriction of user agency to fend off the ennui of the scroll. In other words, the site offers the viewer choice – but not *too much choice* – through categories that are carefully organized to cater to individual viewer preferences.

Furthermore, the platform also has a range of built-in features that help to frame the videos as sleep aids, such as the 'timer mode', which allows users to choose when the video should stop playing, and the 'siesta mode', which rotates the screen on a 180-degree axis, so that viewers can watch from a supine position. But there are other benefits to watching boring content via Napflix, rather than accessing it via one's own playlist on YouTube, for example. One major advantage of the Napflix content selection is that it does not feature ad breaks; for those who want to set the ambiance for sleep to set in, this creation of an uninterrupted stream is a vital part of the site's appeal. In addition, Napflix's minimalist interface design stands in stark contrast to the visually noisy design of platforms like YouTube, which present individual videos alongside an assortment of other data points, such as viewing figures, playback speed options, user comments, and a set of recommended videos and channels listed as thumbnails alongside prompts to 'continue watching' previously accessed content. As Susanna Paasonen notes, 'video sharing platforms, from YouTube to PornHub, comprise vast, unsteady archives where content available today may be gone tomorrow, where historical footage meets video clips just shot, and where novelties fight for attention with popular sticky content garnering millions of views'.[107] On Napflix, by contrast, the user is provided with an interface that helps to drown out the noise from the outset, relieving her just a little bit from experiences of information overload that might otherwise characterize screen engagement. It fights for the viewer's attention, paradoxically, through its embrace of a recessive aesthetic that seems not to demand very much attention at all.

The concept of boredom is thus an important part of Napflix's interface design, sharing conceptual ground with other 'boring' design trends, from BoringPhones – the 'minimalist smartphone with all the useful things, but none of the distracting stuff'[108] – to 'borecore' – a trend for understated fashion amongst the uber-rich, designed to express their 'approachability' and averageness, as popularized by the cast of *Succession* and Gwyneth Paltrow's appearance in a Utah ski crash trial in 2023.[109] Napflix's framing of its content via a comparatively quiet and simple platform design helps to drown out ambient noise, establishing a 'mood-orienting frame' that helps to prime viewers for 'a calming affective experience'.[110] Finally, the discursive framing of the platform within the cosy Spanish cultural tradition of the 'siesta' works to naturalize sleep-directed media and obscure the increasingly chaotic work practices and conditions that make it necessary for some workers to timetable their sleep into ever smaller units.

To date, Napflix has produced a small selection of videos for the site – 'Napflix Originals' – which include a thirty-one-minute video of the sun rising over Central Park, a ten-hour video of an oscillating fan (Figure 3.2), a twenty-three-minute video of a New York subway journey, and a twenty-four-minute video of the crashing ocean waves in San Sebastián, Spain. However, the vast majority of the site's content library is sourced from free, open-access material that exists in other locations on the internet. Napflix's very *raison d'être* thus hinges on its niche content curation; its selection of material that – according to its founders – is so 'repetitive and boring' as to induce sleep.[111] Within these parameters, the site curates a range of material, divided into eleven distinct category options, including Sports, Documental [*sic*], Music, Education, Videogames, Daily, Relax, ASMR, Religion, Originals and New Content.

Figure 3.2 'Oscillating Fan' by Napflix © 2016.

Given its framing as a sleep-inducing platform, most – but not all – of the videos included on Napflix deploy low-intensity aesthetic qualities that lend themselves to ambient atmospheric and mood regulation. As defined by Ulrich Schmidt, ambience is 'the production of a distinctive *effect* characterized by an *intensification of the experience of being surrounded*', with ambient media placing the subject '*in the centre* of a given situation' and 'producing the experience that everything is "going around" the subject and nothing else but the subject'. In contrast to traditional media objects, ambient media are experienced as 'open, formless fields' with no elements that stand out from the rest, no parts calling for attention more than others, and with everything in continuous variation.[112] As Schmidt claims, ambient fields thereby produce a strong feeling of 'ubiquity', dissolving distinctions between figure and ground, and between viewing subject and ambient field.[113] In his philosophical work on the aesthetics of atmosphere, Gernot Böhme similarly points to the essentially 'indeterminate status of atmospheres, between subject and object' when he suggests that:

> One does not quite know whether to attribute them to the objects or environments from which they emanate or to the subjects who experience them. One also does not quite know where they are. They seem to fill the space with a *Gefühlston* (feeling-tone), like a haze, as it were.[114]

At stake in ambient mediation is thus a process whereby the viewing (or listening or reading) subject's strong sense of self is gently dissolved into an ambient field or atmosphere that surrounds the subject and provides protection from unwanted stimuli.

On Napflix, the videos that appear under the 'Relax' category correspond most closely to the hallmarks of ambient mediation as defined by Schmidt. Videos with titles such as 'Tropical Rain', 'Burning Fireplace', 'Tropical Beach', 'The Sound of Rain', 'Birds' and 'Flying Through Clouds' focus on natural elements such as lush jungles, pristine beaches, dense forests, clouds, exotic fish and other wildlife. Sound plays an essential role in these videos, providing the illusion of a stable and continuous background that ensconces the viewer even once they have closed their eyes. Audiovisual cues such as steadily falling rain, lapping waves, bubbling streams, crackling fire and birdsong work to create an 'incubatory space' that provides 'a heightened level of protection from exterior threats'. As Roquet suggests, this allows the individual to 'redirect energies usually devoted to coping with the outside world to the interior task of physical and emotional healing'[115] – at least for the time that they remain within the enclosed incubatory space of ambient media.

Unlike many of the videos featured elsewhere on the site, videos in the 'Relax' category do not tend to foreground temporal processes so much as they create an immersive atmosphere for viewers to experience via sensory means. These videos have a diffuse quality, composed of a minimal set of audiovisual elements that gradually modulate over time, unfolding as 'a steadily smoothing sine wave' rather than as a teleological process.[116] For example, in 'The Sound of Rain', rainfall gently waxes and wanes while the camera position and all other elements within the frame remain fixed for the full two hours and four minutes of the video's unfolding. 'Tropical Rain' provides a similar experience of gently modulating movement through its soundtrack, which includes the sound of rain falling through dense foliage onto a forest floor, mixed with periodic distant bird cries. However, in this video the visual perspective changes intermittently across its duration, with straight cuts revealing different visual details within the setting. The impression is of what Schmidt refers to as a total field, with the camera disclosing elements of the environment gradually, in an unintrusive way, providing minor variations within a structure of continuity that feels predictable and unthreatening.

The visual composition of 'The Sound of Rain' is striking: a six-pane window nested inside the video frame creates a strong contrast between the interior and exterior (3.3). This 'out-the-window' framing that we see in the screenshot below is a staple of many ASMR and ambiance videos, which work to produce a cosy, calming space for viewers to inhabit.[117] Through the window in this video, we can see vivid greens of various tones, textures and hues, but the distinct edges and contours of the foliage are obscured by both the frosted glass in the bottom third of the window and the condensation and fog in its upper two-thirds. While the visual composition thus cues viewers to want to know what is happening in the world beyond the frame, the video does not provide any elements that might cater to this type of visual curiosity. Not only does nothing happen for the full two hours of the video's duration, what we do see appears as a hazy ambient field, with no discrete parts except for the panes of glass that obscure our access to the scene outside. In short, there is a darkened room, there is a smear of vivid green and there is steadily falling rain. Nothing else happens for the full two hours of the video's duration. In keeping with an ambient aesthetic, this video 'does not refer beyond [itself]' in quite the same way that traditional or narrative media do'. Like other ambience videos, 'The Sound of Rain' is not experienced as 'a window onto a world' but rather as an ambient field of 'interrelated yet separate sensory points'.[118] The darkness that surrounds the window helps to blur the boundaries between the viewer's (presumably darkened) surroundings and the video itself, creating the womb-like ambient field for viewers to inhabit (Figure 3.3).

Many of Napflix's videos work as 'ambient events' that take the viewer on a journey, whether literally, as in the example of 'Train Ride from Bergen to Oslo' (which features in the Napflix library under the alternative title 'Cab Ride'), or figuratively, as in 'Car Wash "n" Clean', or 'Meditation Class'. These videos feature processes that are completed from beginning to end and which take place over a set duration. Although they do offer a beginning, a middle and an end, the emphasis in these videos is not on the destination but on a given process in the present of its

Figure 3.3 'The Sound of Rain' by Napflix © 2017.

unfolding. The ambient effect of these videos is thus 'more *temporal* than spatial', creating the experience of a time-space that 'circulates around' and 'surrounds the subject in and with real time'.[119] The videos 'Hourglass with Blue Sand' and 'Ten Hour Timer' take temporality itself as the main focal point. In traditional narrative media, a countdown often functions to activate a sense of tension and to sketch a movement towards a fixed goal. Here, by contrast, the countdown works to involve viewers in the ambient quality of ubiquity, a feeling that Schmidt refers to as being akin to 'a river, a car ride, a digital device, a distant soundscape or a fly on the wall'.[120] The steady temporal flow of these videos aims to produce a feeling of ontological calm against which sleep might set in.

Other videos on Napflix focus more on repetition and monotony rather than processuality or temporality. For example, 'Swiss Chalet's Rotisserie' and 'Doner Kebab Cam' both picture meat rotating slowly but steadily against a cooking heat source. In these videos, there is no sense of progression or change; the meat never actually cooks. Instead, the focus is on the formal principle of rotation and the loop. Indeed, these and other videos on Napflix – such as 'Power Juicer Pro', 'Juice Filling Machine', 'Conveyor Belt Sushi' and 'Oscillating Fan' function essentially as looped white or brown noise videos, emphasizing audiovisual patterns of monotony, repetition and nothing really happening. They hold the viewer in a tempo of repetition and stasis, watching the same low-intensity stimuli repeat itself over … and over-… and over again. In this over-and-over-and-over again pattern, the subject's attention is arrested, and within this space of arrestation, perhaps a little bit of the burden of choice is also suspended, delayed or resolved. Citing Silvan Tomkin's claim that '*I am, above all, what excites me*', Susanna Paasonen speculates that boredom might then stand not just for a 'lack of excitement' but for 'a fundamental lack of appetite that undoes the self'.[121] As I have been arguing in this chapter, the fundamental paradox of boredom-on-demand is its activation of a viewing subject whose agency is understood to be empowered through its embrace of the nothingness that boredom holds within it, its desire for the self-erasure that boring media might bring.

Conclusion

Questions of platform design and personalization are thus key to the re-framing of boredom as a technique of ambient mediation and a technology of self-care in an always-on culture. As we have seen, platforms such as Netflix and

Napflix have worked hard to position this idea of personalization at the heart of user-directed television, framing attentive, rational decision-making as crucial determinants of the viewing experience, even when the goal is just zoning out. While viewers have long fallen asleep in front of their television sets, in the era of streaming platforms viewers are framed as actively involved in choosing the right content according to their taste profiles, and hence as more responsible for achieving their own relaxation and sleep. In this instance, sleep is framed as a state that is not purely biological, but which individuals are required to optimize through their on-demand media.

Streaming services such as Netflix and Napflix help to shore up the fantasy of the viewer as having an active and rational agency over their time and viewing schedule, over their moods, and over their atmospheres of sleep and productivity. But they also mask the hard work of making choices in the era of unlimited choice. Indeed, the privileging of self-determination in a user-directed viewing context produces an uncomfortable friction with the conflicting need that always-on subjects also have, to be released from the din of choices and data, to float off and merge with the background ambiance. If, as Roquet, Schmidt and Böhme suggest, ambient aesthetics can cultivate a desire to subtract markers of identity and 'to *merge* with the atmosphere', they also have the counter-effect, in these examples, of sustaining 'the illusion of an autonomous self' who is in control of these atmospheres. Both of these positions are, as Roquet notes, 'essential to neoliberal biopolitics, working to obscure the everyday back-and-forth of ambient subjectivation'.[122]

Boredom-on-demand promotes a similar paradox of agency by providing a kind of attachment that is somewhere in between self and media object, floating aimlessly in the atmosphere. The low-intensity aesthetics of boredom-on-demand are experienced by always-on subjects as pleasurable not just because they afford a temporary reprieve from the frenzy of digital communication, but because they imply a temporary retreat not just from the external world, but from desire altogether. As Richmond puts it: 'Bored, I am a subject, but not an agent'.[123] While television in a post-network era has been re-framed as an ambient medium, which might afford opportunities for viewers to actively carve out spaces of relaxation, these are always in an uncomfortable tension with competing demands for attentiveness and productivity in an 'always on' culture. While this 'ambient turn' frames viewers as having more control over their own atmospheres and moods, over their time and experience, it also, as Roquet suggests, 'turns the atmosphere into a site of ever-increasing control and modulation', placing increasing demands on subjects to monitor, control and manage their experience continuously, often in ways that make sleep more elusive, productivity even less practicable.

Although they are promoted as such, the trends discussed in this chapter are not alternatives to always-on culture. Rather, they represent important strategies of diversification and expansion, which only further encourage the steady erosion of states of deep relaxation – including profound boredom – in favour of the imperative to keep streaming. As Netflix CEO Reed Hastings famously commented in 2017, the streaming giant's biggest competitor was, at that point, not Amazon Video, YouTube or broadcast television, but rather the human need for sleep: 'You know, think about it, when you watch a show from Netflix and you get addicted to it, you stay up late at night. We're competing with sleep, on the margin. And so, it's a very large pool of time'.[124] The multi-tasking background TV viewers that I have considered in this chapter have helped corporations like Netflix to increase their market share by further eroding any meaningful distinctions between work and leisure, wakefulness and sleep. As we have seen, boredom has been enshrined in this context as offering a means of de-intensifying the frenetic atmospheres of daily life. While it presents boredom as a kind of 'incubatory space' set apart from the frenzied rhythms of more mainstream media consumption, this enclosure serves to bring viewers more fully into what Roquet calls the 'walled-garden logic of platform capitalism'.[125] Through its promises to promote productivity *and* relaxation, and to make televisual spectatorship compatible with an ever-growing range of everyday tasks, boredom-on-demand thus offers a means of extending the window of engagement between the viewer and the platform, chipping away at sleep as the final impediment to 24/7 networked media immersion. As I will consider in the next chapter, during the Covid-19 pandemic, social media platforms such as TikTok tapped into and updated such promises of total immersion and round-the-clock pleasure, by offering users specific tools for managing boredom, organizing attention and interfacing with the strange new temporalities of lockdown life.

4

#BoredintheHouse
TikTok and the rhythms of #lockdownlife

Throughout this book I have developed the claim that boredom has been increasingly instrumentalized in a network culture as a mood that produces value for media corporations by driving users back to entertainment networks. Looking back at this claim from a post-Covid perspective, it is apparent that this optimizing of boredom also played an important role in premediating the Covid-19 pandemic. By providing the training and tools to fend off boredom, the neoliberal culture of networked entertainment also modelled in advance the techniques that would subsequently help users to navigate the newly boring conditions of life under lockdown. But if networked media have long been positioned as technologies for managing and optimizing our attention and moods, they often do so, as this book has shown, in ways that are actively antithetical to our physical and mental flourishing. While the previous chapters of this book have focused on boredom-themed content produced before the coronavirus crisis, this chapter now turns to the context of the pandemic itself, to explore how the 'problem' of boredom and what to do about it would come to dominate as a major preoccupation of #LockdownLife. Focusing on the outpouring of 'pandemic media' during the global Covid-19 lockdowns, the chapter will consider how the complex relationships between boredom, networked media and neoliberal discourses surrounding attention and mental well-being have been further intensified in this context.[1]

In a time when the health and safety of global populations depended on a shared willingness to #StayTheFuckHome, the task of boredom management through digital entertainment took on a renewed urgency. While streaming television continued to play an important role in this context as a technology that was poised to help manage the tedium of #LockdownLife, participatory platforms such as TikTok gained increased visibility as tools for working through the feelings of stuckness, stasis and restriction that boredom indexes. Focusing on the 'Bored in the House' TikTok and the subsequent #BoredVibes hashtag challenge, the chapter considers how TikTok offers one technical means of releasing the cramped stuckness of lockdown boredom into the rhythms and flows of contagious memetic participation. It will consider how networked media capitalized on boredom management in the context of the pandemic as a tried-and-tested technique of both physical and mental optimization, to produce a new understanding of responsible citizenship modelled on the importance of remaining at home, remaining connected and remaining entertained. In doing so, platforms such as TikTok – which have profited massively from the pandemic – offer one means of visualizing what a bored public might look like in an age of digital psychopolitics.

Bingeing in the time of Covid-19

In the introduction to this book, I briefly considered how the emerging effort to contain the very real Covid-19 virus was underwritten by a ramping up of the metaphorical war on boredom, as world governments, mental health charities, public health bodies, cultural organizations and media outlets across the globe began to issue advice documents, tool kits, watch lists and activity recommendations for how to cope with boredom during lockdown. Couched as they were in the reassuringly familiar language of personalized viewing recommendations and listicles, these 'What to do When You're Bored in Quarantine' communications helped to smooth the transition to lockdown life, by modelling ways that people could remain entertained while self-isolating. Back in March 2020, one sentiment that was echoed across a range of media contexts was a sense of thinly veiled delight at the prospect that #StayHome restrictions had freed some students and nonessential workers to indulge in epic stints of binge-watching hitherto incompatible with the rhythms of daily life. In many internet memes that circulated in this context, the pleasures of binge-watching were routinely imagined as the silver lining of the cloud cast by the pandemic. One popular quarantine meme establishes a tongue-in-cheek parallel between an older generation who were called to war, and a new generation of conscripts who have been 'called to sit on the couch' to selflessly perform their patriotic duty through binge-watching Netflix (Figure 4.1).[2]
In another, *The Office*'s Dwight Schrute – a character frequently mobilized by meme creators for his 'realist and survivalist' worldview – appears alongside the

Figure 4.1 Netflix Quarantine Meme by anonymous author © The Chive 2020.

caption 'I don't need the Government to tell me to stay at home all day watching TV'.[3] TikToks made in the context of the pandemic frequently riff playfully on this idea as well. For example, in a TikTok titled 'How to NOT get BORED during lockdown! Enjoy!' posted on 5 April 2020, popular British TikToker Bobby Moore explains in an infomercial-style video how viewers can download a VPN on their streaming devices in order to access 'hundreds of TV shows and movies that you haven't seen because they are only available in America'.[4] Binge-watching as a cultural practice works so well in this context because it responds to a uniquely distressful situation of stuckness and constraint felt *en masse* during quarantine by providing feelings of comfort and safety, and an incitement to embrace the freedom from restrictions on viewing time normally imposed by routines of work and school.

What these examples illustrate is the pivotal role that boredom now plays within the targeting and control of bodies and minds in the context of what philosopher Byung-Chul Han calls 'digital psychopolitics'.[5] In the context of the pandemic, there has been a resurgence of interest in the paradigm of biopolitics as an entry point for responding to the strengthening of surveillant power as it traverses across 'medical, political, technological, economic, social, and psychological spheres'.[6] As one indicative example, Paul B. Preciado claims that the coronavirus has precipitated a transition to a new stage of digital capitalism, giving birth, in his view, to 'the new subject of informatic capitalism: the full-time remote worker and remote consumer of the pharmacopornographic economy, for whom being online is the primary form of existence'.[7] He goes on to suggest that in this regime 'our bodies are the new enclaves of biopower' and 'our apartments are the new cells of biovigilance'.[8] As I explore in what follows, boredom management can be considered as one important form of biovigilance that is outsourced to individuals in the context of pandemic self-isolation. However, in a regime of digital psychopolitics, it is not just the body, but also – and especially – the psyche that is targeted as a productive force, as Han suggests when he writes: 'Now, productivity is not to be enhanced by *overcoming* physical resistance so much as by *optimizing* psychic or mental processes. Physical discipline has given way to mental optimization'.[9] The consolidation of digital psychopolitics thus entails a passage 'from passive surveillance to active steering', where power flows through neoliberal 'performance subjects' who internalize an imperative to constantly manage and optimize their own emotions, well-being and general health.[10] What Han calls 'psycho-power' is underwritten by an ethos of positivity, an incitement to continuous pleasure through digital consumption, and a fantasy of freedom from limits and constraints of any kind.[11] As he notes, the 'psychic constitution' of this performance subject 'is not determined by *should* but *can*'.[12] And where '*Should* has a limit … *Can* has none. Thus, the compulsion entailed by *Can* is unlimited'.[13]

During the pandemic, this understanding of unfettered freedom through digital connectivity has been widely mobilized as a palliative response to the physical restrictions and tedium of #LockdownLife. The concept of binge-watching in particular helps to assuage feelings of boredom and stasis by producing the illusion of freedom – to move through space and time, to consume without limits – from within the cramped space-time of lockdown. The notion of the digital stream lends vital conceptual support to this psychopolitical regime by offering an image of time as unbroken and infinite, producing a corresponding image of the subject as defined by a similarly limitless desire to consume content. But as Han suggests, a paradox emerges here whereby absolute freedom to consume results in coercion and subjection.

This tension between freedom and compulsion is evident in the memes produced later in the context of pandemic. For example, in a series of quarantine-related memes that congratulate viewers for having 'completed Netflix', an earlier delight at being freed to binge-watch without limits begins to shade into a creeping anxiety about whether there is enough TV to stave off the boredom of lockdown.[14] These and similar memes poke fun at the dread of exhausting all binge-worthy media by recasting the streaming platform as a game-based challenge that the dedicated viewer has regrettably completed. As the pandemic progressed, this initial sense of veiled contentment would gradually slide into exhaustion, boredom, despair and the realization that the vaunted freedom to binge-watch is perhaps not all that it was imagined to be. A popular *Family Guy* meme that went viral in the context of the pandemic, 'Quarantine – Day 24: Skin Has Fused to Couch', offers a playful but grim recognition of the limits of bingeing as a long-term strategy, calling attention to the state of abject inertia that the practice of binge-watching both demands and aims to alleviate (Figure 4.2).[15]

This point in the lockdown, when the pleasure of bingeing collapses into desperation and burnout, maps onto what Han calls the 'violence of positivity', a state that emerges not only when there is 'too little' freedom – for example, the freedom of choice and time that binge-watching implies – but also when there is 'too much'. As Han notes, the 'positivity of the ability to do everything'

Figure 4.2 Coronavirus Meme variation by author © Imgflip 2024. Original image from *Family Guy* © Disney Corporation, 1999–2024.

transforms freedom into compulsion.[16] Heeding this incitement to limitless pleasure, the performance subject of digital capitalism 'exploits itself until it collapses completely', leading to burnout, depression and more boredom.[17] While digital entertainment platforms have been promoted in the context of the pandemic as gateways to limitless pleasure and as tools for optimizing mental well-being, they act as a kind of digital enclosure that eventually restricts and depletes. In Han's view, being freed to play and enjoy in this context is not freedom, but a 'new prison ... where one is prisoner and warden all at once'.[18] As Han notes – echoing a range of thinkers such as Franco 'Bifo' Berardi, Jonathan Crary, Mark Fisher and others – this framing of freedom as self-determined psycho-power leads to the emergence of new pathologies that correspond with a neoliberal regime of power, such as burnout, ADHD, depression and anxiety.[19] What the digital capitalist economy absolutizes, for Han, is not the good life, but mere survival and 'bare life'. As Han suggests, this is why it invests so much in the concept of well-being, a paradigm that outsources health to individuals, reducing them to nothing more than their 'exhibition value' and 'health value'.[20]

Bingeing's bored body problem

While the paradigm of binge-watching is in some senses tailor-made for the situation of lockdown, at some point, it eventually comes up against what we might call the 'bored body problem'. At stake here is not just the issue of what to do with one's own body when freedom of movement has been severely curtailed, but, more pointedly, the problem posed by any human body's threshold for sustained attentive engagement. As I have explored in previous chapters, states such as boredom and fatigue point to the limits of the human body's capacity for prolonged attention, and as such they have the potential to expose and trouble digital network culture's fantasies of 24/7 productivity and unbroken attentive engagement. This bored body problem is heightened within contexts of spatiotemporal restriction, as McKenzie Wark suggests, writing that 'boredom is not doing nothing. Boredom is something a body does when space will not let the body enter it in a way that transforms the body into something else, so that the body can forget itself. ... If the triggers in space always point toward the same possibilities, just under different signs, then boredom inevitably returns'.[21] Moral panics around the paradigm of bingeing have long called on the dangers that protracted binge-watching might imply for physical and mental well-being.

This bored body problem becomes even more intractable in the context of lockdown, though, because *it is the central problem of lockdown*: how should individuals organize their daily routines to optimize themselves physically and mentally for the constant grind of days, weeks and months spent in quarantine?

As the pandemic continued to rage across the globe in rolling waves between 2020 and 2022, lockdown-related boredom was frequently framed as a threat to the collective #StayHome effort, and also as a mental health risk, especially among young adults.[22] Advice from health organizations and mental health charities in this period consistently emphasized the need to 'stay connected via social media' and to 'stay positive' as part of the global effort to combat the virus and the mental health impacts of lockdown.[23] Throughout the Covid-19 crisis, media reports regularly speculated that the bored body problem might motivate mass flouting of lockdown restrictions and spark subsequent waves of the pandemic.[24] During the height of the third lockdown in the UK, for instance, news headlines such as 'Partygoer Tells Police "We've Been Bored and We Want to Have Fun" As Student Lockdown Party Broken Up' and 'Covidiots Drive 150 Miles Because "Lockdown Is Boring" and Get Car Seized by Police' presented lockdown breaking as a criminal offense as well as an act of egregious stupidity, with a clear tone of derision aimed at those unable to properly manage the tedium of lockdown life.[25] Boredom management was thus framed as a major problem in the context of Covid-19, not only as an issue of individual well-being, but suddenly a matter of public health and the public good.

As one of the most frequently downloaded and used technologies of the pandemic, the video-sharing social networking app TikTok has played a key role in shaping the affective experience of lockdown, working as a privileged site through which the feelings of stuckness, stasis and restriction that boredom indexes in this context are acknowledged and worked through. Social media platforms such as TikTok thrived in this moment in part, I will suggest, because they offer a means of working through a series of thorny tensions that speak to the condition of lockdown: tensions between limitation and liberation, between staying put and staying entertained, and between the collective labours of social duty and the solipsistic pleasures of digital connectivity and performative play. In what follows, I will develop this argument by focusing on the 'Bored in the House' videos and subsequent #BoredVibes hashtag challenge that went viral on TikTok during the first lockdown, to consider how TikTok invites users to 'play' with their boredom through the wide range of video editing and processing tools, and the vast pool of user-generated content that the platform puts at the disposal of its users. By framing the user as both performative player and always-vigilant spectator, TikTok has further instrumentalized boredom as a key site of discipline in an age of digital psychopolitics.

However, while platforms like TikTok have instrumentalized lockdown boredom, it is important to ask *how else* boredom might operate. As an incipient force of felt intensity, what else might boredom *do* within spatiotemporal structures of enclosure? How else might users respond to the painful negativities that have, to a large extent, disrupted previous ways of organizing life? In *How to Live Together*, Roland Barthes writes that in extreme contexts of isolation, individual subjects are afforded an opportunity to experiment with their own rhythms, to discover their own proper 'idiorrhythmy'.[26] Idiorrhythmy refers to a process of 'finding the right rhythm or balance between different ways of organizing life – a rhythm that neither can nor should be formulaic'.[27] In Barthes's view, spaces of enclosure (such as monasteries, sanitoriums, prisons and domestic interiors), have the potential to act as zones of experimentation, defamiliarizing engrained routines and allowing subjects to produce new rhythms that are in tune with their own individual proclivities and desires. As Barthes suggests, boredom provides an entry point onto this process of experimentation, for it entails a disinvestment that detaches the subject from its prior rhythms and habits of being, from its previously recognized desires. At stake in boredom is 'the repeated, extenuated, insistent moment when you find you've had enough of your way of life, of your relationship with the world … It's repetitive, it goes round and round'.[28] Boredom's negative but active force has the potential to contribute to the positive project of inventing new rhythms, new ways of being interested in, and engaging with, the world. Boredom thus operates as a kind of pivot point, either trapping the subject in a loop of the same habits and rhythms of life or opening onto the new. In what follows, I will consider how the 'Bored in the House' TikToks negotiate these tensions by inviting the user's participation in rhythmic relations that are specific to a regime of digital psychopolitics.

Bored in the house, in the house bored

TikTok is best known for its hashtag-propelled participatory challenges, which encourage TikTokers to perform physical stunts, humorous skits, lip-syncing and dance routines based on tracks that are uploaded to the app's audio library. Challenges on TikTok are often based on popular user-generated content that goes viral. Seeking to capitalize on the popularity of such posts, TikTok will sometimes sponsor an official hashtag challenge through the designation of a hashtag and a campaign designed to promote engagement on the site. Challenges on TikTok act like meme templates, offering 'expressive repertoires that simultaneously enable and limit expression'.[29] This tension is central to understanding how platforms like TikTok have addressed the bored body problem in the context of the pandemic, as I will go on to explore in more detail later in this chapter.

One example of an officially sponsored hashtag challenge is the #BoredVibes campaign that was launched by the platform on 3 April 2020.[30] This challenge was based on the viral 'Bored in the House' TikTok that was uploaded on 4 March 2020, by Detroit-based musician and TikToker Curtis Roach.[31] Described as 'the perfect anthem for lockdown', the track has been used in over 4.1 million videos and counting since Roach's original upload, including in a range of performative re-uses of the track by celebrities and TikTok influencers.[32] As the title of the track indicates, these #BoredVibes TikToks tend to picture people in domestic settings performing or trying to displace the feelings of cramped stuckness that are associated with the experience of quarantine.

Viral content such as Roach's 'Bored in the House' track trades on a kind of affective stickiness that invites participation in the midst of pandemic self-isolation. Originating in a 15-second-long post, the video depicts Roach in the centre of the vertical frame, his body outstretched on a polished wooden floor. Perched on his forearms, and wearing casual attire, Roach beats out a simple 4/4 beat pattern by alternating a strike of his fist on the floorboards with a snap of his fingers in the air. This movement – a simple pivot of the elbow from the horizontal to the vertical – is repeated several times as he raps: 'OK, I'm bored in the house, and I'm in the house, bored; bored in the house, and I'm in the house bored'. At the mid-point of the rap, the fist thump/snap pattern is interrupted by five rapid consecutive beats of Roach's fist, before returning to the original 4/4 fist/snap beat.

Visually, he is surrounded by accoutrements of domesticity: in the screenshot illustration below, we can see a floral-patterned rug under his body; something that looks like a fire alarm on the ceiling behind his head, a white plastic laundry basket, and behind him we can just about make out a Barack Obama 'Hope' poster on the wall. These elements help to position Roach within an everyday setting, which is in some senses generic and relatable, at the same time as it is suggestive of both a specific racial positioning and relative economic privilege. While Roach's persona is based on a particular wholesome relatability that he performs across his TikToks – which tend to focus on mundane observations and experiences – this is held in tension with his appearance, which is striking and highly cultivated. In this screengrab from the video, his bleach-blonde dreadlocks show signs of having grown out over time; he is wearing what look like festival bracelets and has a septum ring (Figure 4.3). These elements help to position him within a youth culture that is specific to TikTok. As Melanie Kennedy notes, TikTok celebrity is often premised on a kind of goofy relatability, which Roach effortlessly exudes; but his positioning as a young Black man

Figure 4.3 'Bored in the House' by @curtistootrill © TikTok 2020.

makes him a notable exception to the typical demographic of young, female and normatively white TikTok stars.[33]

What makes this track work so well as a viral TikTok is its use of a very simple metric and lyrical structure, which lodges itself in the body and invites or even compels participation. As one popular press headline puts it: 'The unofficial anthem of self-isolation is a total earworm and we can't stop listening, send help'.[34] The video is produced in one continuous take, using no editing, and there is very little bodily movement or other performative elements that might take the emphasis away from the track's driving beat and lyrical focus on a condition of being 'bored in the house, in the house bored'. The repetition and inversion of the two discursive elements 'bored' and 'in the house' throughout produce a symmetry or circularity that mirrors an understanding of boredom as a closed system that produces nothing but the same thing, back and forth, over and over. Repetition and circularity are, of course, default features of looping video formats such as Vine and TikTok, with many videos, including this one, making the most of the loop as part of their formal structure.[35]

In Roach's 'Bored in the House' track, the first two stanzas create a kind of ping-pong effect that is comparable to the steady and regulated ticking of a clock, through its repetition of the lines 'I'm bored in the house and I'm in the house bored'. Repetition is clearly a distinguishing feature of this track, but as Carol Vernallis suggests, sonic repetition can elicit different effects depending on how it is deployed in combination with other elements. It can be 'combined with boredom and tedium' to convey a downbeat sense of stuckness and ennui, but it 'can also be paired with a kind of jacked-up, unrelenting excitement'.[36] 'Bored in the House' uses repetition to both ends: to express boredom and to defuse it. After the establishment of the ABBA/ABBA pattern in the first two lines, the track introduces minor variations in phrasing and pacing that introduce dynamism and create interest within an otherwise highly repetitive song structure. The introduction of the phrase 'in the motherfucking' in the middle of the earlier refrain suggests a ratcheting up of boredom's intensity, but it also performs a compression of the beat phrasing, creating the effect of rapidly propelling the track forward. Following on from this, the next two stanzas decelerate the beat phrasing by introducing a variation with fewer syllables: 'bored in the house, bored in the house, bored'. Roach's delivery of these lines places an emphasis on the first syllable of the word bored, extending the vowel sound, and producing a drawn out, rolling rhythm that contrasts with the more staccato syncopation and symmetrical lyrical composition of the first two stanzas. Next, the rap picks up pace again through a return to the accelerated and more syncopated beat pattern from the previous line. These variations of pace and beat phrasing produce a counterpoint to the song's minimal, repetitive lyrical content, creating an internal dynamism that is appealing and infectious rather than stultifying and tedious. In this sense, the song reflects and enacts, but also compensates for and displaces, the feelings of tedium that are specific to #LockdownLife. Enacting tensions between repetitive stuckness and rhythmic dynamism, and alternating between boredom and its release, the track thus produces a particularly strong affective resonance for TikTok users in quarantine, acting as an ideal template for memetic re-iteration and mutation.

This tension between bored stuckness and its release is also a central feature of most of the subsequent videos that take up the #BoredVibes challenge. As I will now consider in more detail, many of these videos place a strong emphasis on TikTok as a performative, ludic space that is able to address the bored body problem by propelling it into different types of physical, participatory action. However, as I will also explore, there are elements of some of the videos that simultaneously pull in the opposite direction, performing a desire for a different rhythmic relation to the affective and embodied intensities of pandemic time. In the following analysis, I am restricting my discussion of the 'Bored in the House' TikToks to those that use Roach's original track, and which have been tagged with #BoredVibes and/or #BoredInTheHouse hashtags.[37] Given their quarantine setting, it follows logically that most of the 'Bored in the House' TikToks that I analysed picture people – often individuals – in domestic settings for the most part.[38] While some of these videos offer an illustration of what lockdown boredom feels like, and others bear a somewhat ambiguous relationship to the title track, most of the time the videos depict activities that are aimed at avoiding boredom during long stretches of domestic self-isolation.

There are a typically diverse range of undertakings pictured in these 'Bored in the House' TikToks, which fall into familiar content genres or 'communicative forms', including comedic, documentary, communal, interactive and explanatory style videos.[39] There are also significant variations in the formal logic and stance of the videos, as I will explore in more detail in what follows. For the purposes of this analysis, I classified them using five main activity categories: performative, stunt, 'boreductivity', creativity and everyday life TikToks. Performative TikToks show people performing the title track, either through lip-synching or dance numbers that are choreographed to the beat. Stunt TikToks feature physical stunts, pranks or tricks performed, for the most part, within the space of the home. 'Boreductivity'[40] TikToks display repetitive boredom-avoidance tasks, senseless or zany activity, or tedious busywork, such as systematically removing all the seeds from a Strawberry using tweezers, producing an elaborate and extensive pattern by making a series of handprints on the surface of a domestic shag carpet, or making a Jenga set out of a watermelon. Creativity TikToks showcase artistic processes, crafting, cooking and beauty tutorials or 'life hacks', while everyday life TikToks picture ordinary activities such as snacking, studying, gaming, napping, watching or touching screens and devices, or simply sitting staring into space. This last category of 'Bored in the House' TikTok uses montage or seriality as a means of illustrating a variety of different typical behaviours that are assigned to the experience of being 'Bored in the House', while also performing particular rhythmic relations to #LockdownLife.

These categories are by no means self-contained; many TikToks combine different elements of each, and this is reflective of the recombinatory logic of meme culture. Each of these categories provides a slightly different set of techniques for addressing the bored body problem. While performance and stunt TikToks place an emphasis on the platform's ability to involve the body in spectacular physical feats and high-intensity energy, creativity and everyday life TikToks typically involve less showy forms of physical expenditure, but nonetheless foreground a kind of technical proficiency or agency, which involves embodied know-how and demands attentive engagement. 'Boreductivity' videos can occupy either end of the spectrum, embodying a high-intensity zany energy, or exemplifying quieter forms of embodied attention and agency. In the following analysis of the 'Bored in the House'/#BoredVibes TikToks, I focus on three categories in particular: performative, stunt, and everyday life TikToks.

Performing boredom

Performative 'Bored in the House' TikToks emphasize the song's lyrical content, with TikTokers miming gestures or facial expressions in time with the track. On a basic level, the track provides both a narrative and rhythmic framework for TikTok users to acknowledge the feelings of boredom and cramped stasis associated with lockdown. But it also gives them a set of networked tools to discharge these feelings through embodied performative play. One of the earliest and most liked of the performative 'Bored in the House' TikToks was made by influencer Charli D'Amelio, who is currently the most-followed creator on the platform, with over 151.9 million followers and 5.9 billion likes at the moment of writing. D'Amelio's rendition is set in a fairly generic domestic bedroom; in the screenshot below, she appears in the foreground of the frame in a medium shot, and in the background we can see a bed, a bedside table and a storage bench.[41] The video unfolds in continuous time with no editing, such that the focus is squarely on D'Amelio's expressive performance. As she lip-synchs the lyrics, she pivots her body from the right side of the frame to the left several times, alternating in time with the lines 'bored in the house' and 'in the house bored'. Although D'Amelio is performing solo, this framing evokes the effect of a TikTok split screen 'duet', giving the impression that she is performing with herself. This performance echoes the back-forth movement of the lyrics; as she moves her body from the right of the frame to the left and back again, she gestures with her fingers as if counting the number of times the 'bored in the house' formula is repeated, as seen in the screenshot below (Figure 4.4). Her performance is lively, exuding an energy that sometimes evokes bewilderment, and sometimes seems angry or even aggressive. Indeed, at the end of the video D'Amelio's performance shifts tenor, through a series of hand gestures and facial expressions that are clearly meant as caricatured enactments of hip-hop/street dance. This is in keeping with the much more widespread practices of Black cultural appropriation by TikTokers – mainly white, mainly female – that are used as a means of bolstering celebrity on the platform.[42] As Jason Parham points out in an article for *Wired* magazine, the 'very tools that have made TikTok into one of the most efficient, visible cultural products of the era – easy to use, hypercustomizable – make instances of digital blackface uniquely personal', with content creators 'taking on Black rhythms, gestures, affect, slang' in order to 'grab hold of our attention'.[43] As Lauren Michele Jackson notes, digital blackface often takes the form of 'displays of emotion stereotyped as excessive: so happy, so sassy, so ghetto, so loud. In television and film, our dial is on 10 all the time – rarely are black characters afforded subtle traits or feelings'.[44] At the heart of such practices is a double logic that spurns boredom and other low-intensity forms of expression, while shoring up a 'cultural propensity to see black people as walking hyperbole'.[45] In this instance, digital blackface performance offers – quite problematically – D'Amelio and other TikTokers like her a means of modulating their normatively middle class white girl boredom (the residue of a certain kind of social privilege) into highly animated affective tones and intensities, all the while augmenting their popularity on the site.

Figure 4.4 'Bored in the House' by @charli d'amelio © TikTok 2020.

Some performative TikToks contain more elaborately or imaginatively composed dance numbers; in their video, brothers James and Jack Wright perform a tightly choreographed, frenetically paced dance performed in what appears to be an expansive entryway or front room. Their choreographed limbs are entirely in synch as they perform, and both brothers smile exuberantly, their eyes fixed continuously on the camera. The video's subject line – 'we'll dance to anything … also do this dance if ur in the house bored' – invites the bored viewer's participation, recommending TikTok dance as an ideal technique for releasing the cramped restriction of lockdown boredom into full-bodied, effortful participation. Another TikTok, made by Leona Stewart, features imaginative foot choreography, with a camera setup focused on the limbs and feet of two subjects who are outstretched on a bed (Figure 4.5). We see three of the four feet initially, each of which has its own hand-drawn paper sign attached bearing the words 'Bored', 'in the' and 'House'. Propelled by the feet, these signs move up and down in time with the lyrics, until a fourth foot with the sign 'motherfucking' crosses into the frame, resting in between 'in the' and 'house', before moving out of it again.[46]

What these examples emphasize above all are the pleasures of synchronization at a distance, of bodily mimicry.[47] According to Dominic Pettman, this 'will-to-synchronize' is a pervasive aspect of human experience, one that takes on different forms in different contexts. In a digital network culture, it is 'deeply colored by the experience of alienation', marked by a fantasy that our smart screens will bring us into synchronicity with other people in a 'banal beyond ... *somewhere out there* ... where life is being lived *as it should be*'.[48] This desire for collective synchronization takes on a special kind of urgency in the context of the pandemic, as individuals are suddenly faced with the task of remaining connected while remaining at home. Being rhythmically synchronized through the pleasures of TikTok dance responds on a very basic level to this condition of pandemic alienation and a desire for connectedness and collectivity. And yet, the notion of 'will' that comes into play in a digital 'will-to-synchronize' is highly ambivalent, indexing a concept of desire that is subjective, expressive and performative at the same time as it is aperspectival and asubjective. Following Byung-Chul Han, what is produced through the ever-accelerating collective rhythms of networked media is a '*collective unconscious*' that operates 'even *faster* than free will' and thus holds the potential to synchronize mass behaviour on 'a level that escapes detection'.[49]

Performance TikToks also offer an obvious means of breaking up the tedium of lockdown life by encouraging users to respond to the song through spectacular or inventive displays of physical movement produced from the confines of the home. In her reading of short-form Screendance videos in the context of the pandemic, Pamela Krayenbuhl discusses how the 'forced vertical or portrait orientation' of TikTok produces a specific kind of choreography that is compacted and constrained, with a focus on the 'face, as well as hands, arms, hips, and butt' rather than on footwork or expansive movements in space. She argues that in the context of the coronavirus pandemic, these 'constrained dances' constitute a '*performance of entrapment*, mirroring our shared experience of being stuck

Figure 4.5 'Bored in the House' by @leonastewart27 © TikTok 2020.

at home'.⁵⁰ Although Krayenbuhl is writing about TikTok dance more generally, this formal analogy between the cramped vertical frame and domestic setting in TikTok dance and the cramped stuckness of lockdown is further intensified in the more specific 'Bored in the House' performative TikToks. However, if aspects of content and form work to articulate this sense of entrapment, their stance or tone is playful, energetic and even joyful. Their aim is not primarily to express the discontents of home confinement, but to acknowledge boredom while moving both TikTokers and viewers past it. Their logic is participatory and connective, aimed at producing feelings of co-presence and social solidarity from within the context of lockdown. As such, these TikToks reinforce a correlation between staying home, staying entertained and staying connected, shoring up an image of #stayhome citizenship in relation to the demands of boredom management.

Playing with boredom

This is in keeping with the widespread use of mobile apps as entry points onto what Larissa Hjorth and Ingrid Richardson call 'ambient play'. As they note, the concept of ambient play foregrounds the potential of digital media to 'move *between* and *across* collocated and networked spaces', blurring 'divisions between public and private/domestic and rethinking how we experience intimacy and copresence'.[51] In the performative TikToks discussed in the previous section, participating in the #BoredVibes challenge provides a pretext for exuberant dances performed inside the home, but it also affords a feeling of moving beyond it, by linking up with other TikTok users who are similarly bored in their homes.

In addition to its ability to create feelings of co-presence, ambient play works on the 'sensory and affective *texture* or *atmosphere* of a place', involving users in the creation of new temporalities as well as new affective tones and rhythms. Ambient play is a helpful concept for thinking about the use of TikTok as a means of managing 'the boredom, impatience, and bodily agitation of waiting' in the context of the lockdown.[52] While mobile media is often deployed 'anywhere and anytime' as a means of filling up empty time, during the pandemic this function has shifted increasingly into the domestic sphere. This points to a key paradox at the heart of ambient play, as Hjorth and Richardson note: while mobile apps allow us to remain entertained while '*unattached* and on the move', they also 'tether us to a sense of being-at-home'.[53] Indeed, in crucial ways, the dream of an untethered 'smartphone life' that is promoted endlessly in a digital network culture is really a story of immobilized mobile media writ large.[54] During the pandemic, this renewed emphasis on ambient play within the space of the home is ambivalent, producing an understanding of the home as alternately a safe refuge from the outside world, or a kind of prison, where one is both entrapped and observed.

These 'oscillations between tethering and freedom' are reflected in many of the 'Bored in the House' stunt TikToks.[55] While performative TikToks typically emphasize the networked body and its capacity for expressive performance against an unremarkable domestic background, stunt videos often focus on the space of the home itself as the object of ambient play, in an effort to transform a space of restriction into one of fun and games. A significant percentage of #BoredVibes stunt TikToks feature playful tricks, stunts and activities that are normally – and more appropriately – conducted outside: there are many examples that feature TikTok users practicing sports such as soccer, basketball, golf or bowling in domestic settings; there are several that feature people riding on hoverboards, skateboards, scooters or even on dirt bikes in their homes. In one short-lived trend that went viral in #BoredVibes and other TikToks at the tail end of the first lockdown in July 2020, some users transformed their home into a kind of extreme sports arena, by dousing the hard surfaces of balconies, kitchens and other rooms with dishwashing liquid and water, and picturing themselves perilously slip-sliding around them.

In another popular variation on the 'Bored in the House' stunt TikTok that incorporates the 'Level Up' challenge, users construct walls or barricades using everyday items such as toilet paper or plastic cups, and film themselves or their pets attempting to jump over them, one level at a time.[56] While this trend predates the period of lockdown, it performs a different symbolic function in the context of quarantine, due to the new resonances that walls or barricades accrue in this context as potential metonyms for feelings of confinement and restriction. In one of the most popular of these level-up jump videos that feature the 'Bored in the House' track, we see one TikToker (@guille.what) perform a virtuosic leap over a tower of toilet paper rolls packed tightly into an interior door jamb, with only the top third of the door unimpeded by tissue.[57] The TikTok uses slow motion to picture the TikToker as he leaps superman-style from one side of the barricade to the other. The video cuts on action as the stunt performer launches himself into space, to reveal his graceful somersault landing onto layered mats on the opposite side, as pictured in the screenshot below (Figure 4.6). What is articulated here is an intense affective longing for escape from a condition of being 'Bored in the House'. The concentrated pleasure that the video activates for viewers comes from the way that it addresses and activates this fantasy of escape. In other words, its appeal lies in the way that it is able to navigate tensions between boredom and entertainment, confinement and freedom, producing a powerful if temporary illusion of liberation from within the cramped space-time of lockdown. Indeed, such feelings of emancipation can only ever be temporary because the temporality of networks involves a constant process of 'updating to remain the same', as Wendy Chun has argued.[58]

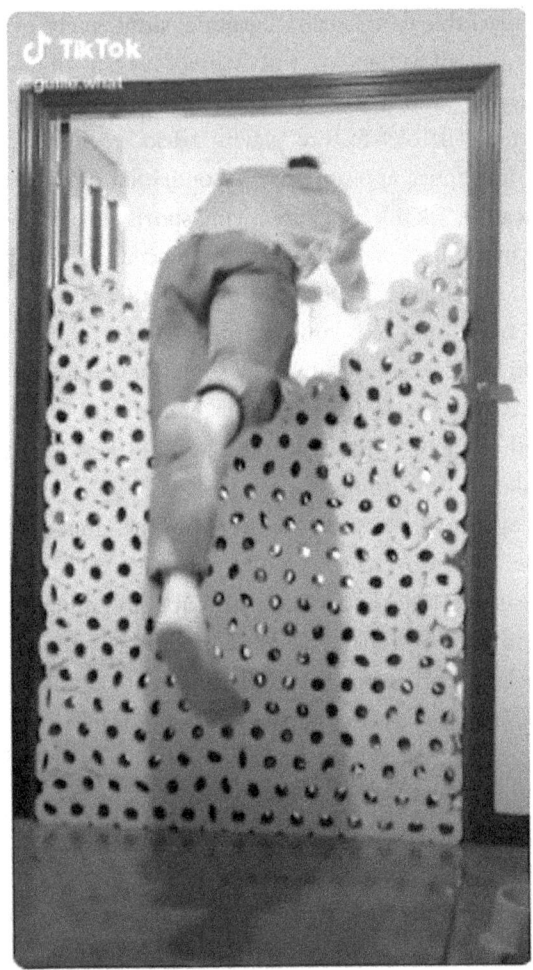

Figure 4.6 'La casa de papel' by @guille_what © TikTok 2020.

While many quarantine memes poke fun at home confinement as an experience akin to incarceration, with jail cells often standing in for bedrooms, as shown in the screenshot below (Figure 4.7), these stunt TikToks re-imagine the home as playground rather than as prison.[59] Mediated through TikTok, the ordinary domestic space of the home affords fun on the condition that we learn to look past habitual ways of using it, to discover creative affordances that have previously been overlooked. This process of creative re-invention echoes Ian Bogost's understanding of play and its relationship with both boredom and limits. While we tend to think of play as a freedom from constraints and obligations,

Figure 4.7 Work From Home Meme, by ZimmerKen © Imgflip 2020.

as Bogost reminds us, play exists in a necessary relationship with structures of restriction, essentially emerging as a result of working through the possibilities contained within limitations: 'Fun comes from the attention and care you bring to something that imposes arbitrary, often boring, even cruel limitations on what you – or anyone – can do with them'.[60] This is reminiscent of the way that meme-based formats such as TikTok challenges work, in that they frame fun within a highly restrictive framework that invites participation, while strongly delimiting the forms that this participation might take. Indeed, as Sabrina Ward-Kimola has persuasively argued, while a TikTok challenge may well '[*look*] very much like a meme, it doesn't *act* like one' to the extent that 'TikTok mimesis exploits an assemblage of working pieces (algorithm, organization, user norms)' to produce something that has already been largely predetermined '*by* TikTok's algorithmic production of culture'. In other words, while all meme templates enable and limit expression, on TikTok these limitations are more rigorously driven by the platform's 'infrastructural conditioning of mimetic possibilities'.[61]

This logic of play as emerging from within the space of boredom and limitation is also at work in the extended version of the 'Bored in the House' track. This extended version was made as a collaboration between Curtis Roach and TikTok rap sensation Tyga, after the latter helped to propel Roach's original track to viral status on the platform by performing his own rendition.[62] Seeking to capitalize on the popularity of the original hook, Tyga invited Roach to collaborate on a single which was released by Columbia Records for streaming platforms on 27 March 2020, with an official video dropping on YouTube on the same date.[63] The video uses the original hook as its opening lines and as the track's central theme, with Roach and Tyga each contributing new lyrical content and crafting performances around it. Through their respective lyrics and performances, the pair comment further on the experience of being bored in home quarantine. They each enumerate a list of things that they do while they are bored in lockdown, referring to everyday activities that are closely associated with the tedious routines of self-isolation, such as 'going through my Netflix' and 'Hulu binge-watchin'' episodes of *Ben 10*', playing 'COD on a PS4', ordering food through 'Door Dash', or eating 'Ramen noodles every night for my din-din'.

However, there are significant differences in the way the pair describe and perform a relationship to lockdown. Lyrically, Tyga raps mainly about the discontents of quarantine, complaining that he is 'Bored [*sic*] than a motherfucker, I ain't doin' shit', and explaining: 'Can't even go on tour, nigga so bored I'm losing my mind', while peppering his account with sexual and financial boasts, perhaps as a kind of compensation. His physical performance of the track reinforces this sense of feeling cooped up or trapped within the confines of his conspicuously luxurious home. Tyga appears in typical lounge attire of sweatpants, a generic white tee-shirt and a baseball cap; at the start of the video, we see him lying upside down on a white leather couch tossing a basketball up and down in the air as if trying desperately to pass the time. A montage cuts to Tyga performing a range of stunts and other mundane activities in and around the space of his opulent home: we see him leaping from one piece of furniture to the next without stepping on the floor, dancing on an ornate marble staircase and on top of a pool table, opening the refrigerator and looking for food, washing his hands while wearing a white decorator's mask, talking on the phone while walking across the top of his mantlepiece, before finally appearing asleep on the sofa. This montage – which replays on a loop throughout the video – pictures the cumulative impact of boredom as a feeling that gradually builds up in intensity until it overwhelms its subject; although Tyga tries to outrun boredom by transforming his home into a space of play and possibility, it eventually wears him down, until he is simply 'bored, bored, bored, bored, bored, bored, bored, bored'.

In his portion of the rap, Roach similarly refers to the tedious discomforts of lockdown life, but while Tyga appears defeated by boredom, Roach turns his self-isolation into a virtue, by rapping: 'I'm a socializin' at a distance/ I'm livin' my best life, mindin' my business ... And my anti-social's for the win-win/Locked down I'm gonna stay stayin' in-in'. Later in the song he professes that 'In quarantine I'm the quarterback/MVP, I'm scoring that'. Roach's physical performance of his lyrics is much more 'constrained' in Krayenbuhl's sense of the term, as if displaying a kind of stay-home virtuosity. As Roach undertakes his part of the rap, his body is literally squeezed into the vertical frame, as he crouches and then sits awkwardly on the floor of his bedroom. He performs the track through a direct-to-camera address where the emphasis is on his facial expression and minimal arm and hand gestures, performed with desultory energy, until Roach signs off with a playful smile at the end. Being bored in the house is thus made to feel almost effortless, taking on a casual ease that might take the edge off of feelings of entrapment and stuckness for viewers.

Through their respective renditions of being 'Bored in the House', Tyga and Roach display what Roland Barthes, in his description of 'extreme-experiences of enclosure' in *How to Live Together*, refers to as a 'kind of athletic performance of asceticism: Who can wall themselves up the most effectively, the longest?' What is staged here is essentially a kind of 'ascetic Olympics, but with reclusion instead of pole-vaulting'.[64] In this battle, the boredom of self-isolation is turned into an expression of civic virtue: who is the MVP of self-isolation? Who has managed to master the art of bored body management that this title demands? What this YouTube video helps to articulate is an understanding of #StayHome citizenship that is modelled on the capacities of subjects to modulate and master the pressures of home confinement, whether by re-invigorating the home as potential playground, or by embracing the condition of being bored in the house as a kind of endurance sport in itself. It is of course significant that this rendition of #StayHome citizenship should be performed by two Black men, given the media headlines that have projected fears about lockdown breaking onto the bored bodies of young men in particular.[65] In this context, boredom management is enshrined as a technique of racialized and gendered pandemic biovigilance, and an expression of virtuous social duty made more palatable through the pleasures of performative play.

By putting on display the myriad possibilities for fun and games that might be contained within private domestic space, these 'Bored in the House' TikToks contribute to an understanding of the home as what Paul B. Preciado calls a 'total inhabitable *ludotopia*'.[66] Writing about architecture and biopolitics during the Cold War, Preciado points to the Playboy mansion and the Barbie Malibu Dream House as exemplifying a new ideal of domestic space, which could contain endless options and possibilities for play. What takes shape through the construction of the home as ludotopia is an 'interior that no longer is characterized by its privacy and in which the inhabitants are conscious of their double theatrical condition: serving at the same time as actors and spectators'.[67] In his more recent responses to the Covid crisis, Preciado argues that the pandemic is precipitating an intensification of this historical process, to the extent that 'what we today call lockdown will probably be considered as a global transition period towards digital capitalism, a sweeping global exercize in informatic pedagogy, which has put an end to the last modern Fordist subjects and to their relation to the Taylorist production machine'.[68] He goes on to suggest that the removal of intersubjective social rituals and their replacement by 'social networks and digital compensations' is generating – and will continue to generate – mental pathologies such as 'anxiety, disorientation and depression' that require new techniques of self-regulation and optimization.[69] Both TikTok and YouTube function in this context as technologies that expose the space of the home as a site of fun, summoning an image of home as ludotopia: a networked space without limits, which yields easily and infinitely to the desires of the inhabitants who are confined within it. In doing so, however, as both Preciado and Han suggest, these platforms reinforce the subject's relationship to digital capitalism and its 'specific forms of submission, surveillance, and control'.[70] Boredom management through digital home entertainment operates in this context as a form of pandemic biovigilance, a new technique of mental and physical self-optimization.

Boredom and the rhythms of #LockdownLife

But as MacKenzie Wark has observed, even the most thrilling game-spaces eventually lapse back into boredom: 'Boredom can be displaced only so far … Boredom always returns'.[71] This has as much to do with boredom's relationship to time as it does with the notion that, as Wark points out, 'what displaces boredom is the capacity to act in a way that transforms the situation'.[72] While TikTok performs a kind of affective modulation that works on – and works over – the space of the home, in the Covid period it performed this transformation within the limitations imposed by quarantine regulations, which required bodies to remain in place for unusually long stretches of time. While TikTok offered one means of addressing the bored body problem by re-potentializing the space of the home into an arena of fun and games, it also advanced a set of tools that allowed users to navigate, and perhaps to better endure, the demanding temporalities and tedious rhythms of lockdown life.

The last category that I classified for this chapter – everyday-life TikToks – speaks to this desire to break up and enliven pandemic time by foregrounding the rituals and routines of everyday life in self-isolation. Of the categories that I analysed for this chapter, everyday-life TikToks make most direct reference to the experience of boredom, often attempting to depict what life in quarantine feels like. As discussed in previous chapters, an important component of the allure of previous video-sharing social platforms such as Vine and YouTube is their ability to picture people in ordinary settings, often depicting 'users simply doing things'.[73] In the wake of Vine, TikTok has taken up this remit of providing access onto the ordinary lives of users, structuring both users and viewers into a shared, temporalized experience of the lived everyday. As one commentator puts it, on TikTok 'you can see kitchens, bedrooms, backyards. It's kind of voyeuristic, in a peeking-around-the-dinner-party-host's-house-on-your-way-to-the-bathroom kind of way'.[74] Because the allure of user-generated social media is based in part on the access it provides to the private lives and daily routines of its users, TikTok has been able to structure a relationship to the pandemic around a promise of showing what life is like in the context of a global pandemic – including what it looks and feels like to be 'Bored in the House'. As one TikToker (@lydialoo121) puts it in a confessional monologue video made during the pandemic in January 2021, TikTok has a particular fascination with 'beautiful montages of boring everyday life, and that's what life is, boring tasks punctuated by moments of excitement'.[75] It is TikTok's ability to visualize this temporalized everyday and to charge it with affective intensity – to make boredom exciting – that has contributed to its success, particularly during the pandemic. In this context, it trades on an affective promise that it can fill up the dead time of solitary boredom by weaving it into the collective rhythms of networked participation.

Unlike performative and stunt TikToks, which attempt to drive lockdown boredom away through effortful bodily participation, everyday life TikToks endeavour to document what boredom looks and feels like in contexts of extended self-isolation. They feature a range of daily activities and habits that typify the tedium of pandemic life, such as snacking, trying on outfits, dusting, browsing for video content, playing video games, staring at art, climbing up walls, cutting or styling one's own hair, sitting on furniture, reclining on sofas or beds, laying on floors, staring into space, sighing heavily, dozing off, doing nothing. For example, in her TikTok from 22 March 2020, captioned 'Ya Bored Yet?' Dominican actress Stephany Liriano (@stephanyliriano) features in a montage that includes a series of very short snippets of what are framed as daily activities in her lockdown routine.[76] Her attire of denim dungarees and black sweatshirt, and her loosely upswept hairstyle help to contextualize the video as providing a window onto Liriano's private domestic life. Firstly, she is pictured yawning while stretching back in a chair; then we see her looking for some food through a point-of-view shot from the inside of her refrigerator; next she stares into space, nods off, catches herself and struggles to stay awake. She then eats dry cereal directly from the plastic lining of an absent cereal box; she studies her image in what is framed as a mirror (but is the device camera); she climbs up the interior of a door jamb and suspends her body there. After this point, the pace of the editing intensifies, in tempo with the second repetition of the accelerated 'bored in the motherfucking in the house bored' stanza. In this portion of the TikTok, we see even quicker cuts of her sitting in a folding chair staring vacantly into space (Figure 4.8); lying on a sofa scrolling through her Samsung smartphone, leaning up against an exterior wall, looking first at the sky and next down into the camera, drumming her fingers on a desk, lying on the floor and trying to roll her tongue and finally bringing scissors up to a section of her hair, in a mock fringe-cutting gesture.

In contrast to Liriano's public persona as a glamorous actress and lifestyle blogger, this TikTok presents a more relatable and behind-the-scenes snapshot of Liriano's everyday life. At 4.4 million views, this is one of the most viewed of the everyday life TikToks, but apart from its particularly skilful use of the platform's video editing tools to keep in precise time with the track's beat pattern, there is nothing particularly out-of-the-ordinary about it. There are many others that use the same montage formula to provide slice-of-life portrayals of users' typical lockdown routines. For example, a very similar TikTok shared on the *Independent* newspaper's TikTok channel (@independent) on 2 April 2020 shows a young white woman seated at a kitchen table stacking rolls of toilet paper, dusting a framed print, doing pull ups in a doorway, seated in the lotus position meditating, looking at a framed photograph of Madonna and Sean Penn, selecting DVDs from an extensive bookshelf, constantly spinning a lighted globe, dressing up in outlandish attire and posing dramatically for the camera, practicing yoga moves, lying on the kitchen floor and finally, eating peanut butter directly out of the tub and pretending to drink red wine directly

Figure 4.8 'YA BORED YET?' by @stefany.liriano © TikTok 2020.

out of the bottle whilst wearing aviator sunglasses and bopping her head to the 'Bored in the House' beat. By providing an insight into the domestic routines of users, these videos work as enactments of public intimacy, which depart from boredom as the basis for a shared acknowledgement of the conventions and clichés of #LockdownLife. Through their knowing deployment of activities such as cutting one's own hair, snacking and binge-watching as widely acknowledged elements of life in quarantine, they have the potential to produce valuable feelings of co-presence, which might mitigate against some of the loneliness and anxiety of self-isolation. As Lauren Berlant has suggested, social media platforms afford a mode of connection that is emphatically 'light impact ... where the bar for reciprocity is so low that anyone could perform it by clicking'. While social media platforms such as TikTok do not work in the 'idiom of the great encounter or the great passion', Berlant suggests it is important to take seriously the space that they might provide for 'calibrating the difficulty of knowing the importance of the ordinary event ... the episodic nature of existence'.[77]

The use of montage plays a key role in the way that these videos frame ordinary life comprising habit, repetition and routine. In contrast with the stunt and performative TikToks, which feature spectacular or zany activities captured for the most part in continuous time, these everyday life videos focus on ordinary activities that are undertaken across the course of a day. Montage privileges a logic of seriality, showing us a presumably sequential series of activities that accrue over an indeterminate period. This allows the videos to compress a dense amount of information into the (then) fifteen-second time constraint, and to characterize boredom as above all a temporal phenomenon that is concerned with duration and endurance.[78] Like Tyga's version of the 'Bored in the House' YouTube, these TikToks insist on boredom as a temporal force that accumulates in intensity, mounting in pressure, often gradually wearing its subjects down. While stunt videos work primarily on the spatial restrictions of lockdown, these everyday life videos address the strange and uncertain temporal dimensions of quarantine. Through an emphasis on desultory gestures and slackened bodily postures, they express feelings of drawn-out ennui that come through long periods of waiting, paradoxically compressing this experience of duration into looping intervals of fifteen seconds or less. They also tend to cycle through a series of in-home solutions for enduring the bored body problem, rather than focusing on activities intended to chase it away, as in the performative and stunt TikToks.

However, while these TikToks express the discontents that come with enduring long-term home confinement, they also offer a means of modulating these feelings in ways that are not always visible. Hjorth and Richardson note, mobile practices have 'adapted to an always-on mode of existence', with mobile devices often catering to 'feelings of anxiety about waiting and productivity', and offering a 'means of occupying what we now regard as dead time'.[79] TikTok is particularly adept at occupying what would otherwise be considered as dead time because it puts at the disposal of users a rich and user-friendly array of sophisticated video editing and production tools, allowing TikTokers to capture little snapshots of their daily lives and to stitch them together into something that feels measured, regulated and cohesive. Although montage can gesture towards the drawn-out temporal force of boredom as it builds and builds, its serial logic also produces a tangible record of movement through time. This emphasis on temporal progress works in tension with the widespread feeling that pandemic time is out-of-joint, a time that has lost its punctual and regulatory character. Everyday life TikToks regulate the out-of-joint tempo of lockdown by providing a more palpable and measured beat: a Tick and a Tock.

These TikToks thus re-temporalize the dead amorphous time of lockdown and help to move the user past boredom's state of protracted suspension by enlisting them in the work and rhythms of 'digital playbor'.[80] Paradoxically, while these videos come closest to showing us what lockdown boredom looks and feels like, they tend also to be the most heavily produced of the five categories of video. In other words, there is a tension between the boredom and 'doing nothing' that they depict, and the time consuming effort they require to make. This tension is directly addressed by one TikToker, Michelle Elman (@scarrednotscared), in her #BoredVibes TikTok from 1 April 2020. Her iteration of the track uses a stop-motion editing technique that makes her stock-still body appear to leap rhythmically between one side of her living room to another, in time with the 'Bored in the House' track's beat. The caption – 'This took way too long to film for it to flop' – recognizes both the time and exertion that this category of TikTok requires. As one *Vice* journalist puts it, the paradox is that while 'effortlessness is the hallmark of a good TikTok … it takes a lot of work to make it look so easy'.[81] The fact that this style of TikTok requires so much time-consuming labour to produce is perhaps part of what has made it so appealing in the context of the coronavirus crisis. Put bluntly, TikTok has succeeded better than most other platforms in providing a space where users can fill up pandemic time in a way that further blurs already fuzzy distinctions between effortful, attentive labour and effortless distracted play. As John Herrman suggests in an article for the *New York Times*, TikTok has pushed further than any other social media company to 'assertively answer' the 'paralyzing' questions '*what should I watch*' and '*what should I post?*' By providing an extensive array of video-processing tools and 'extensive reasons and prompts' that encourage participation, the platform has been able to convert user attention into profit at a massive scale. As Herrman puts it, 'If engagement is how success is measured, why not just design the app where taking up time is *the entire point*?'[82] TikTok has succeeded in this context by providing the tools and nudges that encourage users to 'waste time' in a way that makes that time-wasting feel fulfilling, productive, fun, absorbing.

The app has thus capitalized on boredom as a means of extracting free labour from its users by presenting it as play. However, it is important to understand how the nature of play changes in the context of the performance cultures of platforms such as TikTok. As Byung-Chul Han suggests, '[t]he performance principle removes the ludic element and turns it back into labor', such that playing 'amounts to yoking oneself to the compulsion to perform optimally and achieve maximally ... the utopia of play and leisure yields a dystopia of achievement and exploitation'.[83] Comments such as Michelle Elman's 'This took way too long to film for it to flop' bears witness to the transformation of play into labour, as success and failure is framed through a logic of social media metrics.

Beyond an incitement to shake off the lethargy of lockdown through performance and stunt challenges or by enlivening the tempo of pandemic time, TikTok has also sought to address the bored body problem through an appeal to the pleasures of content browsing.[84] As Shreya Sudarshana and Jonathan Zhou note, a key component of TikTok's success is 'its ability to cater to lurkers – silent users that consume but rarely create content. Lurkers play a critical role in the success of social applications and TikTok has been able to solve lurkers' needs better than any other short-form video or social application'.[85] To compete with on-demand entertainment, social-media companies such as TikTok have repurposed televisual flow into the infinite scroll or stream. By doing so, platforms like TikTok attempt to make good on a long-standing promise that entertainment media can 'stave off the boredom of the banal' by filling up dead time.[86] TikTok and other streaming platforms tap into and update the promise of pleasure that has always been central to previous media technologies, by offering users specific tools for managing boredom, organizing attention and interfacing with the strange temporalities of lockdown.

In a very direct way, the idea of such infinite scrolling echoes the apparent endlessness of on-demand television but upgrades it into the limitless flow of social-media content. In this move, the fear of exhausting bingeworthy shows, of 'completing Netflix', is replaced by a fear of missing something from the never-ending stream. As Ludmila Lupinacci notes, the infinite scroll operates 'under the pressure that, at any time, something worthy of attention – something eventful – might happen, and that social media are the best available resource for us to keep track of this informational flux'.[87] Endless scrolling as cultural practice does not just fill the tedium of pandemic time. It also plays a vital role in providing access to a collective experience of the lived everyday of lockdown in which endless scrolling is always *potentialized* as full-bodied participatory action, even if it isn't acted upon. In the context of Covid-19 lockdown, TikTok made boredom eventful through the promotion of boredom-specific hashtag challenges that potentialized the scroll as a set of scripted actions that might – or might not – propel the bored body into action. This compulsion to remain connected was framed as both a gateway onto pleasurable, solipsistic play and as an expression of social duty, further complicating tensions between work and play in this context.

This is in keeping with the way that mobile technologies operate more widely. In her work on video games and affect, Audrey Anable suggests that casual games 'have particular rhythms and temporalities that are bound up with the blurring distinction between work and play in contemporary culture'. Given their positioning as 'time-filling' activities between other more 'productive' ways of spending time, both casual games and mobile-based platforms like TikTok reflect the positioning of digital subjects as 'increasingly tied to the capture, measurement, and commodification of affect'.[88] Similar to casual games, TikTok mediates the blurred and uncertain boundaries between work and play, boredom and entertainment, by producing 'affectively charged' rhythms that are physically embodied and performed. TikTok's viral patterning of bodies and gestures around popular music tracks evokes Theodor Adorno's well-worn critique of musical standardization and the emergence of what he calls the '"rhythmically obedient" type'. In his view, these 'rhythmically obedient' subjects were drawn dangerously towards a mechanized or even agglutinized collectivism at the expense of what he saw as more socially significant forms of participation.[89] This critique explicitly recognized the fundamental role that boredom – specifically, the 'boredom of mechanized labor' – played in creating the conditions of receptiveness for 'cheap commercial entertainment', framed as a 'relief from both boredom and effort'.[90] In a similar vein, Byung-Chul Han suggests that the 'excess of positivity' in a digital psychopolitical regime induces a state of 'hyperattention' that is at odds with 'profound boredom'. For Han, this regime does not facilitate a substantial shift in rhythmic relations between subjects and digital entertainment, but represents merely an intensification of the same that further erodes our ability to 'grant deep, contemplative attention' to our environment, and to experience duration in general.[91] As Han puts it, hyperattention prompts a speeding up that is 'just accelerated walking' as opposed to the uniquely 'human' forms of rhythmic motion that are expressed through '[d]ancing or gliding'.[92] In a similar vein, Franco 'Bifo' Berardi maintains that a network culture is characterized by its 'sonic hypermachines that besiege ... attention, imposing a rhythm in which singularity is cancelled'.[93]

Anable's work on casual games provides one useful response to these kinds of critiques of boredom and mass entertainment by emphasizing the affective complexities and tensions that flow through the rhythms of digital playbour in the twenty-first century. As she notes, while the rhythms produced through digital play continue to speak to the 'conditions of modern labor' that enact and sustain them, they also 'offer players more than just work disguised as play'. Through their sensual address to the 'conditions of digital labor in the twenty-first century', they mediate our feelings about work and play, and articulate a 'longing for something different'.[94] To adapt this perspective for the context of TikTok, we might say that while the #BoredVibes challenge standardizes individual movement and expression around a collective 'Bored in the House' pulse, it also speaks to the idiorrythmic desires that are embedded within, and arise from, that condition of boredom. What I am claiming is that when approached through Barthes's concept of idiorrhythmy, the notion of ambient play provides one means of re-framing boredom, not so much a problem to be managed through digital entertainment, but as an opening onto a desire for different rhythmic relations that might be forged through the state of suspension experienced during the pandemic. These suppressed desires are difficult to access, for they point to flows of affect that are bound up in, but not fully captured by, the form, logic and conventions of TikTok hashtags and challenges.

However, if many everyday life TikToks tend to use montage to enliven and break up the tedium of pandemic time – endorsing an understanding of TikTok as a technique of boredom management through digital entertainment – there are some that distort or re-frame this logic in subtle ways. I want to conclude by suggesting that it is through these subtle distortions that we might begin to glimpse the hard-to-grasp desires for new rhythms and modes of engaging with pandemic time, which are embedded within participatory platforms such as TikTok – even as they are also often thwarted by them. For example, one TikTok posted on 29 March 2020 captioned 'Quarantine Day 12' (@pizzaslime) features a toddler dressed in a pink top and diaper, who is pictured face down and dangling from a kitchen console. As the toddler's face presses directly into the top of the table, their legs swing rhythmically back and forth in time to the 'Bored in the House' track. At 4.8 million likes, this is one of the most popular video responses to the song. What makes it so compelling is perhaps the way that it perfectly captures the feeling of suspended animation that is a key feature of boredom. This recalls Adam Phillips's definition of boredom as a 'state of suspended animation in which things are started and nothing begins, the mood of diffuse restlessness which contains that most absurd and paradoxical wish, the wish for a desire'.[95] But unlike the previously discussed 'Bored in the House' TikToks, this moment of suspension is not counterbalanced by an impulse for progress, or an attempt to move past boredom. Instead, it keeps the viewer hovering in the time of the precariously dangling child, capturing an image of endurance in a particularly heightened state.

Through its appeal to a condition of boredom that is rooted in childhood, I would argue that this TikTok engages a subtly different understanding of play than is at stake in many other 'Bored in the House' videos. Here, play is not presented as an incitement to participation and performative re-iteration but is instead rooted in something more contingent and specific – something closely linked to Barthes's concept of idiorrhythmy. Rather than presenting a generalized idea of play as a solution to the bored body problem, it depicts *this child's* somatic response to the bored body problem. What captures my attention is the way that this particular child's dangling and swaying limbs enacts an image of calm, a means of marking out a rhythm that soothes and perhaps pacifies the out-of-joint time of childhood and of lockdown. In Anable's terms, it makes visible a different kind of desire, a different affective relation to the intensities of pandemic boredom. It 'leans in' to boredom in a different way.

Conclusion

Through its appeal to the pleasures of participating in synchronized and collectively produced rhythms, TikTok offers one means of addressing the lockdown's bored body problem. What TikTok tends to produce through its promotion of hashtag challenges such as #BoredVibes is a shared rhythm, a metric means of synchronizing individual bodies in self-isolation to a collective pulse. This pulse can and does work to stabilize bodies both temporally and spatially, producing feelings of jacked-up excitement and restorative calm in equal measure.

If the more effortful and 'entertaining' TikToks present digital subjects as 'tied to the capture, measurement, and commodification of affect', as Anable suggests, in a small number of TikToks such as this one, there is something more ambiguous at play.

Everyday-life TikToks sometimes embrace temporal ambiguities, performing a desire for rhythmic relations that could take shape through boredom rather than through an effort to drive it away. This category of TikTok is full of imagery that speaks to a longing for the specific comforts that might be found through embracing duration and the suspension that comes with boredom. They are full of images of lockdown life as a consoling hiatus from the pressures of the intensified digital everyday: a man cradles a sleeping baby, lip-synching to the track with his eyes closed; a young woman lounges back in a face mask and robe, placing cool slices of cucumber over her eyes; humans, dogs and cats are pictured cocooned in blankets. As Barthes suggests in his reading of 'extreme enclosures', it is the blanket that epitomizes above all the pleasures to be found in seclusion: 'The blanket is the veil that envelops and blocks out he light ... providing total isolation'.[96] The repetition of this type of imagery in 'Bored in the House' TikToks – such as soft furnishings, blankets, pillows and other plush textures – also echoes Walter Benjamin's evocative description of boredom as a 'warm gray fabric lined on the inside with the most lustrous and colorful of silks', noting that it is in this fabric that 'we wrap ourselves when we dream'.[97]

While the global Covid-19 lockdowns have intensified the need for boredom management through digital entertainment, they have also given boredom a new kind of publicness – making it visible, following Benjamin, 'as index to participation in the sleep of the collective'.[98] Through a limited number of TikToks that resist the imperative to make boredom eventful, we can perhaps begin to excavate these suppressed desires for new rhythmic and temporal relations that have been writ large in the context of the pandemic.

Epilogue: Unworking entertainment: Public boredom and the next normal

In his work on technical images, the media theorist Vilém Flusser frequently returned to the topic of boredom and its relationship to questions of human agency, creativity and freedom in an increasingly programmed world. Asking whether there is room for human freedom in this context, he writes: 'The essence of freedom is unpredictability. But once co-opted and objectified by apparatus and their programs, all that is left for us is a life of bored contentment within the nauseating technical paradise of a predictable eternal return of the same'.[1] In his later work, Flusser probes this vision of a nauseating technical paradise further, by speculating that in this future 'people will sit in separate cells, playing with their fingertips on keyboards, staring at tiny screens, receiving, changing, and sending images. Behind their backs, robots will bring them things to maintain and reproduce their derelict bodies'. These people, he writes, 'will be in contact with one another through their fingertips and so form a dialogical net, a global superbrain, whose function will be to calculate and compute improbable situations into pictures, to bring information, catastrophes about'.[2] This encroaching universe of a totally programmed future was already looming when Flusser was writing in the mid-1980s. From a post-Covid vantage point, what seemed speculative then today reads more like an accurate portrayal of everyday life for many during the period of lockdown and beyond.

This book has its origins firmly in a pre-pandemic period: a time when, as Mark Fisher, Nicholas Rombes and others surmised, boredom seemed to be under threat. At its inception, this study was inspired by a long-standing fascination with negative affect, or 'bad feelings': emotions that have come to occupy an ambivalent or marginalized position within culture. This project was similarly sparked by a kind of anxiety about whether we have time to experience boredom anymore, in an always-on culture that constantly sells us the promise that if we download the right apps or follow the right feeds, we'll never have to feel bored again. Very quickly, though, what became apparent through my research into boredom-themed hashtags and trends on platforms such as YouTube and Vine was that although we live in a boredom-averse culture, boredom is writ large across digital networks. One of the main paradoxes of networked boredom is that while social media is built on and out of ordinary boredom, it is also the one thing we're not supposed to notice or feel through our engagements with it. Boredom persists as a low-level structure of feeling across the same entertainment networks that promise to remedy it. It remains, to paraphrase MacKenzie Wark, as a kind of sticky lint that clings to all our attempts to outrun dead, uneventful time.

The experience of conducting research for this book in 2020, just as the coronavirus crisis began to unfold, would prove both a challenge and an opportunity. What was formerly on the margins of cultural discourse – easily dismissed as a feeling experienced mainly by teenagers and 'boring people' – would move into the mainstream, appearing not just as a trifling issue of individual concern, but as a matter of collective solidarity and the public good. Navigating this discursive explosion of boredom often felt overwhelming, given the sheer scale of content that was now being generated on a daily basis across both social and traditional media channels. The pandemic period yielded a rich seam of user-generated material; as one news headline put it, these were truly 'boom times for boredom and the researchers who study it'.[3] But while the pandemic would produce its own viral boredom trends – such as the 'BoredVibes' hashtag challenge that I explore in Chapter 3 – ultimately, it would do very little to alter the nature of boredom-themed content, which would largely continue to emulate previous formulae for expressing and displacing boredom. Reflecting on my previous research through the prism of the pandemic, I began to see how the historic moment of lockdown had been premediated by an entertainment-on-demand culture, which has long targeted housebound boredom as a core part of its business model. What took shape through the pandemic was not a massive seismic shift, but a further turn of the screw; it exposed and intensified an existing cultural logic that frames boredom as a domestic problem in need of proper discipline. As I have argued in this book, networked entertainment platforms are, and have long been, technologies of lockdown: both producing and pacifying the bored, housebound subjects that are central to the post-Fordist digital economy.

However, if the global coronavirus would further intensify the relationship between boredom management and digital entertainment, it would also give boredom a new visibility and a new publicness that has the potential to counter its obfuscation through entertainment networks. I want to conclude by suggesting that as we continue to navigate the lessons of the pandemic, we should not be so quick to dismiss the significance of the public visibility that this period has conferred onto boredom as it is entwined with networked media practices. It is precisely this visibility that creates the conditions for political action. As Jonathan Flatley argues, it is in such moments of crisis that the previously hidden or obscured 'social origins of our emotional lives can be mapped out and from which we can see the other persons who share our losses and are subject to the same forces'.[4] While the pandemic has further instrumentalized boredom as an individual feeling that drives media engagement – pushing us further into the nauseating technical paradise that Flusser foresaw – it has also shone a spotlight on boredom as a shared, structural condition that grows out of the 'entertained or else' ethos of digital capitalism.

In my analyses of the range of boredom-themed media that I have considered in this book, I have, on the one hand, shown how networked media have instrumentalized boredom in part through their ability to place it outside the conscious, phenomenological grasp of subjects. Networked media have explicitly capitalized on the differences between human and technological ways of sensing and processing experience in order to engrain the habits and gestures that keep subjects from feeling that they are bored in the moment. But on the other hand, I have also emphasized how the affective intensities at work in experiences of boredom will always exceed their 'plat-formatting' through viral trends and content genres.[5] I have tried to remain alive to the vitality of the affect that lies beneath the forms that boredom takes in concrete networked settings. A key concern for me in attending to the material that I have analysed has been to look for the less visible forms that boredom also takes across entertainment networks; to ask: what *else* does boredom do? How else might boredom operate? While the affordances and cultural norms of platforms shape the form that boredom takes on them, these do not totally determine the way that they will be used. Boredom's unruly affective intensities are never fully captured by the platforms that promise to tame them. For instance, on Vine, boredom might help to set up a prank or punchline, just as easily as it might allow users to self-reflect on the micro-moments of ordinary life, multiplying and augmenting the force of these feelings through loops. On YouTube, boredom might reinforce problematic ideas about girls as shallow and flighty, at the same time that it might inaugurate a space of intimacy and solidarity for aspirational young women to sound out the contours of their inchoate desires. On streaming platforms such as Napflix, boredom is both a casual feeling that can be dipped in and out of, and a durational mode with its roots in avant-garde aesthetics, which may also have the power to cut through some of the noise of always-on living. On TikTok, boredom can synchronize and standardize human expression, or it might reveal desires for a different relationship to digital temporality – opening up a space of public dreaming about what the alternatives to feeling #BoredintheHouse might be. Beneath the boredom that has been instrumentalized and given a concrete shape on these platforms, there is always a remainder. The task of media theory is to look for these remainders and think about how these could be leveraged to disentangle boredom's cooptation by the 'entertained or else' ethos of digital capitalism.

I want to conclude with some questions for future research that grow out of this study: what else might boredom do if we learn to see it differently, not as an individual feeling, but as a collective demand? How might this framing help channel boredom outwards towards something other than entertainment as a solipsistic end in itself? As I have only intimated in this book, while boredom can engrain the gestures and habits that sustain digital capitalism, it can also reveal a desire for other ways of being interested in the world as we try to make sense of the next normal in a post-pandemic world. While it is clearly beyond the scope of this epilogue to expand on the questions raised here, I hope that they will be taken up by future scholars who, like me, believe that the story of boredom and its entanglements with affective networks does not necessarily end in the nauseating technical paradise imagined by Flusser. As I have argued in this book, even though it has been co-opted as a feeling that keeps driving users back to the eternal return of the same, boredom can also clear the way for new desires, opening onto new ways of being interested in the world. There is always more to boredom's wish for a desire than can be captured by the technical apparatuses that would try to instrumentalize it.

Notes

Introduction

1. 'Bored Panda – Apps on Google Play', *Google Play*, n.d., https://play.google.com/store/apps/details?id=com.boredpanda.android&hl=en&gl=US (accessed 21 October 2023).
2. 'Bored Button – Games', *Apple App Store*, 2023, https://apps.apple.com/gb/app/bored-button-games/id1219432055 (accessed 3 November 2023).
3. 'About Us', *Boredom Therapy*, 2022, http://boredomtherapy.com/about/ (accessed 21 October 2023).
4. Lars Svendsen, *A Philosophy of Boredom* (London: Reaktion, 2005), 25.
5. Ibid., 31.
6. Peter Toohey, *Boredom: A Lively History* (New Haven, CT, and London: Yale University Press, 2011), 8.
7. Elizabeth Goodstein, *Experience without Qualities: Boredom and Modernity* (Stanford, CA: Stanford University Press, 2005), 1.
8. Ibid.
9. Ludmila Lupinacci, '"Absentmindedly Scrolling through Nothing": Liveness and Compulsory Continuous Connectedness in Social Media', *Media, Culture & Society* 43, no. 2 (2020): 275.
10. Adam Phillips, *On Kissing, Tickling and Being Bored* (Cambridge, MA: Harvard University Press, 1998), 68.
11. Scott C. Richmond, 'Vulgar Boredom, or What Andy Warhol Can Teach Us about Candy Crush', *Journal of Visual Culture* 13, no. 1 (2015): 32.
12. Roland Barthes, *The Neutral* (New York: Columbia University Press, 2007).
13. Jonathan Crary, *24/7: Late Capitalism and the Ends of Sleep* (London and New York: Verso, 2013), 30.
14. Mark Fisher, 'No One Is Bored, Everything Is Boring', *3:AM Magazine*, 6 November 2018, https://www.3ammagazine.com/3am/no-one-is-bored-everything-is-boring/ (accessed 21 October 2023).
15. Ibid.
16. Nicholas Rombes, *Cinema in the Digital Age* (London: Wallflower, 2009), 20.
17. Fisher, 'No One Is Bored'.
18. Susanna Paasonen, *Dependent, Distracted, Bored: Affective Formations in Networked Media* (Cambridge, MA: MIT Press, 2021), 3.

19 Ibid., 126.
20 Patrice Petro, *Aftershocks of the New: Feminism and Film History* (New Brunswick, NJ, and London: Rutgers University Press), 87.
21 Ibid., 89.
22 Goodstein, *Experience Without Qualities*, 414.
23 Ibid., 405.
24 Siegfried Kracauer, *The Mass Ornament: Weimar Essays*, ed. and trans. Thomas Y. Levin (Cambridge, MA: Harvard University Press, 1995), 331.
25 Ibid., 296.
26 Evgeny Morozov, 'Only Disconnect', *New Yorker*, 21 October 2013, https://www.newyorker.com/magazine/2013/10/28/only-disconnect-2 (accessed 4 December 2023).
27 Walter Benjamin, *Selected Writings: 1935–1938*, ed. Howard Eiland and Michael W. Jennings (Cambridge, MA: Harvard University Press, 2002), 149.
28 Walter Benjamin, *The Arcades Project*, trans. Howard Eiland and Kevin McLaughlin, ed. Rolf Tiedemann (Cambridge, MA: Harvard University Press, 1999), 105.
29 Joe Moran, 'Benjamin and Boredom', *Critical Quarterly* 45, no. 2 (2003): 169.
30 Ibid.
31 Benjamin, *The Arcades Project*, 476.
32 Adorno, 'Free Time' in *The Culture Industry: Selected Essays on Mass Culture*, ed. J. M. Bernstein (London and New York: Routledge, 1991), 197.
33 Martin Heidegger, *The Fundamental Concepts of Metaphysics: World, Finitude, Solitude*, trans. William McNeill and Nicholas Walker (Bloomington: Indiana University Press, 1995), 135.
34 Andreas Elpidorou and Lauren Freeman, 'Is Profound Boredom Boredom?' in *Heidegger on Affect*, ed. Christos Hadjioannou (New York: Springer, 2019), 184.
35 Ibid., 144–8.
36 Fisher, 'No One Is Bored'.
37 Mark B. N. Hansen, *Feed-Forward: On the Future of Twenty-First Century Media* (Chicago, IL: University of Chicago Press, 2014), 8; See also: Shane Denson, *Discorrelated Images* (Durham, NC: Duke University Press, 2020); Crary, *24/7*; Franco 'Bifo' Berardi, *The Soul at Work: From Alienation to Autonomy* (Cambridge, MA: MIT Press, 2009); Bernard Stiegler, *Taking Care of Youth and the Generations*, trans. Stephen Barker (Stanford, CA: Stanford University Press, 2010).
38 Hansen, *Feed-Forward*, 37.
39 Denson, *Discorrelated Images*, 1.
40 Dominic Pettman, *Infinite Distraction* (London: Polity, 2016), 134.
41 Hansen, *Feed-Forward*, 49.

42. Ibid., 58.
43. Ibid., 59.
44. Ibid.
45. See David M. Berry, *Critical Theory and the Digital* (New York and London: Bloomsbury Academic, 2014), 197–205; Martin Hand, '#Boredom: Technology, Acceleration, and Connected Presence in the Social Media Age' in *Boredom Studies Reader: Frameworks and Perspectives*, ed. Martin E. Gardiner and Julian Jason Haladyn (London: Routledge, 2017), 115–29.
46. Mark Kingwell, *Wish I Were Here: Boredom and the Interface* (Montreal, London and Chicago, IL: McGill-Queen's University Press, 2019).
47. Richmond, 'Vulgar Boredom', 21–39.
48. Michael E. Gardiner, 'The Multitude Strikes Back? Boredom in an Age of Semiocapital', *New Formations*, no. 82 (2014): 29–46.
49. Hansen, *Feed-Forward*, 58.
50. Richard Dyer, *Only Entertainment*, 2nd edn (London and New York: Routledge, 2002), 175.
51. Martin Heidegger, *Being and Time: A Translation of Sein und Zeit*, trans. Joan Stambaugh (New York: SUNY Press, 1996), 253.
52. Ibid., 127.
53. Byung-Chul Han, *Good Entertainment: A Deconstruction of the Western Passion Narrative*, trans. Adrian Nathan West (Cambridge, MA: MIT Press, 2019), 74.
54. Ibid., 86.
55. Dyer, *Only Entertainment*, 176.
56. Ibid., 177.
57. Ibid., 178.
58. Ibid.
59. Ibid., 179.
60. Andreas Treske, *Video Theory: Online Video Aesthetics or the Afterlife of Video* (Berlin: Verlag, 2015), 97.
61. Neta Alexander, 'Catered to Your Future Self: Netflix's Predictive Personalization and the Mathematization of Taste' in *The Netflix Effect: Technology and Entertainment in the 21st Century*, ed. Kevin McDonald and Daniel Smith-Rowsey (London: Bloomsbury Academic, 2016), 93.
62. Ibid., 90.
63. Han, *Good Entertainment*, 108.
64. Kingwell, *Wish I Were Here*, 103.
65. James J. Hodge, 'The Subject of Always-On Computing: Thomas Ogden's "Autistic-Contiguous Position" and the Animated GIF', *Parallax* 26, no. 1 (2020): 75.

66 Wendy Hui Kyong Chun, *Updating to Remain the Same: Habitual New Media* (Cambridge, MA: MIT Press, 2017).
67 Hodge, 'Always-On Computing', 76.
68 James Danckert and John D. Eastwood, *Out of My Skull: The Psychology of Boredom* (Cambridge, MA: Harvard University Press, 2020), 20.
69 Kingwell, *Wish I Were Here*, 51.
70 Tung-Hui Hu, *Digital Lethargy: Dispatches from an Age of Disconnection* (Cambridge, MA: MIT Press, 2022), i.
71 Ibid., xxii.
72 Paasonen, *Dependent, Distracted, Bored*, 124.
73 MacKenzie Wark, *Gamer Theory* (Cambridge, MA: Harvard University Press, 2007), 152.
74 Giorgio Agamben, 'Notes on Gesture' in *Means without End: Notes on Politics*, trans. Vincenzo Binetti and Cesare Casarino (Minneapolis: University of Minnesota Press, 2000), 59.
75 Byung-Chul Han, *In the Swarm: Digital Prospects*, trans. Erik Butler (Cambridge, MA: MIT Press, 2017), 78.
76 Byung-Chul Han, *Psychopolitics: Neoliberalism and New Technologies of Power*, trans. Erik Butler (London and New York: Verso, 2014).
77 Thomas Nail, 'What Is COVID Capitalism?', *Distinktion: Journal of Social Theory* 23, no. 2–3 (2022): 327–41.

Chapter 1

1 Blaise Pascal, *Pensées*, trans. A. J. Krailsheimer (London: Penguin, 2005), section 136.
2 Ann Douglas Wood, '"The Fashionable Diseases": Women's Complaints and Their Treatment in Nineteenth-Century America', *The Journal of Interdisciplinary History* 4, no. 1, (Summer 1973): 30.
3 Jonathan Beller, *The Cinematic Mode of Production: Attention Economy and the Society of the Spectacle* (Hanover, New Hampshire: Dartmouth College Press, 2006).
4 See Hansen, *Feed-Forward* and Denson, *Discorrelated Images*.
5 Fisher, 'No One Is Bored'.
6 Kenneth Rogers, *The Attention Complex: Media, Archeology, Method* (New York: Palgrave Macmillan, 2014), n.p.
7 N. Katherine Hayles, *How We Think: Digital Media and Contemporary Technogenesis* (Chicago, IL: University of Chicago Press, 2012); Stiegler, *Taking Care of Youth*, 54–93.

8   Bill Moyers, 'Sherry Turkle on Being Alone Together', PBS, 18 October 2013, television broadcast, https://billmoyers.com/segment/sherry-turkle-on-being-alone-together/ (accessed 1 February 2024).
9   Phillips, *On Kissing, Tickling, and Being Bored*, 68.
10 Mark Kingwell, 'Bored, Addicted, or Both: How We Use Social Media Now' in *Social Media and Your Brain: Web-Based Communication Is Changing How We Think and Express Ourselves*, ed. C. G. Prado (London: Bloomsbury Academic, 2016), n.p.
11 Angela McRobbie, *Be Creative* (Cambridge: Polity, 2016), 95.
12 Jonathan Beller, 'Wagers Within the Image: Rise of Visuality, Transformation of Labour, Aesthetic Regimes', *Culture Machine* 13 (2012): 19 & 10.
13 Beller, 'Wagers Within the Image', 13.
14 McRobbie, *Be Creative*, 94.
15 MayBaby, 'What To Do When You're Bored!', YouTube, 6 July 2014, https://www.youtube.com/watch?v=7edeMtCA6VU&t=424s; MayBaby, 'What To Do When You're Bored', YouTube, 13 December 2014, https://www.youtube.com/watch?v=uqv2ztlLV5s&t=1s; MayBaby, 'What Girls Do When They're Bored' YouTube, 25 April 2015, https://www.youtube.com/watch?v=vEDqATXyM1s&t=422s; MayBaby, 'Weird Things Bored People Do', YouTube, 6 March 2016, https://www.youtube.com/watch?v=mRZ3CCFJQok&t=44s; Maybaby, 'What To Do When You're Bored During Summer Break', YouTube, 18 June 2016, https://www.youtube.com/watch?v=yHt-jEZfVX8&t=11s (All accessed 23 November 2016).
16 @cr3xbly, comment on MayBaby, 'What To Do When You're Bored', 2021.
17 Meg DeAngelis, 'How to Become a Social Media Superstar with Meg DeAngelis', *Film Talk* (podcast), 16 February 2016, http://filmtalkpodcast.com/meg-deangelis/ (accessed 18 December 2016).
18 Gillian Bower, '10 Fun Things To Do When You're Bored! What To Do When Bored!', YouTube, 3 April 2016, https://www.youtube.com/watch?v=swwX2RwBbH4&t=4s (accessed 13 January 2024).
19 Gillian Bower, 'DIY ROOM DECOR To Do When You're BORED! Easy DIY Room Decor Ideas!', YouTube, 27 May 2017, https://www.youtube.com/watch?v=1ub3_ESEKt8 (accessed 13 January 2024).
20 Cassie Diamond, '4 Fun DIY's To Do When You're Bored', YouTube, 14 August 2014, https://www.youtube.com/watch?v=HL44rVSWLfo; 'What To Do When You're Bored This Fall! Treats, Activities & More!', YouTube, 31 October 2015, https://www.youtube.com/watch?v=pdd_S-6rc7s; 'Fun Things To Do When You're Bored!', YouTube, 17 June 2016, https://www.youtube.com/watch?v=t2zCPGnijZQ&t=7s; 'Fun Things To Do When You're Bored!', YouTube, 20 January 2017, https://www.youtube.com/watch?v=MdwxviUctds&t=6s;

'Fun Things To Do When You're Bored!', YouTube, 28 April 2018, https://www.youtube.com/watch?v=4aXxitguzYs&t=7s; 'Fun Things To Do When You're Bored!', YouTube, 5 January 2019, https://www.youtube.com/watch?v=uHz3n3rWUh0&t=19s; 'Fun Things To Do When You're Bored!', YouTube, 20 July 2019, https://www.youtube.com/watch?v=88-75hK_L-Q&t=3s; 'What To Do When You're Bored!', YouTube, 2 December 2019, https://www.youtube.com/watch?v=IShSFYvv5I0&t=3s; and 'What To Do When You're BORED at HOME!', YouTube, 5 April 2020, https://www.youtube.com/watch?v=_57goVdlyNk&t=3s (all accessed 20 January 2024).
21 Angela McRobbie and Jenny Garber, 'Girls and Subcultures' in *Resistance Through Rituals: Youth Subcultures in Post-War Britain*, ed. Stuart Hall and Tony Jefferson (London: Routledge, 2006), 177–88.
22 Anita Harris, *Future Girl: Young Women in the Twenty-First Century* (London: Routledge, 2003), 6.
23 Jacqueline Arcy, 'Emotion Work: Considering Gender in Digital Labor', *Feminist Media Studies* 16, no. 2 (2016): 365.
24 Ibid.
25 Brooke Erin Duffy, *(Not) Getting Paid to Do What You Love: Gender, Social Media, and Aspirational Work* (New Haven, CT, and London: Yale University Press, 2017), 10.
26 Don Slater quoted in Duffy *(Not) Getting Paid*, 17.
27 Amy Shields Dobson, *Postfeminist Digital Cultures: Femininity, Social Media, and Self-Representation* (New York: Palgrave Macmillan, 2015), 1–2.
28 Petro, *Aftershocks of the New*, 89.
29 Allison Pease, *Modernism, Feminism and the Culture of Boredom* (Cambridge: Cambridge University Press, 2012), viii.
30 Pease, *Modernism*, 10.
31 Petro, *Aftershocks of the New*, 89 and Pease, *Modernism*, 7.
32 Pease, *Modernism*, 2.
33 See: Brooke Erin Duffy, 'Gendering the Labor of Social Media Production', *Feminist Media Studies* 15, no. 4 (2015): 710–14; Thomas Poell, David B. Nieborg and Brooke Erin Duffy, *Platforms and Cultural Production* (Cambridge: Polity, 2022).
34 Phillips, *On Kissing, Tickling, and Being Bored*, 74.
35 Tania Lewis, *Smart Living: Lifestyle Media and Popular Expertise* (Oxford and New York: Peter Lang, 2008), 138.
36 Ibid.
37 MayBaby, '10 DIY Room Décor Projects You NEED to Try!', YouTube, 21 May 2015, https://www.youtube.com/watch?v=X1fVlYUxZlE; MayBaby, 'DIY Room Décor Tumblr Room Makeover!', YouTube, 19 June 2014, https://www.youtube.com/watch?v=eho2M6Pxl8E (Both accessed 12 January 2016).
38 Fisher, 'No One Is Bored'.

39 Sun-Ha Hong, 'Hansen – Feed-Forward' (Review), *Untimely: Anachronistic Commentary and Theory*, 2016, https://web.archive.org/web/20160322205547/http://untimely.co/?p=69 (accessed via Wayback Machine 2 February 2024).
40 Hansen, *Feed-Forward*, 40.
41 Ibid., 58.
42 MayBaby, 'What To Do When You're Bored!'
43 danah boyd, *It's Complicated: The Social Lives of Networked Teens* (New Haven, CT, and London: Yale University Press, 2014), 10.
44 Chun, *Updating to Remain the Same*, 17.
45 Ibid., 53.
46 Ibid.
47 Kyra D. Gaunt, 'YouTube, Bad Bitches, and an MIC (Mom-in-Chief): On the Digital Seduction of Black Girls in Participatory Hip Hop Spaces' in *The Hip Hop & Obama Reader*, ed. Travis L. Gosa and Erik Nielson (Oxford: Oxford University Press, 2015), 214.
48 Kimberly Ann Hall, 'The Authenticity of Social-Media Performance: Lonelygirl15 and the Amateur Brand of Young-Girlhood', *Women and Performance: A Journal of Feminist Theory* 25, no. 2 (2015): 129.
49 Fisher, 'No One Is Bored'.
50 Pettman, *Infinite Distraction*, 96.
51 Carol Vernallis, *Unruly Media: YouTube, Music Video, and the New Digital Cinema* (Oxford: Oxford University Press, 2013), 131.
52 Berry, *Critical Theory and the Digital*, 199.
53 Richard Grusin, *Premediation: Affect and Mediality after 9/11* (Basingstoke: Palgrave Macmillan, 2010), 129.
54 Shane Denson, 'Crazy Cameras, Discorrelated Images, and the Post-Perceptual Mediation of Post-Cinematic Affect' in *Post-Cinema: Theorizing 21st-Century Film*, ed. Shane Denson and Julia Leyda (Falmer: Reframe Books, 2016).

Chapter 2

1 WikiHow and Lui, Elvina, 'How to Know if a Person Is Getting Bored of You', *WikiHow*, 4 February 2022, https://www.wikihow.com/Know-if-a-Person-Is-Getting-Bored-of-You.
2 Wendell O'Brien, 'Boredom: A History of Western Philosophical Perspectives', *Internet Encyclopedia of Philosophy*, n.d., https://iep.utm.edu/boredom/.
3 Phillips, *On Kissing, Tickling, and Being Bored*, 82.
4 Svendsen, *A Philosophy of Boredom*, 13–14.

5 Kevin Pocock, 'What Was Dall-E 2 Trained On?', *PC Guide*, 10 May 2023, https://www.pcguide.com/apps/what-was-dall-e-2-trained-on/.
6 Dominik Maeder and Daniela Wentz, 'Digital Seriality as Structure and Process', *Eludamos. Journal for Computer Game Culture* 8, no. 1 (2014): 143.
7 Goodstein, *Experience without Qualities*.
8 Agamben, *Means without End*, 51.
9 Deborah Levitt, 'Notes on Media and Biopolitics: "Notes on Gesture"' in *The Work of Giorgio Agamben: Law, Literature, Life*, ed. Justin Clemens and Nicholas Heron (Edinburgh: Edinburgh University Press, 2008), 197.
10 Ibid., 198–9.
11 Agamben, 'Notes on Gesture', 51.
12 Benjamin, *The Arcades Project*, 108.
13 Goodstein, *Experience without Qualities*, 144.
14 Ibid., 146.
15 Ibid.
16 Émile Tardieu, *L'Ennui: Étude Psychologique*, 2nd edn (Paris: Librairie Félix Alcan, 1913), 4 & 240 (all translations mine).
17 Ibid., 240; 4–5.
18 For a discussion of boredom in the context of nineteenth-century painting, see Jason Haladyn, *Boredom and Art: Passions of the Will to Boredom* (Alresford, Hants: Zero Books, 2014).
19 Goodstein, *Experience without Qualities*, 184.
20 Gustave Flaubert, *Madame Bovary* (London: Vintage Digital, 2012), n.p.
21 'Although he does not make great gestures or great cries,/He would gladly make the earth a shambles/And swallow the world in a yawn;/It is boredom! his eyes weeping an involuntary tear,/He dreams of gibbets as he smokes his hookah'. Charles Baudelaire, *The Flowers of Evil & Paris Spleen: Selected Poems*, ed., Suzanne E. Johnson (New York: Dover Thrift Editions, 2012), 4.
22 Agamben, 'Notes on Gesture', 53.
23 Janet Harbord, *Ex-Centric Cinema: Giorgio Agamben and Film Archaeology* (London: Bloomsbury Academic, 2016), 77.
24 Ibid., 72.
25 Agamben, 'Notes on Gesture', 56.
26 Agamben cited in Levitt, 'Notes on Media and Biopolitics', 207.
27 Agamben, 'Notes on Gesture', 59.
28 Ibid.
29 Ibid., 58.
30 Lucia Ruprecht, 'Introduction: Towards an Ethics of Gesture', *Performance Philosophy* 3, no. 1 (2017): 4–22, https://www.performancephilosophy.org/journal/article/view/167/185.

31 Levitt, 'Notes on Media and Biopolitics', 203.
32 Ibid., 56.
33 Agamben, 'Notes on Gesture', 56.
34 Giorgio Agamben, *The Open: Man and Animal*, trans. Kevin Attell (Stanford, CA: Stanford University Press, 2004), 67.
35 *The Oxford English Dictionary* (Oxford: Oxford University Press, 2019).
36 John D. Eastwood et al., 'The Unengaged Mind: Defining Boredom in Terms of Attention', *Perspectives in Psychological Science* 7, no. 5 (2012): 482.
37 Haladyn, *Boredom and Art*, n.p.
38 See, for example: Berardi, *And: Phenomenology of the End* (Los Angeles, CA: Semiotext(e), 2015); Crary, *24/7*; Hansen, *Feed-Forward*; Jonathan Beller, *The Message is Murder: Substrates of Computational Capital* (London: Pluto Press, 2018).
39 See Crary, *24/7* and Gardiner, 'The Multitude Strikes Back'.
40 Andrew McStay, *Emotional AI: The Rise of Empathic Media* (London: Sage, 2018), n.p.
41 Natasja Bodgers, 'Why You Want to Know if Your Customers Are Bored, and How to Find Out', *Noldus*, 26 October 2017, https://www.noldus.com/blog/facereader-affective-attitudes (accessed 17 February 2024).
42 Noldus, 'What Facial Action Units Look Like', *Noldus*, 2023, https://www.noldus.com/applications/facial-action-coding-system (accessed 17 February 2024).
43 Affectiva, 'In Lab Biometric Solution', *Affectiva*, 2024, https://www.affectiva.com/product/individual-product-page-imotions/ (accessed 17 February 2024).
44 Luke Dormehl, 'AI Educational Software Knows When Students Are Bored, Can Adjust Lessons Accordingly', *Digital Trends*, 13 December 2016, https://www.digitaltrends.com/cool-tech/emotion-sniffing-learning-apps/ (accessed 17 February 2024).
45 Mark H. Myers, 'Automatic Detection of a Student's Affective States for Intelligent Teaching Systems', *Brain Sciences* 11, no. 3 (2021): 331.
46 Ibid.
47 Hayles, *How We Think* and Sherry Turkle, *Alone Together: Why We Expect More from Technology and Less From Each Other*, 3rd edn (New York: Basic Books, 2017).
48 Andrew McStay, *Automating Empathy: Decoding Technologies that Gauge Intimate Life* (Oxford: Oxford University Press, 2023), 120.
49 Ibid., 116.
50 Jason Eppink in Tim Maughan, 'Six GIFs about Things You Didn't Know about GIFs', *New Scientist*, 16 March 2016, https://www.newscientist.com/article/2080686-six-gifs-about-things-you-didnt-know-about-gifs/ (accessed 17 Feburary 2024).
51 Jason Eppink, 'The Reaction GIF: Moving Image as Gesture', *Jason Eppink's Catalogue of Creative Triumphs*, https://jasoneppink.com/the-reaction-gif-moving-image-as-gesture/ (accessed 17 Feburary 2024).

52 See: Hampus Hagman, 'The Digital Gesture: Rediscovering Cinematic Movement Through Gifs', *Refractory: A Journal of Entertainment Media* 21 (2012), https://web.archive.org/web/20200313214310/http://refractory.unimelb.edu.au/2012/12/29/hagman/ (accessed 17 February 2024 via Wayback Machine); Iris Cuppen, '#GESTURE', *I Have Nothing to Say, Only to Show: Towards an Archaeology of the Animated GIF*, https://www.ihavenothingtosayonlytoshow.com/#essays (accessed 17 February 2024); Maeder and Wentz, 'Digital Seriality'.
53 Pasi Väliaho, *Biopolitical Screens: Image, Power, and the Neoliberal Brain* (Cambridge, MA: MIT Press, 2014), 103.
54 Top Vines, 'What are those Original', YouTube, 16 September 2015, https://www.youtube.com/watch?v=HNtz05bhI1k (accessed 22 November 2023).
55 Ryan McHenry, 'Ryan Gosling Won't Eat His Cereal (2013–2014 Vine Compliation)', YouTube, 21 April 2014, https://www.youtube.com/watch?v=FkpCP9R1Jjc (accessed 22 November 2023).
56 Treske, *Video Theory*, 97.
57 Goodstein, *Experience without Qualities*.
58 Agamben, 'Notes on Gesture', 58.
59 Nathan Jurgenson, 'Vine, Vinepeek, and Visual Efficiency', *Cyborgology*, 27 January 2013, https://thesocietypages.org/cyborgology/2013/01/27/vine-vinepeek-and-visual-efficiency/ (accessed 17 February 2024).
60 Top Vines, 'When Happy Cloud Gets Bored!', YouTube, 25 November 2013, https://www.youtube.com/watch?v=H_FZPrDk7CI (accessed 23 November 2023).
61 JÄY, 'Ghetto Names', *Vine Archive*, 18 December 2013, https://vine.co/v/h0n9np6PxO9 (accessed 23 November 2023).
62 BlackBo, 'When Boredom Strikes w/Izzy Dinma', *Vine Archive*, 19 May 2014, https://vine.co/v/MHqgVW5QIzp/ (accessed 24 November 2023).
63 Nadia Whitehead, 'People Would Rather Be Electrically Shocked Than Left Alone with their Thoughts', *Science*, 3 July 2014, https://www.science.org/content/article/people-would-rather-be-electrically-shocked-left-alone-their-thoughts (accessed 17 February 2024).
64 Sianne Ngai, *Our Aesthetic Categories: Zany, Cute, Interesting* (Cambridge, MA: Harvard University Press, 2012), 12.
65 Ibid.
66 Giorgio Agamben, *Potentialities: Collected Essays in Philosophy*, trans. Daniel Heller-Roazen (Stanford, CA: Stanford University Press, 2000), 253.
67 9,999,999 Views, 'Bored as Shiiiiii Vine', YouTube, 3 December 2017, https://www.youtube.com/watch?v=XDot1OgqJNQ (accessed 24 November 2023).
68 Jacksepticeye, 'VINE VIDEO | BORED IN CLASS!!', YouTube, 14 October 2013, https://www.youtube.com/watch?v=3zvJziucK9k (accessed 24 November 2023).

69 Loveableheartshere3900, comment on MelissaDelBye, 'Bored as Shiiiiii Vine', YouTube, 28 October 2016, https://www.youtube.com/watch?v=VxOtcxDN4Fs&lc=UgyzqkO4Vi1yyNPqFKB4AaABAg (accessed 17 February 2024).
70 Blackfox147, comment on 'Bored as Shiiiiii Vine'.
71 Anna Munster, *An Aesthesia of Networks: Conjunctive Experience in Art and Technology* (Cambridge, MA: MIT Press, 2013), 103.
72 Ibid.
73 Agamben, 'Notes on Gesture', 56.
74 Annarigatoni, 'Bored', Vine Archive, 12 February 2014, https://vine.co/v/MWEZAdBKmLh (accessed 28 December 2023).
75 Elena Gorfinkel, 'Weariness, Waiting: Endurance and Art Cinema's Tired Bodies', *Discourse* 34, no. 2–3 (2012): 312.
76 Laura Mulvey, 'Cinematic Gesture: The Ghost in the Machine', *Journal for Cultural Research* 19, no. 1 (2015): 7.
77 Agamben, 'Notes on Gesture', 58.
78 Ibid., 57.
79 Ibid., 58.

Chapter 3

1 See M. J. Robinson, *Television On Demand* (New York and London: Bloomsbury Academic, 2017); Chuck Tryon, *On-Demand Culture: Digital Delivery and the Future of Movies* (New Brunswick: Rutgers University Press, 2013).
2 Tyron, *On-Demand Culture*, 59.
3 Chuck Tryon, 'TV Got Better: Netflix's Original Programming Strategies and Binge Viewing', *Media Industries* 2, no. 2 (2015), https://doi.org/10.3998/mij.15031809.0002.206 (accessed 17 February 2024).
4 Ibid.
5 Ibid.
6 Elena Pilipets, 'From Netflix Streaming to Netflix and Chill: The (Dis)Connected Body of Serial Binge-Viewer', *Social Media + Society* 5, no. 4 (2019): 2.
7 Tryon, 'TV Got Better'.
8 Crary, *24/7*, 30.
9 Napflix, 2016, https://napflix.tv/ (accessed 25 July 2023).
10 Anna McCarthy, *Ambient Television* (Durham, NC: Duke University Press, 2001); Malcolm McCullough, *Ambient Commons* (Cambridge, MA: MIT Press, 2013); Paul Roquet, *Ambient Media: Japanese Atmospheres of Self* (Minneapolis: University of Minnesota Press, 2016).

11 McCarthy, *Ambient Television*, 209.
12 John Ellis, *Visible Fictions* (Milton Park: Taylor & Francis, 1992), 162.
13 Ibid.
14 Ibid., 137.
15 Theodor Adorno, 'How to Look at Television', *The Quarterly of Film, Radio, and Television* 8, no. 3 (1954): 213–35.
16 Tung-Hui Hu, 'A Brief History of Disengagement, From Couch Potatoes to Users', *The MIT Press Reader*, https://thereader.mitpress.mit.edu/a-brief-history-of-disengagement-from-couch-potatoes-to-users/ (accessed 26 July 2023).
17 Ibid. Hu points out that the couch potato is a racially marked category, helping to reinforce distinctions between the lazy couch potato who was imagined as white, and the unemployed person on benefits whose racial position is marked as non-white.
18 Laurence Scott, 'What Ever Happened to the Couch Potato?', *The New Yorker*, 6 July 2016, https://www.newyorker.com/tech/annals-of-technology/what-ever-happened-to-the-couch-potato (accessed 26 July 2023).
19 William Uricchio, 'Television's Next Generation: Technology/Interface Culture/Flow' in *Television after TV: Essays on a Medium in Transition*, ed. Lynn Spigel and Jan Olsson (Durham, NC: Duke University Press, 2005), 171.
20 Scott, 'Couch Potato'.
21 Ibid.
22 Kayleigh Day, 'Psychology of Concentration: Why the World is Now Addicted to "Background TV"', *Stylist* (2021), https://www.stylist.co.uk/entertainment/tv/psychology-concentration-background-tv/547752.
23 Hu, 'A Brief History of Disengagement'.
24 Ibid.
25 Ibid.
26 Pilipets, 'Netflix and Chill', 2.
27 Scott, 'Vulgar Boredom', 33.
28 Ibid., 32.
29 Ibid., 35.
30 Neta Alexander, 'From Spectatorship to "Survivorship" in Five Critical Propositions', *Film Quarterly* 75, no. 1 (2021): 52–7, https://online.ucpress.edu/fq/article/75/1/52/118473/From-Spectatorship-to-Survivorship-in-Five (accessed 17 February 2024).
31 Sharday C. Mosurinjohn, *The Spiritual Significance of Overload Boredom* (Montreal: McGill – Queen's University Press, 2022).
32 Søren Kierkegaard cited in Svendsen, *A Philosophy of Boredom*, 25.
33 Michael E. Gardiner, 'Not Your Father's Boredom' in *Boredom Studies Reader: Frameworks and Perspectives*, ed. Michael E. Gardiner and Julian Jason Haladyn (London and New York: Routledge), 241.

34 Petro, *Aftershocks of the New*, 95.
35 Eva Hoffman, *How to Be Bored* (London: Palgrave Macmillan, 2016), 4.
36 'Learning to Listen to one's Own Boredom', *The School of Life*, n.d., https://www.theschooloflife.com/article/listening-to-own-boredom//?/ (accessed 23 February 2024).
37 'About', *The Boring Conference*, 2014, https://boringconference.wordpress.com/about-boring/ (accessed 23 February 2024).
38 Hoffman, *How to Be Bored*; Sandi Mann, *The Upside of Downtime: Why Boredom is Good* (Boston, MA: Little Brown, 2017); Jenny Odell, *How To Do Nothing: Resisting the Attention Economy* (Brooklyn and London: Melville House, 2019); Manoush Zomorodi, *Bored and Brilliant: How Time Spent Doing Nothing Changes Everything* (London: Pan Macmillan, 2017); Manoush Zomorodi, *Bored and Brilliant: How Spacing Out Can Unlock Your Most Productive and Creative Self* (London: Picador, 2018).
39 Tom Hodgkinson, *An Idler's Manual* (London: The Idler, 2021).
40 Hoffman *How to Be Bored*, 8.
41 Tiago de Luca and Nuno Barradas Jorge, eds, *Slow Cinema* (Edinburgh: Edinburgh University Press, 2016), 3.
42 Emre Çağlayan, *Poetics of Slow Cinema: Nostalgia, Absurdism, Boredom* (Cham: Palgrave Macmillan, 2018).
43 NRK, 'Slow TV' (Press Release), n.d., https://www.nrk.no/presse/slow-tv-1.12057032 (accessed 19 July 2023).
44 Ibid.
45 BBC, 'BBC4 Goes Slow', BBC iPlayer 2023, https://www.bbc.co.uk/programmes/p02q34z8 (accessed 21 July 2023).
46 Cassian Harrison in John Plunket, 'Gently Does It: From Canal Trips to Birdsong, BBC4 to Introduce "Slow TV"', *Guardian*, 1 May 2015, https://www.theguardian.com/media/2015/may/01/gently-does-it-from-canal-trips-to-birdsong-bbc4-to-introduce-slow-tv (accessed 17 February 2024).
47 Helen Wheatley, *Spectacular Television: Exploring Televisual Pleasure* (London: I.B. Taurus, 2016), 15.
48 Lefebvre, Martin, cited in Wheatley, *Spectacular Television*, 16.
49 Pilipets, 'Netflix and Chill', 2.
50 Thomas Hellum, 'Norway's Slow TV: Fascinating Viewers for Hours or Days at a Time', *CBS News*, 7 May 2017, https://www.cbsnews.com/news/norways-slow-tv-fascinating-viewers-for-hours-or-days-at-a-time/ (accessed 18 July 2023).
51 Thomas Hellum, 'The World's Most Boring Television … And Why It's Hilariously Addictive', TEDxArendal, 2014, https://www.ted.com/talks/thomas_hellum_the_world_s_most_boring_television_and_why_it_s_hilariously_addictive/transcript?language=en (accessed 18 July 2023).
52 NRK, 'Slow TV'.

53 Kenneth Goldsmith, 'A Week of Blogs for the Poetry Foundation' in *Postscript: Writing After Conceptual Art*, ed. Andrea Andersson (Toronto: University of Toronto Press, 2018), 149.
54 Pamela M. Lee, *Chronophobia: On Time in the Art of the 1960s* (Cambridge, MA: MIT Press, 2004), 283.
55 Erika Balsom, 'Watching Paint Dry' in *Unwatchable*, ed. Nicholas Baer, Maggie Hennefeld, Laura Horak and Gunnar Iversen (Cambridge, MA: MIT Press, 2019), 197.
56 Balsom, 'Watching Paint Dry', 198.
57 Ibid.
58 Roel Puijk, *Slow TV: An Analysis of Minute-by-Minute Television in Norway* (Bristol: Intellect Books, 2021), n.p.
59 See for example Gernot Böhm, *Critique of Aesthetic Capitalism* (Berlin: Mimesis International, 2017); Ulrik Ekman, *Throughout: Art and Culture Emerging with Ubiquitous Computing* (Cambridge, MA: MIT Press, 2013); McCullough, *Ambient Commons*.
60 Roquet, *Ambient Media*, 18.
61 Ibid., 13.
62 McCarthy, *Ambient Television*.
63 Helle Breth Klausen in Eliza Brooke, 'The Soothing, Digital Rooms of YouTube', *The New York Times*, 16 February 2021, https://www.nytimes.com/2021/02/16/style/ambience-videos-asmr-youtube.html (accessed 18 July 2023).
64 Ibid.
65 On White Noise videos, see João Francisco Porfírio, 'YouTube and the Sonification of Domestic Everyday Life' in *YouTube and Music: Online Culture and Everyday Life*, ed. Holly Rogers, Joana Freitas and João Francisco Porfírio (London: Bloomsbury Academic, 2023), 209–29. On Brown Noise Videos, see Dani Blum, 'Can Brown Noise Turn Off Your Brain?', *New York Times*, 23 September 2022, https://www.nytimes.com/interactive/2022/09/23/well/mind/brown-noise.html (accessed 18 July 2023).
66 Derek Johnson, 'Pluto TV: Channels, Portals, and the Changing Television Cosmos' in *From Networks to Netflix: A Guide to Changing Channels*, ed. Derek Johnson (Milton Park: Taylor & Francis, 2022), n.p.
67 Hodge, 'The Subject of Always-On Computing', 67.
68 Roquet, *Ambient Media*, 51.
69 Ibid., 51–2.
70 Ibid., 17.
71 Channel 4 News, 'Slow Going: Why "Slow TV" Is Catching on Fast', *Channel 4*, 24 June 2014, https://www.channel4.com/news/slow-tv-nrk-train-journey-ship-video-125 (accessed 30 July 2023).

72 Sabienna Bowman, 'These Very Relaxing Netflix Programs Are Leaving Soon, But Here's How to Fill That Void', *Bustle*, 25 July 2019, https://www.bustle.com/p/netflixs-most-relaxing-genre-is-leaving-in-august-but-heres-where-you-can-still-get-your-slow-tv-fix-18235886 (accessed 30 July 2023).

73 Carina Wolff, 'People Are Loving Netflix's New Meditative TV Shows', *Simplemost*, 13 October 2016, https://www.simplemost.com/people-loving-netflix-new-meditative-tv-shows/ (accessed 30 July 2023).

74 Lottie Woodrow, 'Take It Slow … The TV Trend That Will Chill You The F Out', *The Handbook*, 25 January 2021, https://www.thehandbook.com/take-it-slow-how-to-explore-the-world-virtually-with-slow-tv/#:~:text=The%20TV%20Trend%20That%20Will%20Chill%20You%20The%20F%20Out&text=When%20things%20get%20too%20much,back%20and%20admire%20our%20surroundings> (accessed 30 July 2023).

75 Jaime Fuller, 'Slow-Watching Slow TV: All Aboard the Train from Bergen to Oslo', *MTV*, 30 August 2016, https://www.mtv.com/news/7xtkaz/slow-watching-slow-tv-all-aboard-the-train-from-bergen-to-oslo (accessed 15 July 2023).

76 Mark Lawson, 'What's the Point of BBC4?', *Guardian*, 8 March 2017, https://www.theguardian.com/tv-and-radio/2017/mar/08/from-a-place-to-think-to-background-activity-bbc4-turns-15 (accessed 3 August 2023).

77 Luis Gallardo, 'How to Enter the State of "Soft Fascination" and Ultimate Healing', *World Happiness Foundation*, 28 January 2022, https://worldhappiness.foundation/blog/happiness/how-to-enter-the-state-of-soft-fascination-and-ultimate-healing/ (accessed 3 August 2023).

78 Stephen Kaplan, Rachel Kaplan and Robert L. Ryan, cited in Roquet, *Ambient Media*, 111.

79 Roquet, *Ambient Media*, 111.

80 Daniel Bukszpan, 'Slow TV: Netflix's Chill, Mesmerizing Antidote to the Madness of 2016', *The Daily Beast*, 13 April 2017, https://www.thedailybeast.com/slow-tv-netflixs-chill-mesmerizing-antidote-to-the-madness-of-2016 (accessed 3 August 2023).

81 Tania Modleski, 'The Rhythms of Reception: Daytime Television and Women's Work' in *Regarding Television: Critical Approaches – An Anthology*, ed. E. Ann Kaplan (Frederick, MD: University Publications of America, 1983), 67–75.

82 Isobel Moore, 'Easiest Shows to Watch While You Work from Home', *Immortal Wordsmith*, 28 October 2021, https://www.immortalwordsmith.co.uk/easiest-shows-watch-while-working/ (accessed 2 August 2023).

83 Roquet, *Ambient Media*, 112.

84 LilyNova, 'Peaceful, Slow Films to Have on While Falling Asleep?', *Reddit r/NetflixBestOf*, 17 January 2015, https://www.reddit.com/r/NetflixBestOf/comments/2spwrq/peaceful_slow_films_to_have_on_while_falling/ (accessed 3 August 2023).

85 See: ADPXEROX, '[Request] Something for When You're Woken Up in the Middle of the Night from a Night Terror and Need Something to Ease the Anxiety', *Reddit r/NetflixBestOf*, 11 January 2022, https://www.reddit.com/r/NetflixBestOf/comments/s1mait/request_something_for_when_youre_woken_up_in_the/ (accessed 3 August 2023); Natmcoy, 'Peaceful, Slow Films to Have on While Falling Asleep?', *Reddit r/NetflixBestOf*, 17 January 2015, https://www.reddit.com/r/NetflixBestOf/comments/2spwrq/peaceful_slow_films_to_have_on_while_falling/ (accessed 3 August 2023); Mascoot_scootma, 'Looking for Suggestions for Netflix Shows to Fall Asleep to That Have a Consistent Volume, No Laugh Tracks Or Loud Noises', *Reddit r/netflix*, 16 April 2022, https://www.reddit.com/r/netflix/comments/u4olcu/looking_for_suggestions_for_netflix_shows_to_fall/ (accessed 3 August 2023).

86 ZamrosX, 'What is the Best "Background Noise" TV Show?', *Reddit r/television*, 18 September 2014, https://www.reddit.com/r/netflix/comments/u4olcu/looking_for_suggestions_for_netflix_shows_to_fall/ (accessed 2 August 2023).

87 Whatsatool, 'Ambient TV: Boring Shows That Put You to Sleep', *Primetimer* [Forum], 28 November 2015, https://forums.primetimer.com/topic/35120-ambien-tv-boring-shows-that-put-you-to-sleep/ (accessed 2 August 2023).

88 Shannon Fielder, '11 Netflix Shows to Help You Fall Asleep, Since You Already Know What's Going to Happen', *Romper*, 7 January 2016, https://www.romper.com/p/11-netflix-shows-to-help-you-fall-asleep-since-you-already-know-whats-going-to-happen-3554 (accessed 17 February 2024).

89 Alison Foreman and Jason Adams, '20 Best Netflix Shows to Fall Asleep to Because Wow We Need Some Zzzzzs', *Mashable*, 8 June 2023, https://mashable.com/article/best-netflix-shows-to-fall-asleep (accessed 17 February 2024).

90 Nicole Mello and Peter Mutic, '50 Best Shows on Netflix to Fall Asleep To', 26 June 2023, https://screenrant.com/netflix-relaxing-shows-fall-asleep-to/ (accessed 17 February 2024).

91 TheRossEverett, 'Best Netflix Shows To Fall Asleep To', 6 December 2012, https://web.archive.org/web/20150310222508/http://sourcefed.com/best-netflix-shows-to-fall-asleep-to (accessed via Wayback Machine 10 January 2024).

92 Linda Stone, 'What Is Continuous Partial Attention?', *Lindastone.net*, https://lindastone.net/faq/ (accessed 11 July 2023).

93 Michael Savio, '8 Netflix "Chorecore" Shows to Watch While Doing Something Else', 15 March 2023, https://www.pastemagazine.com/tv/netflix/8-netflix-chorecore-shows-to-watch-while-doing-something-else (accessed 2 August 2023).

94 Day, 'Psychology of Concentration'.

95 Caetlin Benson-Allott, 'The Ennui of the Scroll', *Film Quarterly* 75, no. 2 (2021): 84–8.

96 Derek Kompare, 'The Benefits of Banality: Domestic Syndication in the Post-Network Era' in *Beyond Prime Time: Television Programming in the Post-Network Era*, ed. Amanda D. Lotz (Milton Park: Taylor & Francis, 2010), 56.
97 Benson-Allott, 'Ennui', 85.
98 Miranda Larbi, 'Napflix is Netflix for People Who Need to Get to Sleep and It's [sic] Genius', *Metro*, 1 November 2016, https://metro.co.uk/2016/11/01/napflix-is-netflix-for-people-who-need-to-get-to-sleep-and-its-genius-6226043/ (accessed 4 August 2023).
99 Ibid.
100 Tara Jessop, 'Napflix: The World's Most Boring Channel', *Culture Trip*, 3 November 2016, https://theculturetrip.com/europe/spain/articles/introducing-napflix-the-worlds-most-boring-channel-on-purpose (accessed 4 August 2023).
101 Harriet Mallinson, 'Napflix and … Nap: The New Online TV Channel So BORING It Will Send You to Sleep with Hours of Latin Mass and Quantum Physics', *Mail Online*, 22 October 2016, https://www.dailymail.co.uk/travel/travel_news/article-3858974/Napflix-nap-new-online-TV-channel-BORING-send-sleep-hours-Latin-mass-quantum-physics.html (accessed 4 August 2023).
102 Karissa Bell, 'Napflix Will Help You Sleep with the Internet's Dullest Videos', *Mashable*, 3 November 2016, https://mashable.com/article/napflix-boring-videos (accessed 2 August 2023).
103 'Napflix – Case Study (English)', YouTube, 15 June 2017, https://www.youtube.com/watch?v=hkM1aNvHRpY (accessed 4 August 2023).
104 Victor Guitérrez de Tena, quoted in Larbi, 'Napflix is Netflix for People Who Need to Get to Sleep'.
105 Michaela Zee, 'Netflix Quietly Drops Its "Surprise Me" Shuffle Button', *IGN*, 17 February 2023, https://www.ign.com/articles/netflix-drops-surprise-me-button (accessed 4 August 2023).
106 Catherine Johnson, *Online TV* (Milton Park: Taylor & Francis, 2019), 109.
107 Paasonen, *Dependent, Distracted, Bored*, n.p.
108 'BoringPhone', *BoringPhone*, 2019, https://boringphone.com/ (accessed 4 August 2023).
109 Saskia O'Donoghue, 'Borecore: It Costs a Lot of Money to Look This Dull', *Euronews*, 1 April 2023, https://www.euronews.com/culture/2023/04/01/borecore-it-costs-a-lot-of-money-to-look-this-dull (accessed 4 August 2023).
110 Roquet, *Ambient Media*, 168.
111 Charryy Chauhan, 'Napflix: A Website with Sleep Inducing Videos to Help You Doze Off Peacefully', *ED Times*, 23 November 2016, https://edtimes.in/napflix-a-website-with-sleep-inducing-videos-whichll-help-you-doze-off-peacefully/ (accessed 3 August 2023).

112 Ulrik Schmidt, 'Ambience and Ubiquity' in *Throughout: Art and Culture Emerging with Ubiquitous Computing*, ed. Ulrik Ekman (Cambridge, MA: MIT Press, 2012), 176–9.
113 Schmidt, 'Ambience and Ubiquity', 177.
114 Gernot Böhme, *Atmospheric Architectures: The Aesthetics of Felt Spaces* (London: Bloomsbury Academic, 2017), 14.
115 Roquet, *Ambient Media*, 162.
116 Ibid., 167.
117 Paul Roquet, 'In the Mood: Toward the Full Commodification of Ambience', *Real Life Mag*, 26 April 2021, https://reallifemag.com/in-the-mood/ (accessed 4 August 2023).
118 Nikos Papastergiadis, Amelia Barikin and Scott McQuire, 'Conclusion: Ambient Screens' in *Ambient Screens and Transnational Public*, ed. Nikos Papstergiadis (Hong Kong: Hong Kong University Press, 2016), 220.
119 Schmidt, 'Ambience and Ubiquity', 177–8.
120 Ibid., 178.
121 Paasonen, *Dependent, Distracted, Bored*, n.p.
122 Roquet, *Ambient Media*, 15.
123 Richmond, 'Vulgar Boredom', 32.
124 Alex Hern, 'Netflix's Biggest Competitor? Sleep', *Guardian*, 18 April 2017, https://www.theguardian.com/technology/2017/apr/18/netflix-competitor-sleep-uber-facebook (accessed 10 January 2024).
125 Roquet, 'In the Mood'.

Chapter 4

1 Philipp Dominik Keidl, Laliv Melamed, Vinzenz Hediger and Antonio Somaini, eds, *Pandemic Media: Preliminary Notes Towards an Inventory* (Lüneburg: Meson Press, 2020).
2 'Curb Your Cabin Fever with these Quarantine Memes and Tweets', *The Chive*, n.d., https://thechive.com/humor/curb-your-cabin-fever-with-these-quarantine-memes-tweets-29-photos/ (accessed 24 February 2024). Variations on this same joke have been repeated in different global contexts, including in one controversial public information video clip sponsored by the German Federal Government, which urges German citizens to 'do their patriotic duty in the war against the coronavirus by staying at home and being couch potatoes'. Reuters, '"Be Lazy, Save Lives," Germans Urged in COVID Video', YouTube, 16 November 2020, https://www.youtube.com/watch?v=FS1DDn2eklU (accessed 14 July 2021).
3 'Schrute Facts', *Know Your Meme*, 25 June 2018, https://knowyourmeme.com/memes/schrute-facts (accessed 14 July 2021).

4 Bobby Moore (@BobbyMoore44), 'How NOT to Get BORED During Lockdown! Enjoy!', TikTok, 5 April 2020, https://vm.tiktok.com/ZMdxVMC7A/ (accessed 14 July 2021).
5 Han, *Psychopolitics*.
6 'The Philosophical Debate about Biopolitics in Times of CoVid-19', *Crisis and Communitas*, 5 April 2020, https://crisisandcommunitas.com/?crisis=the-philosophical-debate-about-biopolitics-in-times-of-covid-19 (accessed 18 July 2021).
7 Paul B. Preciado, 'Le confinement … numérique', *Libération*, 11 December 2020, https://www.liberation.fr/debats/2020/12/11/le-confinement-numerique_1808432 (accessed 18 July 2021, translation mine).
8 Paul B. Preciado, 'Learning from the Virus', *Artforum*, 26 March 2020, https://www.artforum.com/print/202005/paul-b-preciado-82823.
9 Han, *Psychopolitics*, 25.
10 Ibid., 11 & 28.
11 Ibid., 1.
12 Byung-Chul Han, *Topology of Violence*, trans. Amanda DeMarco (Cambridge, MA, and London: MIT Press, 2018), 89.
13 Han, *Psychopolitics*, 2.
14 'Quarantine Memes', *MemeZila*, n.d., https://memezila.com/Quarantine-day-13-Congratulations-you-have-completed-netflix-meme-1330 (accessed 19 July 2021).
15 'More Painful Than It Looks', *Imgflip*, n.d., https://imgflip.com/i/3tx9dp (accessed 24 February 2024).
16 Han, *Topology of Violence*, 82.
17 Ibid., 89.
18 Ibid.
19 See Berardi, *And: Phenomenology of the End*; Crary, *24/7*; Mark Fisher, *Capitalist Realism: Is there No Alternative?* (Ropley: Zero Books, 2009).
20 Han, *Topology of Violence*, 19. It is important to point out here how Han's claim differs from Giorgio Agamben's widely ridiculed response to government restrictions as a biopolitical process aimed at reducing citizens' rights and existence to a form of 'bare life' in the context of Covid quarantines. A key distinction between these two positions relates to a difference in the nature of power between a biopolitical and a psychopolitical regime. In the former, a bare life emerges as a result of disciplinary power enacted by state or government forces. In the latter, a bare life emerges as a result of a more diffuse kind of power that is enacted through the compulsion to freedom and self-determination in a digital neoliberal culture.
21 Wark, *Gamer Theory*, 171.

22 A recent publication by the mental health charity Mind lists boredom as the number one concern during the pandemic amongst young people, with 83 per cent of respondents noting that boredom had negatively impacted on their mental health. Mind, *The Mental Health Emergency: How Has the Coronavirus Pandemic Impacted our Mental Health?* (Report) June 2020, https://www.mind.org.uk/media-a/5929/the-mental-health-emergency_a4_final.pdf (accessed 17 July 2021). Similarly, in a survey commissioned by the Office for National Statistics, it was found that just under two-thirds of sixteen- to sixty-nine-year-olds were more worried about their mental health (including boredom, stress and anxiety) than their general health. Office of National Statistics, *Coronavirus and Anxiety, Great Britain: 3 April 2020 to 10 May 2020* (Report) 15 June 2020, https://www.ons.gov.uk/peoplepopulationandcommunity/wellbeing/articles/coronavirusandanxietygreatbritain/3april2020to10may2020 (accessed 18 July 2021).

23 See, for example, World Health Organization, 'Mental Health and Psychosocial Considerations During the COVID-19 Outbreak' 18 March 2020, https://www.who.int/docs/default-source/coronaviruse/mental-health-considerations.pdf.

24 See Arwa Mahdawi, 'Quarantine Fatigue Has Well and Truly Set In – And That Could Spell Trouble', *Guardian*, 20 May 2020, https://www.theguardian.com/commentisfree/2020/may/20/quarantine-fatigue-has-well-and-truly-set-in-and-that-could-spell-trouble, and Corinna S. Martarelli and Wanja Wolff, 'Too Bored to Bother? Boredom as a Potential Threat to the Efficacy of Pandemic Containment Measures', *Humanities and Social Sciences Communications* 7, no. 28 (2020): 1–5, https://www.nature.com/articles/s41599-020-0512-6 (both accessed 18 July 2021).

25 See April Roach, 'Moment Partygoer Tells Police "We've Been Bored and We Want to Have Fun" as Student Party Broken Up', *Evening Standard*, 3 February 2021, https://www.standard.co.uk/news/crime/student-lockdown-party-partygoer-lancashire-police-fines-b918487.html and Matthew Lodge and Lorraine King, 'COVIDiots Drive 150 Miles "Because Lockdown Is Boring" and Get Car Seized by Police', *The Mirror*, 9 February 2021, https://www.mirror.co.uk/news/uk-news/COVIDiots-drive-150-miles-because-23472469 (both accessed 7 June 2021).

26 Roland Barthes, *How to Live Together: Novelistic Simulations of Some Everyday Spaces*, trans. Kate Briggs (New York: Columbia University Press, 2103), 6.

27 Knut Stene-Johansen, Christian Refsum and Johan Schimanski, eds, *Living Together: Roland Barthes, the Individual and the Community* (Bielefeld: Transcript Verlag, 2018), 18.

28 Barthes, *How to Live Together*, 22.

29 Asaf Nissenbaum and Limor Shifman, 'Meme Templates as Expressive Repertoires in a Globalizing World: A Cross-Linguistic Study', *Journal of Computer-Mediated Communication* 23 (July 2018): 294.

30 Alexa Lisitza, 'The Viral TikTok Song "Bored in the House" Turned 1 Year Old and Changed Creator Curtis Roach's Life', *BuzzFeed*, 8 March 2021, https://www.buzzfeed.com/alexalisitza/bored-in-the-house-curtis-roach (accessed July 19 2021).

31 Curtis Roach (@curtistootrill), 'Bored in the House', TikTok, 4 March 2020, https://www.tiktok.com/@curtisroach/video/6800471860761971974?lang=en&is_copy_url=1&is_from_webapp=v1 (accessed 19 July 2021).

32 Celebrity and influencer re-uses of the track include TikToks made by American rapper Tyga, stylist Chiara Ferragni and by TikTok stars Charli D'Amelio, BeastEater and others. See 'Bored in the House', *Know Your Meme* 1 April 2020, https://knowyourmeme.com/memes/bored-in-the-house (accessed 19 July 2021).

33 Melanie Kennedy, 'If the Rise of the TikTok Dance and e-girl Aesthetic has Taught Us Anything, It's That Teenage Girls Rule the Internet Right Now', *European Journal of Cultural Studies* 23, no. 6 (July 2020): 1071. I will return to the significance of Roach's social positioning and its significance for thinking about the psychopolitics of boredom management later in this chapter.

34 Allison Shoemaker, 'The Unofficial Anthem of Self-Isolation is a Total Earworm and We Can't Stop Listening, Send Help', *AV Club*, 23 March 2020, https://www.avclub.com/the-unofficial-anthem-of-self-isolation-is-a-total-earw-1842453496 (accessed 15 July 2021).

35 TikToks often aspire to circularity as a formal quality through an embrace of the 'Infinite TikTok Loop' aesthetic. Online instructional tutorials that teach TikTokers how to achieve the perfect TikTok loop abound. See for example: Josh Martin, 'Infinite Loop TikTok Tutorial', YouTube, 23 January 2019, https://www.youtube.com/watch?v=duDrvzoiIaE; Peter Drazy, 'How To Create the Perfect Loop (Tik Tok Tutorial)', YouTube 9 May 2020, https://www.youtube.com/watch?v=yL7LU3Xudug (accessed 17 July 2021).

36 Vernallis, *Unruly Media*, 186–7.

37 It is worth pointing out that there are many other TikToks that use the hashtag #BoredInTheHouse without re-using Roach's track, some of them made long after the launch official #BoredVibes challenge (often in later stages of the coronavirus quarantines and aftermath). This suggests that the idea of being #BoredInTheHouse has attained widespread currency and that although it has a special relationship to the pandemic, it is able to traverse different contexts.

38 Although the title of the track invites users to perform their boredom in domestic settings under quarantine, there are a few notable exceptions of 'Bored in the House' TikToks made in non-domestic settings. For example, one 'Bored in the House' TikTok takes place in a hospital setting and pictures a woman in scrubs performing a kind of contortionist stunt with a piece of medical equipment. The TikTok uses Roach's track and features the line 'When You Work in a [*sic*] OR and Have No Surgeries', Megan Sutherby (@megansut) TikTok, 26 March

2020, https://www.tiktok.com/@megansut/video/6808569471507139845 (accessed 19 July 2021).
39 Andreas Schellewald, 'Communicative Forms on TikTok: Perspectives from Digital Ethnography', *International Journal of Communication* 15 (2021): 1437–57.
40 One entry in *Urban Dictionary* defines the term 'boreductivity' as 'a state in which one accomplishes a large number of important everyday tasks out of sheer boredom'. I am widening this term out here to include unimportant or meaningless tasks. Szechwean, 'Boreductivity', *Urban Dictionary*, 1 February 2011, https://www.urbandictionary.com/define.php?term=boreductivity (accessed 19 July 2021).
41 Charli d'Amelio (@charlidamelio) 'Bored in the House', TikTok, 22 March 2020, https://www.tiktok.com/@charlidamelio/video/6807164365993757958 (accessed 17 July 2021).
42 For a wider discussion of D'Amelio's TikTok performances and 'digital blackface' see Cienna Davis, 'Digital Blackface and the Troubling Intimacies of TikTok Dance Challenges' in *TikTok Cultures in the United States*, ed. Trevor Boffone (London: Routledge, 2022), 28–38.
43 Jason Parham, 'TikTok and the Evolution of Digital Blackface', *Wired*, 4 August 2020, https://www.wired.com/story/tiktok-evolution-digital-blackface/ (accessed 17 July 2021).
44 Lauren Michele Jackson, 'We Need to Talk about Digital Blackface in Reaction GIFs', *Teen Vogue*, 2 August 2017, https://www.teenvogue.com/story/digital-blackface-reaction-gifs (accessed 13 August 2021).
45 Jackson, 'We Need to Talk about Digital Blackface'.
46 Leona Stewart (@LeonaStewart27), 'BORED IN THE HOUSE', TikTok, 31 March 2020, https://vm.tiktok.com/ZMdtHtLJX/ (accessed 12 April 2020).
47 Jack Wright (@jack.wright) 'We'll Dance to Anything', TikTok, 22 March 2020, https://www.tiktok.com/@jack.wright/video/6807153631469571333 (accessed 12 April 2020).
48 Pettman, *Infinite Distraction*, 56–9.
49 Han, *Psychopolitics*, 63 & 65.
50 Pamela Krayanbul in Alexandra Harling et al., 'TikTok and Short-Form Screendance Before and After Covid', *The International Journal of Screendance* 12 (12 March 2021): 199.
51 Larissa Hjorth and Ingrid Richardson, *Ambient Play* (Cambridge, MA: MIT Press, 2020), 9 & 38, kindle.
52 Ibid., 9.
53 Ibid., 38 & 41.
54 Thanks to Peter Conlin for this insight about immobilized mobile media.
55 Hjorth and Richardson, *Ambient Play*, 83.

56 'Level Up Jumps', *Know Your Meme*, 12 April 2020, https://knowyourmeme.com/memes/level-up-jumps (accessed 17 July 2021).

57 @Guille.what, 'La casa de papel', TikTok, 6 May 2020, https://www.tiktok.com/@guille_what/video/6823719906106805509 (accessed 24 February 2024).

58 Chun, *Updating to Remain the Same*.

59 'Work from Home Prisoner', *Imgflip*, n.d., https://imgflip.com/i/3urs6j (accessed 24 February 2024).

60 Ian Bogost, *Play Anything: The Pleasure of Limits, the Uses of Boredom, and the Secret of Games* (New York: Basic Books, 2016), 13.

61 Sabrina Ward-Kimola, 'A Vaguely Erotic Mime: Mimetic Text vs. Optical Tactility' in *Critical Meme Reader: Global Mutations of the Viral Image*, ed. Chloë Arkenbout, Jack Wilson and Daniel de Zeeuw (Amsterdam: Institute of Network Cultures, 2021), 40 & 43.

62 Chuck Arnold, '"Bored in the House" by Tyga and Curtis Roach is your new Coronavirus Anthem', *New York Post*, 30 March 2020, https://nypost.com/2020/03/30/bored-in-the-house-by-tyga-and-curtis-roach-is-your-new-coronavirus-anthem/ (accessed 19 July 2021).

63 Tyga, 'Tyga x Curtis Roach – Bored in the House (Official Video)', 27 March 2020, YouTube video, https://www.youtube.com/watch?v=YBsPE6yHH9c (accessed 14 April 2020).

64 Barthes, *How to Live Together*, 60.

65 A study in May 2020 found that 'Over 50 per cent of men aged 19–24 have met with a group of friends during lockdown, and 20 per cent have been reprimanded by police', citing boredom as one of the motivating psychological factors for flouting lockdown restrictions. See Covid-19 Psychological Research Consortium, *Initial Research Findings on the Impact of COVID-19 on the Well-Being of Young People aged 13 to 24 in the UK* (report) 7 May 2020, https://drive.google.com/file/d/1AOc0wCPqv2gfFSQ_DVmw12vrqQK01z0V/view (accessed 20 August 2021). Another study conducted in May 2020 by the youth charity Connect Stars, which surveyed people aged between thirteen and twenty-four in the London borough of Brent, found that 'the majority of those questioned said they were not staying indoors because they were living in overcrowded homes, or because they were bored or suffering from a lack of physical activity'. See Léonie Chao-Fong, 'Young People In One of UK's Worst-Hit Coronavirus Areas Are Flouting Lockdown. Here's Why', *Huffington Post*, 14 May 2020, https://www.huffingtonpost.co.uk/entry/why-are-young-people-not-following-the-lockdown-rules_uk_5ebea66fc5b6fac96c967360 (accessed 20 August 2021). The press reception of these sorts of studies has further consolidated links between the boredom of young men and the risk of a second or third wave of the virus.

66 Paul B. Preciado, *Pornotopia: An Essay on Playboy's Architecture & Biopolitics* (New York: Zone Books, 2014), 65.
67 Ibid., 81.
68 Preciado, 'Le confinement … numérique', my translation.
69 Ibid.
70 Ibid.
71 Wark, *Gamer Theory*, 167.
72 Ibid., 162.
73 Treske, *Video Theory*, 97.
74 Carina Chocano, 'Not So Bored in the House: Charli and Dixie D'Amelio, Tyga, Chase Hudson, and TikTok's Other New Stars are Having a Blast (At Home)', *Vanity Fair*, 20 July 2020, https://www.vanityfair.com/style/2020/07/not-so-bored-in-the-house-with-tiktok (accessed 20 August 2021).
75 Lydia Keating (@lydialoo121), 'Stitched with @ …', TikTok, 23 January 2021, https://www.tiktok.com/@lydialoo121/video/6921026887070371077?lang=en (accessed 13 April 2022).
76 @stephanyliriano, 'Ya Bored Yet?', TikTok, 22 March 2020, https://www.tiktok.com/@stephanyliriano/video/6807127510057323781? (accessed 14 April 2021).
77 Lauren Berlant, 'Faceless Book', *Supervalent Thought*, 25 December 2007, https://supervalentthought.com/2007/12/25/faceless-book/ (accessed 14 August 2022).
78 In July 2021, TikTok expanded its maximum video length from 15 seconds to 60 seconds. See Drew Kirchhoff, 'More Tok on the Clock: Introducing Longer Videos on TikTok', *TikTok U.S.*, Product Newsletter 1 July 2021, https://newsroom.tiktok.com/en-us/longer-videos (accessed 16 August 2021).
79 Hjorth and Richardson, *Ambient Play*, 45.
80 See Trebor Schultz, ed. *Digital Labor: The Internet as Playground and Factory* (New York and London: Routledge, 2013).
81 Hannah Smothers, 'I Spent Two Days and a Lot of Beers Trying to Recreate this Viral TikTok', *Vice*, 21 January 2021, https://www.vice.com/en/article/5dpjdn/how-much-time-and-effort-does-it-take-to-make-a-viral-tiktok (accessed 23 August 2021).
82 John Herrman, 'How TikTok Is Rewriting the World', *New York Times*, 10 March 2019, https://www.nytimes.com/2019/03/10/style/what-is-tik-tok.html (accessed 23 August 2021).
83 Byung-Chul Han, *In the Swarm: Digital Prospects*, trans. Erik Butler (Stanford, CA: Stanford University Press, 2017), 33.
84 See Kennedy, 'If the Rise of the TikTok Dance and E-Girl Aesthetic Has Taught Us Anything', and Mona Khattab, 'Synching and Performing: Body (Re)-Presentation in the Short Video App TikTok', *Widerscreen*, 16 January 2020, http://widerscreen.fi/numerot/2019-1-2/synching-and-performing-body-re-presentation-in-the-short-video-app-tiktok/ (accessed 17 February 2024).

85   Shreya Sudarshana and Jonathan Zhou, 'To Win Short-Form Video, Look Away from the Creator', *Femstreet*, 11 September 2020, https://femstreet.substack.com/p/to-win-short-form-video-look-away (accessed 17 February 2024).
86   Mary Ann Doane, 'Information, Crisis, Catastrophe' in *New Media, Old Media: A History and Theory Reader*, ed. Wendy Hui Kyong Chun and Thomas Keenan (Milton Park: Routledge, 2006), 264.
87   Lupinacci, 'Scrolling through Nothing', 277.
88   Audrey Anable, *Playing with Feelings: Video Games and Affect* (Minneapolis: University of Minnesota Press, 2018), 73.
89   Theodor Adorno, 'On Popular Music' in *Cultural Theory and Popular Culture: A Reader*, ed. John Storey (Athens: Prentice Hall, 1998), 207.
90   Ibid., 205.
91   Byung-Chul Han, *The Burnout Society* (Stanford, CA: Stanford University Press, 2015), 13.
92   Ibid., 14.
93   Franco 'Bifo' Berardi, *Breathing: Chaos and Poetry* (Pasadena: Semiotext(e), 2018), 28.
94   Anable, *Playing with Feelings*, 73 & 96.
95   Phillips, *On Kissing, Tickling, and Being Bored*, 71.
96   Barthes, *How to Live Together*, 61.
97   Benjamin, *Arcades Project*, 105.
98   Ibid., 108.

Epilogue: Unworking entertainment: Public boredom and the next normal

1   Vilém Flusser, *Post-History*, trans. Rodrigo Maltez Novaes, ed. Siegried Zielinski (Minneapolis: University of Minnesota Press, 2015), xii.
2   Vilém Flusser, *Into the Universe of Techical Images*, trans. Nancy Ann Roth (Minneapolis: University of Minnesota Press, 2011), 161.
3   Michael S. Rosenwald, 'These Are Boom Times for Boredom and the Researchers Who Study It', *The Washington Post*, 28 March 2020, https://www.washingtonpost.com/local/these-are-boom-times-for-boredom-and-the-researchers-who-study-it/2020/03/27/0e62983a-706f-11ea-b148-e4ce3fbd85b5_story.html (accessed 24 February 2024).
4   Jonathan Flatley, *Affective Mapping: Melancholia and the Politics of Modernism*, (Cambridge, MA: Harvard University Press, 2008), 3.
5   Adrian MacKenzie and Anna Munster, 'Platform Seeing: Image Ensembles and Their Invisualities', *Theory, Culture, and Society* 36, no. 5 (2019): 3–22.

Index

adolescent boredom 25–6
Adorno, Theodor 9, 13–14, 74, 129
aesthetics of boredom 72, 78, 97
Affectiva 59
affective computing 19, 49, 57
affective labour 16, 24, 26–44
Agamben, Giorgio, 'Notes on Gesture' 19, 49–51, 55–6, 60, 62, 64, 66, 68–70, 155 n.20
Alexander, Neta 15
always-on entertainment 73, 77–8
always-on media 16–17
always-on subjectivity 17, 76, 83, 89–97
ambient media 73, 82–9, 93–4, 96
ambient play 116–17, 130
Anable, Audrey 129–32
Arcy, Jacqueline 30
attention economy 24, 26, 30–2, 41, 49, 57–70, 73, 75
Attention Restoration Theory 85
Auto Tutor 59

background TV 4, 72–7, 87–8, 98
Balsom, Erika, 'Watching Paint Dry' 80–1
Barthes, Roland 5, 106, 121, 130–2
Baudelaire, Charles, 'To the Reader' 53
BBC Four Goes Slow season 79, 85
Beller, Jonathan 26
Benjamin, Walter 7–8, 51, 132
Benson-Allott, Caetlin 88–9
Berardi, Franco 'Bifo' 130
Berlant, Lauren 126
Berry, David M. 43
binge watching 100–5, 126
biopolitics 5, 18–19, 50–6, 101, 121
Bogost, Ian 118–19
Böhme, Gernot 93, 97
Bonet, Francesc 90
bored body problem 20, 49, 51–2, 60–1, 104–7, 110–11, 121–2, 126, 128–9, 131

Bored Button app 1
#BoredintheHouse 2, 20, 99–132, 136, 157 n.37
boredom
 and attention 11–12, 24–7, 30–4, 41–2, 44, 49, 57–70, 73–5, 85–7, 92–3, 99, 128
 and the body 49, 51–2, 55, 69, 102, 104, 109, 111
 and computational media 6–12
 and creativity 8, 111, 118
 and criticality 9, 21
 definition 3, 57
 and domestic space 118, 121–2
 and entertainment on-demand 13–16
 and gender 24, 26, 30–2, 37–8, 41–4
 and gesture 10, 16, 19, 33, 38, 40–1, 45, 49–62, 64, 66–70, 111–12, 126–7, 129, 135–6
 history of 13, 19, 23
 and labour 12, 16–17, 20, 24, 26, 31–2, 38, 42–3, 86, 89, 105, 127–8
 management 12, 24, 26–44, 99–100, 102, 105, 116, 121–2, 130, 132, 134
 and negativity 34, 42, 57
 and performativity 19, 64–5
 and race 26, 32, 107, 121, 148 n.17
 and repetition 7, 43, 68, 96, 109, 124, 126, 132
 and sleep 88–93, 96–8
 and temporality 8, 14, 25, 33–8, 65–9, 78–9, 81, 84, 86, 89, 94, 96–8, 116–17, 123, 126–9, 136
boredom-on-demand 18, 71–3, 96–8
 and ambient media 82–9
 couch potato 72, 74–7
 multi-tasking background TV viewer 73–7
 Napflix and always-on culture 89–96
 and slow media 77–82
#boredom Vines 49–50, 60–4, 67

Index

'boreductivity' 111, 158 n.40
boyd, danah 40

casual games 1, 83, 129–30
Chorecore TV 88
Chun, Wendy 17, 40, 117
compulsory continuous connectivity 4, 13, 15, 17
couch potato 72, 74–7, 148 n.17
Covid-19 pandemic 2–3, 7, 15, 20–1, 28, 59, 86, 98–105, 107, 110, 114, 116, 121–3, 127–36, 156 n.22, 157 n.37. *See also* lockdown (#LockdownLife); quarantine
Crary, Jonathan 72, 80

Dall-e Mini (AI image generator) 46–8
D'Amelio, Charli 111–12, 158 n.42
Danckert, James 17
DeAngelis, Meg 27, 33–40
de Luca, Tiago 78
Denson, Shane 10, 43
de Tena, Víctor 90
digital blackface 112
digital capitalism 4–5, 75–6, 89, 102, 104, 122, 135–6
digital psychopolitics. *See* psychopolitics
Dobson, Amy Shields 31
Dyer, Richard 13–15

Eastwood, John 17
Ekman, Paul 58
Ellis, John 73–4, 77
Elman, Michelle 127–8
entertainment 13–16
    always-on 73, 77–8
    mass 9, 11, 24, 130
    networked 1, 4, 17, 19, 34, 68, 71, 99, 134
    on-demand 13–17, 128, 134
Eppink, Jason 59

FaceReader (facial expression analysis software) 58
Fisher, Mark 6–7, 10, 25, 37, 41–2
Flatley, Jonathan 135
Flaubert, Gustave, *Madame Bovary* 52–3, 55

Flusser, Vilém 133, 135–6
Friesen, Wallace 58

Gaunt, Kyra D. 41
GIFs 49, 59–61
glance theory 74
Goldsmith, Kenneth 80
Goodstein, Elizabeth, *Experience Without Qualities* 3, 50–1
Gorfinkel, Elena 68
Grusin, Richard 43

Haladyn, Julian Jason 57
Hall, Kimberly Ann 41
Han, Byung-Chul 14–16, 19–20, 101–4, 114, 122, 128–30. *See also* psychopolitics
    excess of positivity 129
    Good Entertainment 13
    psycho-power 102, 104
    Topology of Violence 155 n.20
    violence of positivity 103–4
Hansen, Mark B. 10–12, 38–40, 43
Harbord, Janet 55
Harris, Anita 30
Harrison, Cassian 79
Hastings, Reed 98
Hayles, N. Katherine 25
Heidegger, Martin 9, 11, 13–14, 24
Hellum, Thomas 79–80
Herrman, John 127–8
Hjorth, Larissa 116, 126
Hodge, James J. 17, 83
human movement and gesture 49–51
Hu, Tun-Hui 148 n.17
hyper/short-term attention 25–6, 59

idiorrhythmy 106, 130–1
Instagram 37–8, 66

Jackson, Lauren Michele 112
Jorge, Nuno Barradas 78
Jurgensen, Nathan 62

Kaplan, Rachel 85
Kaplan, Stephen 85
Kennedy, Melanie 108
Kingwell, Mark 17, 25

Klausen, Helle Breth 82
Kompare, Derek 89
Kracauer, Siegfried 7–9, 11, 24
Krayenbuhl, Pamela 114–15, 121

Lawson, Mark 85
Lee, Pamela M. 80
Levitt, Deborah 50
lockdown (#LockdownLife) 2, 4, 14, 20–1, 28, 98–107, 110–11, 113–17, 120–34, 159 n.65
Lupinacci, Ludmila 4, 128

mass entertainment 9, 11, 24, 130
McCarthy, Anna 82
McRobbie, Angela 26
McStay, Andrew 59
mobile media 116
Modleski, Tania 86
montage 36, 111, 120, 124, 126–7, 130
Mulvey, Laura 68
Munster, Anna 66

Napflix 4, 72, 89–97, 136
  'Oscillating Fan' 92–3
  'The Sound of Rain' 94–5
  'Tropical Rain' 94
Netflix 4, 72, 76, 96–7, 100
  Quarantine Meme 101
  slow TV on 79, 84, 86
  survivorship 77
networked entertainment 1, 4, 17, 19, 34, 68, 71, 99, 134
Ngai, Sianne 64
Noldus Information Technology corporation 58
Norwegian Broadcasting Corporation (NRK) broadcast 78–81, 84

O'Brien, Wendell 45

Paasonen, Susana, *Dependent, Distracted, Bored* 6–7, 18, 92, 96
Parham, Jason 112
Pease, Allison 31
Petro, Patrice 7, 31
Pettman, Dominic 10, 40, 114
Phillips, Adam 4, 25, 33, 40, 45, 131

Pilipets, Elena 72, 76–7
Pluto TV 83
Preciado, Paul B. 101–2, 121–2
private boredom 16
profound boredom 8–9, 11–13, 56, 76, 78, 80, 98, 129
psychopolitics 5, 16–21, 100–2, 106
psycho-power 102, 104
public boredom 133–6, 161

quarantine 100–2, 107, 110, 117–18, 120, 122–3, 126, 157 n.38

Richardson, Ingrid 116, 126
Richmond, Scott C. 17, 76–7, 83, 97
Roach, Curtis 107–10, 119–21, 157 n.33, 157 n.37–157 n.38
Rombes, Nicholas 6–7
Roquet, Paul, *Ambient Media* 82–5, 94, 97–8

Schmidt, Ulrich 93–4
Scott, Laurence 75
scrolling 42, 89, 124, 128–9
self-care 18, 78–9, 82, 85
self-medicating media 82–3, 89
short-form videos 19, 49, 114–15, 128. *See also* Vine videos
Sickert, Walter, *Ennui* 54–5
Simmel, Georg 7
slow cinema 78, 81
slow media 77–82, 85–6
slow TV 78–87
social media 2, 5, 14–16, 18, 20, 30–1, 37–8, 40, 42, 49, 56, 60–1, 81, 83, 98, 105, 123, 126–8, 134
soft fascination 85–6
Solanas, Valeria 6
#StayHome citizenship 100, 105, 116, 121
Stiegler, Bernard 10, 25
Stone, Linda, 'continuous partial attention' 88
streaming platforms 4, 11, 15–16, 18, 20, 43, 71–2, 75–7, 81–5, 89–91, 97–9, 101, 103, 120, 128, 136
Sudarshana, Shreya 128
survivorship (Netflix) 77
Svendsen, Lars, *A Philosophy of Boredom* 3, 45–6

Tardieu, Émile, *L'Ennui* 51–4
televisual spectatorship 18, 72, 74, 76, 98
TikTok 20, 98, 131–2, 136, 157 n.35
  'Bored in the House' 99, 105–13, 115–17, 119, 121, 123, 125–7, 130–2, 157 n.37–157 n.38
  #BoredVibes 99–100, 105, 107, 110, 116–17, 127, 130–1, 157 n.37
  challenges on 106–7, 119
  dance 113–16
  everyday life 110–11, 123–4, 126–7, 130, 132
  during lockdown (*see* lockdown)
  performative 105–7, 109–11, 113–17, 121, 123, 126, 131
  split screen 'duet' 112
  stunt 106, 110–11, 116–18, 120, 123, 126, 128, 157 n.38
  synchronization 114
Toohey, Peter 3
'Train Ride from Bergen to Oslo' (slow TV) 78, 80–1, 83, 95
Treske, Andreas 14
Tryon, Chuck 71
Turkle, Sherry 25
24/7 capitalism 72–7, 80–1, 83–4, 98, 104

Ulrich Schmidt 93–4, 96
unboring boredom 80–1
Uricchio, William 74–5

Vebert, Jean, *Fleurs du Mal* 53
Vernallis, Carol 43, 109
Vine videos 19, 49–50, 56–70, 123, 134–5
Viveport app 1
vulgar boredom 7–8, 76–8

Ward-Kimola, Sabrina 119
Wark, MacKenzie 18, 104, 122, 134
well-being 19–20, 77, 99, 102, 104–5
Wheatley, Helen 79
WikiHow (instructional website) 45

YouTube 12, 23–44, 61, 66, 82, 91–2, 120–3, 126, 134–5
  MayBaby 27–8, 30, 34, 36, 38–43
  #StayHome citizenship 100, 105, 116, 121

zany performances 63–4, 111, 126
Zhou, Jonathan 128